Dynamic Psychotherapy with Adult Survivors

Dynamic Psychotherapy with Adult Survivors

Living Past Neglect

Lori Bennett, LCSW

JASON ARONSON
Lanham • Boulder • New York • Toronto • Plymouth, UK

Published by Jason Aronson
A wholly owned subsidiary of The Rowman & Littlefield Publishing Group, Inc.
4501 Forbes Boulevard, Suite 200, Lanham, Maryland 20706
www.rowman.com

10 Thornbury Road, Plymouth PL6 7PP, United Kingdom

British Library Cataloguing in Publication Information Available

Library of Congress Cataloging-in-Publication Data

Bennett, Lori, 1956–
Dynamic psychotherapy with adult survivors : living past neglect / Lori Bennett.
p. cm.
Includes bibliographical references and index.
ISBN 978-0-7657-0892-2 (cloth : alk. paper) — ISBN 978-0-7657-0893-9 (electronic)
1. Adult child abuse victims. 2. Psychotherapy. I. Title.
RC569.5.C55B44 2012
616.85'822390651—dc23

2011051274

∞™ The paper used in this publication meets the minimum requirements of American National Standard for Information Sciences—Permanence of Paper for Printed Library Materials, ANSI/NISO Z39.48-1992.

Printed in the United States of America

This book is dedicated to Barbara Mantel, LICSW,
who opened the doors to my internal home,
turned on the lights,
and helped me to refurnish.

And to my husband, who taught me the meaning of unconditional love.

Contents

Acknowledgments

This book is a testament to the healing power of psychotherapy. It is a testament to the tenacity of the human spirit, and to the incredible ability of women and men to strive to overcome their histories of neglect.

Living in the past can create our futures. Yet, how do young adults climb out of their histories of neglect? How do they hope to feel loved if they never experienced the love they needed in their families of origin? How do they combat the damage to trust? How do they learn to stop the self-blame over circumstances, to move past the past, and embrace a new future?

These questions are answered in *Dynamic Psychotherapy with Adult Survivors*. With the hope that other people will benefit, I have asked former clients to write about their recovery processes. First, I have asked them to describe what their lives were like prior to therapy, and the tasks they challenged themselves to complete in their first years of treatment. I have asked them to describe living with the aftereffects of neglectful childhoods. Second, I have asked them to describe their processes of healing and recovery. What worked for them, and why?

Some clients chose to describe their autobiographies of healing to me in person, as we evaluated our time together in psychotherapy. I have written their stories for them, and disguised some of their circumstances, to protect their privacy. Others chose to write their own stories for this anthology. I am very grateful for their participation.

This book is dedicated to them—to their wisdom and courage.

Preface

I'll admit it: I am a dinosaur. I am a strong proponent of long-term psychodynamic psychotherapy. I have seen drastic changes in therapeutic interventions and priorities in the last three decades.

I currently supervise a graduate student in social work at a local university. She has recently informed me that the only course taught at her school on the *DSM IV-TR* is now offered as an *elective.* This is not unusual. At graduate schools throughout the country, students are learning less about theorists from the last century, less about diagnosis, and more about short-term interventions. These new priorities are insurance-driven. They have little to do with choice.

Don't get me wrong—I have seen enormous personal growth in clients who chose to try EMDR and brainspotting. And although these techniques are wonderful for melting frozen trauma in the brain, they do little to examine or manage the deep-rooted and pervasive daily mini-traumas that are experienced in the lives of clients with neglect histories.

The focus on short-term work, as well as the exaggeration of its value, began in the early 1990s, with the onset of managed care—or, as a colleague calls it: *mangled care*. During those years, I worked as a Utilization Reviewer for a commercial insurance company. My day consisted of speaking with therapists about their clients' diagnoses and treatments, measurable goals, and outcomes, and of assigning a quota of treatment sessions based on diagnosis. We were assigned a book to read during our first week of orientation to the job: *Single Session Therapy,* by Moshe Talmon. Talmon points out that therapists are accustomed to defining one session of therapy, followed by a discontinuation of treatment, as "resistance." He discusses his research into this phenomenon, and we are led to believe that many clients actually get what they need in that one session. Termination after one session is not considered "resistance"; but instead, a good treatment outcome![1]

During orientation, we were welcomed to an auditorium where a speaker named Bill O'Hanlon informed us about the intervention known as the "miracle question." Here is the miracle question: "Suppose tonight while you sleep a miracle happens. When you awake tomorrow morning, what will you see yourself doing, thinking, or believing about yourself that will tell you a miracle has happened in your life?"[2]

Exploring the answers to that question can certainly assist you in helping some clients to change their quality of life in very positive ways. But for many clients with abuse and neglect histories, the question is nearly irrelevant. At worst, the question backfires. After using this technique, one client told me: "I've had a lobotomy and I can't think anymore." The concept of waking up and feeling good about herself was not in her frame of reference.

Many HMOs and commercial insurance companies have chosen to make clinicians accountable for their work with clients. This new accountability, however, never considered the impact on our clients. One large national insurance company used to require the completion of "Outpatient Treatment Reports" (OTRs), to monitor clients' progress session by session. Not only were we required to diagnose our clients, but also, to detail the process of treatment, setting measurable goals, and meeting those goals in a pre-determined number of sessions. The number of sessions was determined by the severity of the client's diagnosis. If a client had a history of substance abuse, we were expected to move that person quickly from individual to group therapy as the primary modality of treatment. Can you see how this could lead a neglected client to feel even more abandoned by the system, and by her therapist? The more she improved in treatment, the sooner she had to say goodbye.

And I don't know about yours, but my clients were not exactly thrilled about their personal mental health issues being broadcasted to their employer's insurance carrier. Especially for clients with histories of sexual abuse, the over-exposure felt like ongoing re-victimization and violation. This is not what we want to replicate as we try to assist clients with healing! More recently, some insurance companies are requiring practitioners to enter diagnostic information online, by electronically submitting mental health claims. Even though the diagnosis may only appear as a five digit code, several of my clients have questioned the need for online access to that information.

A former client is also a Ph.D. candidate in psychology. She returned to therapy recently for a "tune-up," to re-examine some negative internal voices that had resurfaced. Melinda told me that although she learned about the concept of transference, there was no training or coursework whatsoever regarding how to utilize the transference between therapist and client throughout treatment, to assist with the healing process. To me, there are few things more crucial to facilitating healing than an understanding of the dynamic of transference.

It takes time, trust. and history together to enhance introspective ability. The examination of one's defensive structure, one's introject, and one's transference in relationships requires a great deal of introspection.

My friend Rindi is a virtuoso at meditation. She had a daily meditation ritual for five years, and during the fifth year, she saw a bright white light during her meditation. The illumination was accompanied by a blissful feeling of unconditional love and awareness, and a profound inner peace. Rindi had a spiritual awakening that day, through her meditation practice. If someone had told her that this awakening would eventually occur, I'm not so sure that Rindi would have believed it. After all, her first year of meditation practice was spattered with frustration and doubt, and an inability to quiet her internal voices.

The same is true for therapy practice. The healing becomes deeper and more profound over time. We can see behavioral changes in a short while, and we certainly start to feel better about ourselves, but attitudes and beliefs are more obstinate, more pervasive, and more covert than behaviors. Some beliefs about ourselves, including those associated with a negative introject, feel too dangerous to let surface. They remain buried very deeply, and sometimes, only the passage of time, the enhancement of introspective ability, and the trust and safety in a therapeutic relationship can allow lasting healing to occur.

Introduction

The intentions of this book are threefold: to expand the definition of neglect to include emotional neglect, to create a more profound understanding of the impact of childhood neglect on adult survivors, and to contribute to the training of clinicians who are serving survivors of neglect.

Neglect is the most neglected form of child abuse. Mandated reporters of neglect are taught to look for the obvious signs, as noted at www.childwelfare.gov:

Signs of Neglect

Consider the possibility of neglect when the *child*:

- Is frequently absent from school
- Begs or steals food or money
- Lacks needed medical or dental care, immunizations, or glasses
- Is consistently dirty and has severe body odor
- Lacks sufficient clothing for the weather
- Abuses alcohol or other drugs
- States that there is no one at home to provide care

Consider the possibility of neglect when the *parent or other adult caregiver*:

- Appears to be indifferent to the child
- Seems apathetic or depressed
- Behaves irrationally or in a bizarre manner
- Is abusing alcohol or other drugs[1]

The bad news is that there are plenty of children who are victims of neglect and emotional abuse that do not display the above symptoms. Often, parents function well enough outside of the home to appear to be good caregivers. This dynamic can be both confusing and crazy-making to a child, and a precursor to self-blame.

Neglect exacerbates abuse. It also sets up a foundation for continued abuse to occur. If a child has no comparison to being treated with respect, that child will be more likely to become victimized. That child will be less capable of trusting adults, and will be more likely to keep abuse a secret. Without a trustworthy adult to process the experience of neglect and abuse, or to provide a comparison for the child, that child is the most likely candidate to develop aftereffects of neglect and symptoms of Post-Traumatic Stress Disorder as an adult.

Dan Siegel, a psychiatrist and the executive director of the Mindsight Institute, believes that neglect can lead to other diagnostic symptoms as well. In a lecture at the Garrison Institute on March 2, 2011, he discussed how the brain of a child develops in response to the parents' interactions with the child. If the child is neglected, critical connections in the brain do not occur. These are physiological connections that allow emotions such as empathy, security, the desire to experience new things rather than shrink away from them, and even morality to be integrated in the child's personality. He believes that "every mental disorder in the DSM" can be seen as the result of a lack of attention, or "attunement" between a parent and a child. Dorothy, whose story is later discussed in this book, listened to this lecture. She was most impressed with a wonderful observation that Dr. Siegel made. He spoke about the mind being more like a verb than a noun, and noted that it is never too late to build these connections in the brain, through therapy and other types of interaction.[2]

Dr. Siegel's words ring true for the clients discussed in this book. Through frustration, introspection, and hard work, they have created the lives they desired, despite their neglect histories.

There is no map for healing, and each individual journey is different. Since healing is not linear, its path is usually jagged. Perhaps we walk two steps forward, and one step back. Some of us make behavioral change and wait for our emotions to catch up. Some of us succeed at deep introspective therapy before seeing any behavioral change at all. This book interweaves stories of neglect survivors during the beginning, middle, and end of their journeys. *Dynamic Psychotherapy with Adult Survivors* is meant to replicate a real journey, not a step-by-step map to success. Although it may open wounds, there are numerous success stories and tools offered to gain insight into your particular road, and to close those wounds forever. No one will feel your pain for you if you don't. There is no way to compensate for childhood losses, or to fill the void left in the wake of neglect. Losses need to be grieved, and reparenting is possible. With experienced clinicians who support and encourage us, we can all cry our last tears about our histories.

Change does not happen overnight. In order to make profound change in our lives, we need to know what we will be losing. Survival skills, aftereffects, and defenses have served us well. They often produce secondary gains.

This book serves to educate adult children of neglect, as well as their therapists. If you are an adult child of neglect, this book will assist you in deciding what you want to take from your history, and what you want to leave behind, in order to become the best you can be in this life.

Although there are other books available to adult children of neglect and their therapists, none of them emphasize the following four crucial components of healing. The first component is the *resolution of negative self-talk.* Resolution of self-criticism is a prerequisite to the development of the compassion toward the self that is necessary to resolve the next three components.

The second component is the disclosing of the *introject*—or, the internalized neglectful parent. Helping clients to let their introjects surface involves reading between the lines of their conversations. Introjects can be slippery and elusive. Therapists can assist clients with neglect histories to disclose their deepest fears of becoming like their neglectful parents.

The third topic is *transference*—or, the ways in which we repeat old patterns of neglect in order to bring them to the surface. This book will assist clients and therapists in allowing old patterns to surface, so that self-discovery and emotional evolution can occur. The by-products of this introspective work are the ease in which we are soon able to attract loving, supportive, trustworthy people into our lives; the enhanced ability to achieve true intimacy in relationships; and the capacity to break the cycle of neglect with our own children.

The fourth component is for therapists and beginning clinicians in the mental health field: utilize your supervision time to *process your own countertransference issues*. If you are a clinician with your own neglect history, it is crucial that you are aware of your own aftereffects, whether they are completely resolved or not, to work with survivors. Your awareness will prevent the clouding of your lenses as you seek to help others.

I have written this book in honor of the former clients who walked this road with me. Their memory retrieval redefined their histories in their conscious minds. They took difficult and brave actions toward resolution. They overcame their childhood neglect and trauma histories with fidelity and tenacity. And they have all broken the cycle of neglect in their own families, with the help of therapy.

Lori Bennett, LCSW
August, 2011

Part I

LISTENING FOR NEGLECT

Chapter One

"But Nothing Happened!": Redefining Childhood Neglect

SUN'S UP

One of the first memories that I have is of waking up early in the morning. I can remember getting up in my crib and standing with my hands on the bars looking down at our two big dogs lying on the floor in my bedroom. I would try to reach down through the bars to pet them and usually they would get up and lick my hands and thump their tails on the floor. My parents' bedroom was right next to mine so I would start to call, "Mom, Dad, sun's up," over and over until one of them came in and let me out of the crib to be with the dogs. Usually one of them would just come in, set me on the floor, and tell me that breakfast would be later. They either told me to be quiet or I just knew because I tried to stay as silent as possible, even placing a pillow or blanket under where the dogs' tails might hit the floor. I really loved the time I got to spend with "Basil" and "Todd" in the mornings. I didn't realize until much, much later that the need for quiet in the early hours of the day in our house was due to my mother's hangovers and depression.

I'm not sure if there was a particular incident that forced the change in my sleeping arrangement with the dogs, or if it was just one of my mom's mood swings, but eventually my parents took the sun and the dogs away. My father constructed some kind of light-blocking shades out of cardboard and tin foil and secured them to the outside of my bedroom windows one night after I had fallen asleep. I remember being confused when I woke up, just waiting for the sun to come up. I was still and quiet for what seemed like a really long time and I could not understand why the sun wasn't doing its usual thing. That's the first time that I remember getting that sick, anxious feeling in my stomach. I thought something was really wrong, like it could have been the end of the world. I said the dogs' names very quietly, just to make sure they were with me. They were. I heard them rustle and I felt Basil's breath go by the bars looking for me. Soon after, my dad made a big dog bed so that the dogs could start sleeping downstairs. My mom said that they had been panting too loudly. I stayed in that dark, silent, dogless room until my brother was born. It was then that I began to understand that everything that I cared about could be taken away on a whim, depending on my mother's mood, and that I was a nuisance.[1]

Sarah's Story

The first-born daughter of two alcoholic parents, Sarah was confined in her crib in a darkened room for hours at a time when she was a toddler. Although her parents had a great deal of money, Sarah was often hungry, learning to feed herself breakfast on her own while her parents recovered from drinking the night before. When Sarah couldn't reach the cereal, she improvised by eating cat food. Sarah became the primary caregiver for her brother when he was born, and started drinking "wine water" with support from both parents when she was twelve years old. Sarah was told that the "wine water" would calm her nerves. She was offered the drink on the first day of a new school year, and could never find her classes without assistance. She was offered the drink before a big test, with disastrous results. Sarah would force herself to sit in the front row of class, to try to prevent herself from falling asleep from the effects of the wine-water mixture. One time when her efforts failed, Sarah was found asleep in the front row. Her teacher contacted Child Protective Services after smelling alcohol on Sarah's breath. Although a case worker conducted monthly visits to Sarah's home, the agency eventually closed the case. Sarah's comfort came from her family's pets. She learned unconditional love from the two large dogs that lived in her home, and as an adult, she has chosen a career that allows her to rescue abused and neglected animals.

Sarah's story is unique, but she is not alone. There are countless women like her, who are coping with their neglect histories in every aspect of their adult lives. The focus of this book is not on the adult who was so severely neglected in childhood that s/he was removed from the home. The focus of this book is on the adult whose story never made headlines, but who was subjected to a persistent lack of empathy, emotional distance, and abuse throughout childhood, to the extent that s/he felt unwanted, unloved, ignored and invisible.

Although the details of the case stories told throughout this book are varied, the aftereffects of each child's neglect history are similar. Some men may relate well to many of the aftereffects listed in this chapter, but it is especially true for women who have been neglected by their mothers.

Although things have changed in recent years, there is still some unwillingness to acknowledge that women can be neglectful parents. It is sometimes the nature of neglect, however, that forces the repetition of it. If women become mothers prior to resolving their own histories of abuse or neglect, there is a possibility that patterns from their own childhoods might be repeated. More often, women learn "what not to do" in their families of origin, and can heal from their own upbringings while raising their children. The process of parenting can be healing in itself. The variables that determine the repetition of a pattern of neglect are countless, and this book is not written to define them more clearly. This book emphasizes that especially in cases of same-gender neglect, the "introject," or "internalized neglectful parent," must be explored as one of the most relevant factors in resolution and healing.

If a female child is introduced to her world by a woman who respects herself and her daughter, that child will have no concerns about an *introject* as an adult. The concerns come about as a result of neglect, abandonment, and abuse. Women begin to fear as young adults that they are fated to transform into their neglectful mothers. They often hear the very beliefs in their own heads that their mothers described to them years ago. Although these women may make valiant attempts at ignoring these beliefs, the voices in their heads are persistent, and the beliefs often seem to interfere in their daily lives nonetheless.

When women are neglected as children, they sometimes do not trust that they exist at all. As young adults, many women suffer with eating disorders, or carrying extra weight, simply to prove to themselves that they are here. Neglected young adults tend to abuse themselves in order to relieve the emptiness of their lives. Some cut themselves; some use drugs or alcohol to numb the pain; some enter into relationships with partners who continue to treat them in neglectful ways.

The pain of neglect is often obscured. Sometimes, women are not abused, but merely forgotten. It is difficult to measure how damage occurs, but in listening to hundreds of adults describe their histories, I have learned that neglect may have an even more insidious effect than abuse. The pain of feeling abandoned by those who are supposed to love us is often unmatched by physical wounds that can heal.

Being ignored can cause an intelligent child to look for reasons that her life is the way it is. We are not born with good self-esteem. It is developed over time, with the integration of positive feedback from the nurturing people around us. If there is a lack of nurturing in a child's environment, the child does not learn to nurture herself. She begins, instead, to blame herself for the neglect. She may develop specific reasons why the neglect is occurring, or she may have a generalized feeling of being bad in some way. The little girl cannot become angry with her family for the neglect. She has too much hope that they will love her someday. So, she turns that anger inward, against herself. Internalized anger becomes a means of self-expression and self-hate. It becomes a survival skill that allows this child to make some sense of a world that is too chaotic and painful to conceptualize in any other way.

There are some similar aftereffects for men with neglectful fathers, but boys tend to externalize their anger more than girls do, and internalize their pain. Women in our culture are raised to be other-oriented. We define ourselves through others, and we think of our loved ones' needs before our own. When young girls are neglected, this cultural foundation of other-orientation evolves and festers within us. We learn to care for our neglectful mothers in the hope that they will someday return the favor. Women are seldom able to access our anger about how we were treated as children, and so we are more likely than men to turn that anger against ourselves, under the guise of depression, overeating, anxiety, self-blame, even panic. In therapy, many of us need to learn to let our anger surface about a neglectful past. The anger is usually buried beneath the pain. It is easier and more acceptable for women to express sadness about abandonment than anger about neglect.

Men, on the other hand, are still raised differently in our culture. It remains more likely that boys will express their anger and bury their pain. Boys are more likely to act out their anger behaviorally, especially if they have witnessed their father's rage. It is more acceptable for young boys to fight back and defend their need to be treated with respect. But at the same time, the anger can accumulate about their neglect, and boys may find themselves pushing people away with their anger rather than bringing them closer with their pain. In therapy with men, anger can appear almost like a defense against their pain. The therapeutic work becomes about accessing the pain buried beneath their rage. For this reason, many men tend to have a different experience with resolution of their neglect histories than women. Men may need to learn to define themselves as victims, while women may need to learn to separate from their "victim identities."

Of course, there are always exceptions to these stereotypical responses to neglect. Women may be angry and men may blame themselves. An example follows from Alice Miller's book, *The Drama of the Gifted Child:*

> A young man, Bob, dreamed: "I see a green meadow, on which there is a white coffin. I am afraid that my mother is in it, but I open the lid and, luckily, it is not my mother but me." If Bob had been able as a child to express his disappointment with his mother—to experience his rage and anger—he could have stayed fully alive.[2]

Healing from a neglect history is about finding balance. It is about allowing the full range of emotions to exist within you, without judging yourself or using self-blame as a means of coping.

Self-blame can begin very early in life as a result of neglect. Some young girls overcompensate for feeling evil inside. They become *parentified,* or *pseudo-mature,*[3] and begin to provide nurturing and care to their own parents, or to their siblings. This is done in the hope that the nurturing will become mutual, but it usually backfires. This particular way of coping may lead to a future selection of partners that are needy and dependent, and in this way, the pattern of neglect continues to repeat itself.

Most neglected children, regardless of gender, develop a system of defenses in order to block their emotions. The discovery and examination of one's defensive structure plays a crucial and pivotal role in healing from neglect. An exploration of defenses, as well as assistance in letting go of those childhood defenses that are most unproductive for us as adults, appears in more detail in chapter 9.

Eventually, if young adults seek therapy to examine their defenses and life patterns, they may discover that the process of treatment will need to include an *un-learning* of what they taught themselves, and a learning of new behaviors. The process of un-learning and re-learning can take a lot longer than simply integrating a new lesson, and neglected adults need to be patient with themselves as a result.

A detailed list of aftereffects follows. If you have a neglect history yourself, you may find some increased understanding and validation in the following pages:

Guilt

It is very difficult for each woman to discuss the true extent of the neglect by her mother without a cloud of guilt. Sometimes, the guilt can be paralyzing. Neglected women feel that they betray their mothers by admitting the truth. Many women come from families where secrets are commonplace, and it is understood that the neglect shall remain a secret as well. Our society often contributes to this difficulty in speaking the truth by perpetuating the myth that all women are inherently nurturing and cannot be neglectful. A psychotherapist and colleague of mine told me a sad story about her own maternal neglect history. She remembers bravely choosing to discuss her history in a group of other therapists at a conference she attended years ago. After she concluded, another therapist responded that her "perception could not be accurate."

Adult women also suppress strong fears of becoming like their neglectful mothers. They may believe that their mothers exist inside of them—the concept called the *introject,* mentioned earlier, will be discussed in more detail later. Self-esteem is often damaged greatly by the internal voices and negative beliefs that have been integrated regarding this introject.

Anger

Once women learn in treatment that guilt can be anger turned inward, against the self, it may become more tolerable for them to cope with the guilt that remains. Women with neglect histories, however, have tremendous difficulty accessing their anger. It is important to note that it is never necessary for women to experience their anger directly at the source of the neglect. Although many women choose to try to renegotiate their relationships with their mothers later in life, this healing work can all be done without that dynamic present. It is only necessary to externalize the anger in some way. Absolutely any way will work. From keeping a journal to punching a pillow—there is no limit to the creativity I have witnessed in helping women to access their anger. One woman sewed a life-sized doll to batter at her whim. Another bought ceramic plates at yard sales, and later, screamed as she hauled them against her garage wall. She reported that even the clean-up felt therapeutic. Others roll up their car windows and have imaginary conversations about what should have been. Men may need to do some similar work to access their pain.

Physical and Emotional Needs

Prior to accessing anger, it is necessary to acknowledge that one's needs were not met. This seems like a simple concept, but the idea of having needs is very alien to women with neglect histories. They learn to ignore and bury their needs, and they tend to do a very good job at it. Women attend initial therapy sessions with numerous presenting problems. Rarely does a woman approach therapy with the notion that "I'm not getting my needs met in my life because I was neglected as a child." This theme is often present, however.

Neglected women are often told that they are "too sensitive," "faking," or they are simply ignored, when they express emotion. Unfortunately, they often cope with painful circumstances, including physical injury, without speaking. One former client remembers playing in her backyard alone, when she was about six years old. She fell from her jungle gym. She landed on her back, scared and shocked. She had broken her wrist, and the pain in her right arm was building. She turned her head slowly toward her house, and saw her mother washing dishes through the kitchen window. Her mother had apparently seen the fall, looked up at her daughter, and looked down again to proceed with her washing. She did not come outside to attend to her daughter's needs. Slowly, it dawned on my client that she would have to get up and walk inside on her own. She rose cautiously, entered the kitchen, and began to cry. When the tears started, her mother responded, "You're faking." The arm around the area of the wrist had started to swell, and grew redder in color. My client pleaded with her father to take her to the hospital the next morning, but he went to work instead. He had difficulty standing up to my client's controlling mother as well. Finally, two days after the injury occurred, my client's father consented to take her to a doctor, who was able to place her arm in a cast. This incident left lasting scars on many levels. Children are often blamed for their injuries, and treated as if they are purposely being annoying to their neglectful parents.

Hygiene

Often, neglected children learn about hygiene from school, friends, or television. Young friends can be cruel, and I have heard many stories about children who were singled out and embarrassed in school because, for example, they were not yet using deodorant. One woman remembers attending fifth grade ashamed, because some children had used spray paint to write "Jill Jones stinks" on the outside wall of the elementary school.

Young women entering puberty find that time of life difficult in the best of all possible worlds, but neglected young women are often especially lost and confused during this time. There is no education at home about sexuality and menstruation. One woman rode her bicycle to the pharmacy to buy sanitary pads when her period started. Her mother was a college professor, but she had no time or energy to teach her own daughter what she needed to know.

Work Ethic

Neglected women tend to shine in their work environments, as they often did as children in school. Work is a place to prove oneself, and sometimes, to be appreciated. Unfortunately, it can be a place to be exploited as well. Many women who were neglected as children become perfectionists who have trouble delegating work to others. They believe that they are not replaceable, and often, they produce more work than their peers. Frequently, other people take credit for their hard work. Of course, men may have a similar experience regarding work ethic, especially if they never received guidance, validation or approval from their fathers.

One severely neglected former client took on much of the workload of her critical female boss. During her therapy, my client realized how much her work ethic was a symbolic replaying of the role reversal with her own mother. After five years in the same position, she was doing her manager's job, while her manager worked part-time, from home. It was not long before my client started to explore her talents more fully, with the goal of self-employment.

If a neglected woman has an inappropriately critical boss, chances are she will not respond to the criticism with anger. She may have some inner resentment, but usually, she will respond to criticism by doing even more, working even harder, and taking on more and more responsibility. Because the extra work is not usually adequately compensated, the work dynamic becomes very familiar to the neglected woman. It is often very similar to the dynamic from childhood.

If a neglected man has an inappropriately critical or exploitive male boss, chances are better that he will express anger about his exploitation. It is also more likely that his neglect history will display itself as a "problem with authority." He may take less time than a woman in a similar work situation to branch out on his own, to avoid the dynamic with his boss altogether. He is much less likely to appease a male authority figure by working harder.

Chores

Many young children take care of responsibilities well beyond their capacity when there is neglect at home. They may cook for the family when their mothers are sick, or clean for the entire household on a regular basis. They may be responsible for making breakfast for themselves and their siblings, and getting others ready for school. One former client remarked that she took care of absolutely everything around the house, while balancing her schoolwork and her younger brother's needs. She remembers her mother's friends arriving at the house, and remarking that they had never seen such a young girl handling such a large vacuum. Other people would comment about my client's cleaning, by saying, "I wish my daughter would do that in my house!" but my client's mother never thanked her for her efforts.

Creating a Home

Neglect, like other forms of trauma and abuse, can produce opposite effects. In creating a home environment, some women become hoarders, while others' homes are chaotic and messy, while still others struggle with purchasing even one piece of furniture. One former client used to "personify" all of her belongings. Personification is a defense that enables children to universalize their pain and abandonment. It is the ability to give a voice to inanimate objects—a voice that a neglected child can relate to. My former client began collecting antiques when she was young. She had started babysitting at the age of eleven, and she saved her money in order to purchase old furniture. She learned about the different styles of antiques, her favorites being Mission and Victorian furniture. She remembers having a beautiful old oak table with a tooled copper top, originally from an English pub. When she had difficulty with insomnia, she would turn to face the table near her bedside, and tell herself: if this table made it through the last hundred years and it still survives in such good condition, then I can survive too. This was a self-soothing behavior that continued into my client's adulthood. She still assigns traits to inanimate objects, and her husband sometimes bears the consequences. One of her biggest pet peeves, for example, is when her husband places plates in the dishwasher that touch each other. She believes, in her child self, that the plates could be hurt during the wash cycle. Although she has reached the point where she can joke about this with her husband, personifying objects served as a strong defense and survival skill when this client was small.

Money

Women who were neglected as children have trouble spending money on themselves. They find it too easy to convince themselves that they don't need whatever it is that they're thinking about purchasing. They can justify the frugality, but often, underneath, is the sense that they remain undeserving. The frugal nature of these women seems to be prevalent regardless of how much money is available to be spent. Contrary to this behavior, is the generosity and thoughtfulness that exists when neglected women spend money on other people. One woman currently offers a room in her home to a roommate, without charge. Another has financially supported several of her ex-boyfriends. Money is often symbolic of needs. Many men with neglect histories may also relate to this category.

Trust

After the experience of maternal neglect, trust is always damaged. Again, as with other trauma, extreme opposite effects occur. Some women trust indiscriminately, others do not trust anyone at all. Some waver between the two avenues. They trust until they are betrayed, and then may resort to total withdrawal from people. When withdrawal becomes isolating and lonely, they trust with no boundaries once again. Therapy can be extremely helpful in establishing criteria for trust.

Friendships

More often than not, women with maternal neglect histories experience similar dynamics in their friendships, as they resonate with the mother-daughter relationship. They are often perceived as very "together," with no problems. They are the "givers," the soothers and comforters, the nurturers of others. It is not necessarily a choice for women to play this role, until the pattern of behavior is explored. Often, women wish for someone to "swoop in" to help them in the ways they are so willing to help. Unfortunately, no one ever does. There is no replacement in adulthood for a lack of good mothering in childhood. The loss needs to be grieved at last, which creates the opportunity to move beyond the past.

Hypervigilance

Children who are accustomed to monitoring the moods of their parents become adults who can read people with ease. Adult children of alcoholics, especially first-born adult daughters, are exceptionally skilled in this area. Most can walk into a room and detect the moods of its inhabitants within seconds. This hypervigilant observance becomes so ingrained in the individual that it requires no work—it is simply like a sixth sense. The problem exists when neglected women believe that everyone has this skill. They expect to be read in the way that they are able to read others. When this seldom occurs in their lives, women feel abandoned and alone. It appears that no one can understand them.

Although hypervigilance can lead to feeling isolated and alone, it can also be developed and utilized in many aspects of one's life, as a clear advantage. It is one of the few aftereffects of neglect and abuse that can be worn as a badge of courage and survival.

Food

Neglected women may use food to deprive themselves in some way. One client has re-examined her need to eat the same thing every day. "It's cheap and nourishing," she reports. She will open a can of tuna fish, make a salad, and bake a potato. Another former client reported a history of living between two homes, after her parents' divorce. Her mother ate only "seeds and sprouts," while her father served meat and potatoes. This client would become sick frequently, after leaving her father's home and feeling nearly starved at her mother's home. She would stash candy from her father's house, and her mother would go through her knapsack upon her return, depriving her of each piece. Not surprisingly, this client married (and later divorced) a man who controlled the food she cooked for her family. She could only buy the groceries that he deemed appropriate. One of the greatest freedoms following this client's divorce was being able to cook her favorite meal, salmon with mushrooms and vegetables. She will never again deprive herself of the food she loves to eat.

For some women and men, the opposite reaction to food is evident. Neglected children often eat to comfort themselves as adults. Nurturing oneself with food is sometimes a replacement for a loving relationship. To assuage their guilt, comfort foods are often offered by neglectful and abusive parents after an incident of abuse or neglect occurs. Children may accept ice cream, for example, after a sexual assault by someone they know and love. The mixed messages and associations that are created between food, abuse, neglect, and love are extremely confusing throughout life.

Pregnancy

Some women with neglect histories have terrible fears of becoming pregnant. This may have to do with the concept of the *introject*—the fear of transforming into one's mother if one chooses to parent. Some may feel repulsed by the idea of childbirth. One former client felt that she could never give birth to a daughter, although she had less anxiety about having a son. Another client was so afraid that she was pregnant when her period was late, that she purchased four pregnancy tests at the pharmacy. She used each kit, and each reported negative results. This was not enough to quell her anxiety, so she made an appointment at Planned Parenthood. The staff there reiterated that she was not pregnant, but it was only the arrival of menstruation that calmed her fears. I am unsure if this client's anxiety had more to do with her fear of pregnancy, her fear of becoming her mother, or her lack of trust.

Gifts and Compliments

It is difficult for a woman with a neglect history to accept a compliment without negating it in some way. The negation can happen internally ("If they only knew me, they wouldn't think I was intelligent"), or it can be verbalized directly ("This dress? It's so old it has wrinkles!"). One of the tasks of therapy is to unlearn this behavior, and learn to accept a compliment, however counterintuitive it may feel, with a "thank you," and later, with the addition of a statement of pride.

Gifts were often non-existent for neglected children, and sometimes, birthdays and holidays were forgotten. As a result, gifts and surprises have negative connotations in neglected women's lives. Gifts may also have been thoughtless. I have a client whose mother recently bought her a size 14 blouse for her birthday. My client is a size 2.

Partners

Women with maternal neglect histories may have sexual abuse histories as well. Neglect sets a foundation for a lack of affection and attention, and often, there is no education about appropriate touch. These women are used to appeasing others, and sacrificing their own needs to do so. Neglect histories can serve as a backdrop for future victimization.

When women have been neglected as children, they may not recognize continued neglect from a partner. If they have also been abused, then neglect can actually appear safe and familiar, as it is perceived as the absence of abuse. Women may choose partners who neglect them because their standards for mutuality in relationships are so low. The patterns of neglect in intimate relationships are crucial to explore.[4]

This book is about healing and recovery. It is designed to help adult children and their therapists to combat the aftereffects of neglect histories. Not every story that follows has a happy ending. Each story is unique and similar at once.

It is my sincere hope that the following *History of Parental Neglect Questionnaire* will help struggling adults to recognize themselves more clearly on their journeys to live past their neglect. For therapists working with neglected adults, chapter 19 details the use of this questionnaire in treatment.

HISTORY OF PARENTAL NEGLECT QUESTIONNAIRE

- Were you ridiculed or criticized for expressing feelings as a child?
- Did you feel invisible, or transparent?
- How did you learn about good personal hygiene?
- Do you find yourself feeling envious or sad when you see a loving relationship between a mother and her child, or a father and his child?
- Do you have difficulty making life decisions because of a lack of guidance from your parents?
- Are you conscious of your own emotional needs? If you are, do you have trouble expressing them to the people you care about?
- Do you blame yourself for everything? Do you justify feeling unloved in your own mind?
- Do you overeat when you are feeling angry, upset, or afraid?
- Do you have trouble spending money on yourself, even when you have expendable income?
- Do you neglect your own physical needs, or push your body past its limits?
- Do you try to bury your fears, anxieties, or sadness, because there is no one you trust to listen?
- Do you choose partners who need you, so they won't abandon you?
- Do you take care of your partner better than you take care of yourself?
- Do you overachieve at work? Does your boss take credit for the work you do?
- Can you "absorb" another person's pain?
- Do you believe the negative feedback you get, while thinking any positive feedback is inaccurate?
- Can you "read" other people's moods better than your own?
- Do you prefer negative attention to no attention at all?
- Do you sabotage your success because you believe you don't deserve it?
- Do you deprive yourself of happiness, for fear that it will be taken away?

Chapter Two

Post-Traumatic Stress Revisited

Rock-a-Bye baby on the treetop,
When the wind blows the cradle will rock,
When the bough breaks the cradle will fall,
And down will come baby, cradle and all.

—*Lullaby, Origins Uncertain*[1]

Rumors exist about the origins of the lyrics of this popular lullaby from as far back as the 1500s. It is thought that the lyrics were written by a pilgrim who sailed to America on the Mayflower, after his observation of Native American mothers who rocked their babies to sleep in birch bark cradles, suspended from the branches of trees. There is also a rumor that the lyrics were written by a frustrated babysitter in 1872. Regardless of their origin, the lyrics of the first stanza of this lullaby speak volumes about the instinctive nature of an infant's relationship with mortality.

In the *Diagnostic and Statistical Manual of Mental Disorders, DSM IV-R*, the differential diagnosis of Post-Traumatic Stress Disorder (PTSD) is written with the reminder that "the stressor must be of an extreme (i.e., life-threatening) nature."[2] It is much easier to diagnose clients who have been raped, or robbed, or physically assaulted and victimized, with PTSD. There is an event that occurred, a tangible stressor. On the contrary, with adult survivors of neglect, there is no one event that occurred. There is an accumulation of rejection, abandonment, and hurt from childhood that creates the foundation for every future interaction.

Children are so much more vulnerable than adults, partly because they have scarce resources available to them. In *Why Love Matters*, Sue Gerhardt reminds us that children "are much closer to the possibility of death. They cannot survive alone and are highly dependent on adults to provide for their basic needs of food, shelter, warmth and comfort. Without the goodwill of adults, they could indeed die. In this sense, experiences that would not be a matter of life and death for an adult may well be experienced as such by a child."

Gerhardt goes on to clarify that "childhood trauma may also result from a much wider and more innocuous seeming range of circumstances. From an adult perspective, 'abuse' tends to mean the more gross and visible examples of maltreatment such as hitting and injuring children, or violating them sexually. It is much harder, I think, for some adults to appreciate that being told you are 'a stupid waste of space' or being left unattended and alone are also traumatic for dependent children. The essential aspect of trauma is that it generates doubts about surviving—either as a body, but equally as a psychological self."[3]

When we read the initial criteria for PTSD, we must be sure to acknowledge the fear, desperation, and loneliness of the neglected young child:

> A. The person has been exposed to a traumatic event in which both of the following have been present:
>
> (1) the person experienced, witnessed, or was confronted with an event or events that involved actual or threatened death or serious injury, or a threat to the physical integrity of self or others (2) the person's response involved intense fear, helplessness, or horror.
>
> **Note:** In children, this may be expressed instead by disorganized or agitated behavior.

Neglect is traumatic. Yet, it is much more difficult to diagnose. Few clients will acknowledge a neglect history as their presenting problem. Men and women with neglect histories will most likely use minimization as a coping strategy, or defense. You will need to know how to explore their histories, and what to look for, as you guide your clients on their journeys through the painful awareness of neglect. Clients may also present with a complex defensive structure. Some of these defenses may be results of a neglect history that led to physical abuse or sexual trauma. There is a great deal of overlap between PTSD criteria and defensive structure, including the use of denial or avoidance. I approach this overlap in chapter 9. There is also overlap between PTSD and the phases of grief. Trauma is always about loss. I approach this overlap in more detail in chapter 13.

There are also many ways that our bodies remember childhood trauma. Jasmin Cori (2007) describes physical symptoms that may appear as aftereffects for adults, in her book *Healing from Trauma:*

> Which of the following do you see in your body?
>
> - A sense of contraction with chronically tight muscles?
> - A tendency to hold your breath at times, and to breathe shallowly most of the time?

- Pain at the base of your neck, often causing headaches?
- Cold hands and feet?
- Poor posture from trying to protect your heart area?
- Back pain from trying to protect your soft underbelly?[4]

Cori discusses how this physical contraction helps survivors of trauma to feel safe in the world. Although the contraction protects us, it also makes our world smaller. We accept fewer challenges; we take fewer risks. Cori reminds us that "a universal response to trauma is pulling in and contracting. All life forms do this. When you contract, you're a smaller target."[5]

Cori describes this need to contract as a way of coping that keeps us safe, while simultaneously limiting us in our lives. She refers us to trauma experts Diane and Laurence Heller: "Everything is contracted—your relationships, your emotions, your senses, your body. Your life may become very narrow in an attempt to stay safe."[6]

When we work with survivors of trauma and neglect, we must gently assist our clients to extend themselves—to expand, instead of contract. Building trust in therapeutic relationships combats PTSD by allowing individuals to expand, despite their fears of rejection, anger, criticism, violence, and re-victimization.

I currently supervise a graduate student in social work whose name is Lindsey. Lindsey has an innate skill in engaging clients, but she is often doubtful about her abilities. Although she reports learning a great deal in school, Lindsey has enormous difficulty integrating theory with practice. Recently she acknowledged to me that "I find the theory very interesting, but I just don't understand how it applies to my clients. Maybe it's because we're learning theory about children, and I'm working with adults. Maybe it's because my adult clients have been through so much trauma, and the theories don't seem to address that."

If you are familiar with Lindsey's dilemma, this book can help. When we learn about different theorists and their respective ideas, we are taught about those theories as they apply *in the best of all possible worlds.* We need to take what we learn and reapply those theories as they relate to people with neglect histories.

Chapter Three

Magical Thinking: Finding Power in Helplessness

As young children transition from toddlers to preschoolers, we know that their language skills advance greatly. Simultaneously, they begin to develop different modes of thinking. Swiss psychologist Jean Piaget thought of preschool children as "preoperational"[1]—meaning they do not yet use logic. Instead, children between the ages of about four and seven years old often understand the world through the use of "magical thinking."

For a young child raised in a healthy environment, magical thinking can be associated with healthy narcissism. The world revolves around the child—not because the child is selfish, but because there is no perception of another's perspective. If a young girl is sad, she may cry. In her perception, when it rains, the sky may also be crying. She may personify objects, or develop imaginary friends. Her dolls may have character traits that she sees in herself. This is part of why play therapy is so widely used in working with children, and why it produces such substantial outcomes.

The child believes in magic. Sometimes, the child perceives that he is all-powerful. Recently, my husband and I discovered www.kideo.com, a website where one can purchase videos of children's favorite cartoon characters and superheroes. A "Kideo" DVD, however, transposes the face of your little loved one onto the cartoon character or superhero. A child can star in his or her own animated DVD. We purchased a Spiderman video and personalized it with the adorable face of our nephew Leo. Each time Spiderman removes his mask in the video, Leo's face appears.[2]

We sent the video to Leo's parents for his birthday. We heard immediately that Leo would not stop watching it. He requested a Spiderman costume for Halloween, Spiderman T-shirts and sweatshirts, and began to pose like Spiderman in the video. He demanded that his parents call him "Spiderman."

The Kideo DVD manufacturers have successfully capitalized on the ability of children to utilize magical thinking.

The innocence of magical thinking, however, can sometimes take a tragic turn. In Eric Clapton's autobiography, for example, he recalls his terrible heartache and grief after the death of his son, Conor. On the night before his tragic death, Clapton had taken Conor on a one-on-one outing to the circus. The next day, Conor fell to his death—he fell forty-nine stories from a high-rise window.[3] Is it possible that this innocent little boy thought he could fly, like the acrobats on the flying trapeze at the circus?

When magical thinking takes place in the mind of a child with an abuse or neglect history, it takes on a different, more insidious flavor. A little girl of four might tell herself that if her room were cleaner, for example, her father might stop hurting her at night. Magical thinking can be compounded by threats or intimidation by our physical or sexual abusers. If an adult woman was abused between the ages of four and seven, she will undoubtedly need to revisit her beliefs from that time. The ability to think magically also allows the victim of abuse to believe that she is responsible. It gives the child an explanation, and may help that child to feel a sense of power in a world of helplessness. It is a false belief that is also associated with grief. We blame ourselves after our loved ones die, for similar reasons. It is too difficult to see ourselves as helpless and unable to do anything to change the situation. So, we find power through blaming ourselves. It is a very common and insidious lie that children tell themselves in order to cope with the pain of neglect and abuse. *If I do this differently, it will stop happening to me.* Although it is not a defense, magical thinking can take on the role of a defense for an abuse or neglect survivor. It is a preferable fantasy world that can easily become a child's reality.

If we were forced to live in fear, for example, magical thinking can assist us in blocking that fear. I worked with a survivor of sexual abuse who believed that the color yellow could protect her from harm. She wore a bright-yellow sweatshirt on a regular basis.

I worked with another survivor whose thinking in adulthood remained magical. She believed that nothing could hurt her. This woman was abused by all of the males in her family of origin, both physically and sexually. She had successfully blocked her sense of fear, and continued to prove to herself that she was powerful as an adult. She challenged herself to cope with danger. Once, she told me a story of how she casually walked into an unfamiliar house with the front door ajar, during a robbery. Another time, she tried to befriend two large attack dogs that guarded an outdoor business from behind a tall fence.

A very explicit example of magical thinking occurs below, in Heide's story. She was able to utilize her imagination and fantasy world to survive her abuse, as well as to maintain a loving relationship with her father. It was only after she started individual therapy, over twenty years ago, that the magical beliefs were confronted and put to rest.

Here is Heide's story: I started therapy with Lori after my daughter was born. I hadn't even wanted to have a baby out of fear that I would hate my own child, not be able to love it. How could I? I had no experience of being loved by a parent. I didn't voice my fears to my husband because I didn't want him to think I was a horrible person. He wanted a child, and so I became pregnant. I loved my pregnancy and felt very connected to my baby as she was growing inside me. But whether I would feel the same when she was born haunted me the whole nine months.

I was extremely relieved and stunned at how easy it was to not only love my daughter, but also nurture and protect her. All of that was easy, but at the same time, memories of my own childhood were emerging in very disturbing ways. I felt as though my daughter was in constant danger. I was not comfortable allowing anyone else to hold her. If she was in someone else's arms, my anxiety would build until I couldn't take it anymore and I would snatch her back. I would put her in her crib at night and be overwhelmed with thoughts that someone was in her room about to harm her. I spent my nights going in to check her room, going back to bed for only a few minutes before having to get up and check her again. I don't know how she did it, but she always slept straight through the night. I started spying on my husband while he was downstairs watching television; I was certain he was up to some devious behavior. During sex, I would think he was my father, and at that point I knew it was time to get some help.

It was a bold move to make. My mother's approval of me depended on my behaving in a very certain way. Starting therapy was going to cause some family discord. But I was an adult with a family of my own and I didn't need her approval anymore. In fact, it had become very difficult to spend any time with her. Any contact with her made me feel badly about myself. When I was a child, my mother made it no secret to me that I was a burden, that I was ugly, an idiot, and that she couldn't "stomach" me. She would say these things on a fairly regular basis with such a look of disgust on her face that I knew she really meant it. She would smirk with pleasure when I was sad or upset, and so I learned not to show my feelings. I knew other mothers who hugged their children, made sure they were clean and fed. I remember thinking that if my mother didn't love me, then who possibly could?

Well, my father did. He gave me some attention, compliments, and he would spend time with me. And he was fun! He would make up these elaborate games and teach me to paint on canvas, or make other creative projects. He always said I was just like him. That was the father I loved. But there was another side of him. Both of my parents were terrible alcoholics. My mother would drink all day and my father would drink all night. My father's mood could change without warning. He could be fun and loving in one instant and then, without provocation, turn angry and dangerous. My mother would just lock herself in her bedroom with her vodka, leaving me and my two sisters to fend for ourselves. I learned about my father's moods very quickly, and stayed close to him even when he was angry because I didn't like being taken by surprise. My sisters avoided him—which is why I think I got less of the physical abuse. But he would make me sleep naked with my mattress on the floor and I never understood why my bottom was so sore the next morning. I remember telling my mother of my discomfort and she grudgingly slapped some Vaseline on me and sent me to school. It wasn't long before I would just get the Vaseline out myself because it was easier to do that than ask my hung-over mother to help me—knowing she didn't even like me.

I was able to explain away the night happenings as something separate from my father. The house was very old and surely haunted. I knew if I woke up in the same position I had fallen asleep in, that the evil in the house didn't get me. I would have a recurring dream that a demon was after me and I would try to hide inside the walls. But even in my dreams I was always found. There was no escape from the danger when it was the house itself that possessed it. And that was how I was able to believe for so long that I had a good father. But in therapy, all that changed. I had to face the reality of my childhood. It was devastating and painful to realize that not only was he *not* a good father; he was my abuser. That my mother not only didn't protect me, but allowed him to do what he did. When I told her that I was addressing sexual abuse in therapy she became animated by the fact that I was going to acknowledge what an awful parent he was. She told me that she knew all along that he had an inappropriate fixation with me and accused me of enjoying it. I knew then that in order for me to heal, I had to end all contact with her.

Taking a break from my mother also meant taking a break from my younger sister, who was my mother's defender. My sister was extremely angry with me for bringing up the past, for "attacking" our mother, and she constantly accused me of lying. My older sister, on the other hand, was my biggest supporter. Only eleven months older than me, she had no choice but to take on a parental role when we were children. She remembered things that were too painful for me to stand, and as my memories unfolded, she would back them up with her own recollections. Without her, my healing would have been so much more difficult. She was my hero through all my therapy and though she was not in therapy herself, I think we both healed together.

My whole life, I felt as though I was not deserving of anything. Not even the most basic of needs, such as food or protection. I had been taught never to ask for anything. As a child I had stepped on a rusty nail and my foot had become very infected. I guess I was limping around because my neighbor, Linda, had stopped me to take a look at it. My stomach sank when she said, "Tell your mother if she doesn't bring you to the doctor immediately, I will." I was brought to the doctor, and my foot was scraped out, disinfected, and bandaged. The whole time I wished Linda brought me instead, because then I wouldn't have been yelled at the whole way there and back and made to feel as though I had created a problem. It was easier to keep quiet about such things and to this day, although I have gotten better at it, I have a very difficult time asking for anything.

I had to learn in therapy how to set up boundaries for myself. I had always been very aware of other people's boundaries but had a difficult time setting up my own. Being sexually abused by my father and men he brought home from the bar made me an easy mark to be molested in later years by my best friend's father and a high school monitor. I had sex with boys I didn't care for because I felt I couldn't say no. I married at a young age, a man I knew I didn't love. And of all of the horrors in my life, the worst was leaving that marriage without my daughter because my husband convinced me that I had no right to take her. I was reduced to seeing her once a week for dinner, and every other weekend. She is a grown woman now, with children of her own. I watch her with my grandchildren and see how loving and attentive she is with them. She is a beautiful mother, one her children are lucky to have. My daughter grew up surrounded by people who loved, encouraged, and nurtured her and now she is passing that legacy on to her children. I can't help but take some pride in the fact that a cycle has been broken.

I ended up getting married for a second time, to a man I did love. For most of that marriage, I worked at a job caring for developmentally delayed adults. It was a high burn-out job, challenging both mentally and physically. While working there I studied to become a personal fitness trainer, something I had great passion for. When I passed the exam, I was ready to move on to a job in the fitness field. I worked full-time at my current job and took on a training job part-time in the evenings. My hope, though, was to become a trainer at the gym I was a member of. It was a year before an opening came up. When I got the call, I told my husband I wanted to quit my full-time job so I could spend time building up a clientele at the gym. He was very resistant to that idea and so I worked at all three places for a while. I was hardly spending any time at the gym, making it impossible to get any real business. When I would explain this to my husband, he would tell me that we couldn't afford to have me quit that job and if the training didn't work out, it wasn't meant to be. But I knew I had to give this every effort if I were to succeed. And so without his blessing, I quit my job and spent all my free time working at the gym. It took about six months for me to build up a strong client base. My husband openly doubted that I could make this work and constantly asked me how much money I was bringing in. Had I not been through therapy, I never would have dreamed of going against my husband's wishes to do something that I wanted. Even when I became a successful trainer, my husband never acknowledged it. He never once congratulated me or said he was proud of my accomplishment.

He once told me that, because of my history, I didn't have the same capacity for happiness that he did. I remember it being so hurtful at the time, but maybe it is a true thing. I don't know; I feel pretty happy! I have a strong following as a trainer, I live in a beautiful apartment on my own and am young enough to enjoy my grandchildren thoroughly! I look back on my year of therapy (twenty years ago, really?) as the greatest investment in my life that I ever made. I always tell my daughter that she saved my life. It was because of her that I walked through Lori's door, sat on a chair, cried for an entire hour, and began my journey of healing.

Heide's ability to think magically about her father may have saved her from a childhood of constant fear. She felt unloved and unprotected by her mother. Heide was unable to dissociate from her pain and her longing for a mother's love. Because she could pretend that her father was not a demon, Heide was able to cope with feeling abandoned by her mother on a daily basis. Magical thinking helped Heide to make sense of her world. She was too vulnerable to admit that both parents were causing harm. Magical thinking was not just a clever survival skill that Heide mastered. Her ability to pretend may have kept her sane.

The Glass Castle

There are surprisingly few widely read books about parental neglect that are written for the general public. The *New York Times* bestseller *The Glass Castle,* by Jeannette Walls (2005), is an exception. This masterful memoir is written through a child's eyes, and although parental neglect is never addressed directly, it is evident on every page. Ms. Walls never called her mother narcissistic or addressed her hoarding directly. Although she did confront her father's alcoholism, she never judged his paranoia. In this loving memoir, Jeannette Walls described the circumstances that led to her family's homelessness with compassion and forgiveness. Even when confronted by a case worker from social services who made a surprise visit to her home, Jeannette held tightly to her loyalty to her parents. Her major concern was not the lack of heat and food and emotional support, but rather the fear of being removed from her home and having to live separately from her siblings. It is clear to the reader that her siblings saved Jeannette from repeating the pattern of neglect in her adulthood.

Near the beginning of *The Glass Castle*, Jeannette Walls described a conversation with her father that was very touching. The conversation occurred with each of her siblings as well. During the holiday season when Jeannette was a young girl, her parents could not afford to buy Christmas presents. Jeannette's father compensated for the lack of presents by enhancing his children's ability to think magically.

Jeannette's father gathered his three children, one by one, under the stars. He told each of them to "pick out your favorite star." Jeannette remembered: "He told me I could have it for keeps. He said it was my Christmas present."

Later that evening, after Jeannette and her siblings had each designated a star as their own, Jeannette recalled: "We laughed about all the kids who believed in the Santa myth and got nothing for Christmas but a bunch of cheap plastic toys." "Years from now, when all the junk they got is broken and long forgotten," Dad said, "you'll still have your stars."[4] Maybe we can forgive Jeannette's dad's grandiosity in creating this lasting memory for his children.

Play Therapy

The content of play in children with abuse and neglect histories can be very revealing. I worked with an adult survivor named Dana. Dana successfully repressed a trauma and sexual abuse history by her grandfather. He would bathe her, sexually abuse her, and then hold her head under water as a threat against telling the secret. Once this memory was retrieved, she was able to date her abuse back to the age of five.

Dana remembers playing with matches in her backyard. She would light her dolls on fire. She had learned about Joan of Arc being burned at the stake, and Dana would destroy her dolls by "killing" them in the same way. At Christmastime one year, Dana stole the baby Jesus from her church's nativity scene. Despite suspicion and ridicule, Dana never acknowledged her theft, and never returned the baby to the scene. I imagine that the baby met with the same fate as Dana's other dolls. How is a child to grapple with the notion of a loving God and savior, when she has had to cope with such an evil world? She may take control of that world, through play.

During the early 1990s, I studied with an author named Bobbie Kaufman. She wrote a book entitled *Silent Screams and Hidden Cries*, about the drawings of children who have witnessed abuse, or who have been victims themselves. In some of the drawings in the book, there is evidence of magical thinking. One drawing in particular has fascinated me for many years. It is a pencil drawing of a small girl whose neck is depicted as long and thin, like a giraffe's neck. Kaufman explained in one of her presentations that young children under the age of eight do not often draw necks at all. They draw round heads atop round bodies, or they draw stick figures. The neck in children's drawings is often unaccounted for.[5] This drawing, however, was strikingly different than the usual style that Kaufman described. The neck in this drawing represented the separation of head and heart. This little girl had witnessed the physical abuse of her mother by her alcoholic father. She had been a victim of sexual abuse as well. Although she created this drawing when she was six years old, not only is the neck present in the drawing, but it is also adorned with a necklace. There is no other clothing or accessory depicted. Perhaps in believing that she had the neck of a giraffe, this little girl became more capable of detaching from her feelings and living in her head. This is another example of magical thinking, externalized through drawing. The drawing is reprinted here, with the author's permission.

Chapter Four

Weight Matters: Using Food for Comfort

> *I thought I wasn't good enough, but I realize that my ability to choose the right guy is what's not good enough. How can you pick someone who will really love you when you have enormous unresolved pain and fear? When you feel unworthy from lack of love? When you have a phony love for food and no trust in real people? I've noticed that biting and chewing is important to me in emotional eating, and I think that is about rage . . . biting and destroying.*
>
> —Megan, 37

Food can become very comforting to those who have been neglected by their parents. The weight issues that follow these children into adulthood are complex and confusing. Extra weight for some women can feel like a shield to protect them from intimacy.

In *Feeding the Hungry Heart* (1982), Geneen Roth explains:

> When my mother's discontent was directed at me, I convinced myself that she didn't love me. Because she was, at the same time, critical of my body, I told myself her lack of love was because I was fat. . . .
>
> Fat becomes your protection from anything you need protection from: men, women, sexuality (blossoming or developed), frightening feelings of any sort; it becomes your rebellion, your way of telling your parents, your lovers, the society around you, that you don't have to be who they want you to be. Fat becomes your way of talking. It says: I need help, go away, come closer, I can't, I won't, I'm angry, I'm sad. It becomes your vehicle for dealing with every problem you have . . . Eventually it gets so painful that you may be willing to listen to what your fat is saying.[1]

Especially for incest survivors, extra weight can serve as a way to avoid sexuality. But anorexia can also help women to reach this same goal. With neglect as a foundation, and incest following, a young girl may utilize magical thinking in relation to food, by thinking: *If I am not perceived as attractive, then maybe he will leave me alone. . . .*

The problem with this underlying assumption is the belief that the way the young girl looked actually contributed to her abuse. It is another way that incest survivors blame themselves for their circumstances, while attempting to take control of the future. Some women with incest histories were encouraged to turn to comfort foods by their abusers, as a way to bury the secret of sexual abuse. They were "rewarded" after the abuse, with ice cream, or candy. Thus, the child learns to associate comfort foods with nurturing herself, as well as with self-blame. The most famous of these women is Oprah Winfrey.

In a biography about Oprah entitled *Oprah Winfrey: Just the Facts* (2002), by Katherine Krohn, the author discusses Oprah's early childhood. Oprah was raised on a Mississippi farm, by her grandmother, Hattie Mae Lee, until she was six years old. Hattie Mae is credited with teaching Oprah to read by the age of three, and with encouraging her love of books. Oprah read the Bible at a young age, memorized verses and performed them, and started kindergarten at five—way ahead of her classmates in reading and writing.

Oprah was sent to live with her mother and half-sister when her grandmother became ill. Her mother worked long hours, and spent little quality time with Oprah. After only a year, Oprah moved again, to live with her father and stepmother. In third grade, she moved again, back to her mother's home in Milwaukee.

It was here that Oprah was left with her nineteen-year-old cousin, who raped her, took her out for ice cream, and told her not to tell anyone. Oprah was nine years old at the time. She was re-victimized by an uncle and a family friend just a few years later. The abuse by her uncle was ongoing—she kept silent about all of the abuse throughout her childhood.

Oprah began to skip school, steal money from her mother, and run away. She became pregnant at fourteen, and in her seventh month, she delivered a baby boy who lived less than two weeks.

Despite the secrecy surrounding her abuse history, Oprah was able to excel in school and discover her many talents. She received a four-year college scholarship.[2] We are all blessed by her generous nature and the facility in which she speaks to our culture, bringing crucial issues into the public light.

It is much easier to rediscover a sense of self that was already established, then to form a strong identity later in life—from a foundation of emptiness and loss. Oprah developed her intelligence, her value in the world, and her pride in her talents during her early years with her grandmother. She wove her grandmother's love into her identity.

Still, Oprah struggles with her weight. We all witness her struggle, and many of us can empathize. Many incest survivors are threatened about speaking their truths. Many are fed comfort foods after the abuse is over. The connection between food and abuse can have a lasting, devastating impact. Weight can symbolize safety in the world. Weight loss can increase vulnerability. Oprah has amassed a fortune. She can afford the best personal trainer. Yet, this aftereffect of sexual abuse may have plagued her for decades.

For neglect survivors, weight can acknowledge to the world: "I am here—and I have a right to be seen!" To some, it feels powerful to be big. To others, extra weight can be an excuse to continue internal battering and repetition of negative voices.

Food does not cause pain and betrayal like humans do. It can be trusted, at least temporarily, to help us to numb ourselves from the reality of our neglect and abuse. And, it is usually less dangerous than using other substances. For most of us, food is readily available, and easy to access. For those neglected children who were indigent, however, who lived with the feeling of constant hunger on a daily basis, emotional eating can be associated with nurturing the self, with stopping the physical deprivation that accompanied the emotional neglect.

Megan, a current e-therapy client, has been coping with a physical and emotional neglect history for all of her life. She was born into poverty, and there was seldom enough food for her parents and siblings. Megan's parents were both emotionally neglectful, her father was physically abusive, and she was sexually abused by her brother when she was five years old. Megan has been coping more recently with a neglectful, unfaithful husband, a divorce, and becoming a single parent. She has returned to college and has begun to feel less isolated and alone. In therapy, Megan has been working on combating her self-blame and internalized anger with successful attempts to let her rage surface. A chronology of our work together follows:

> *E-therapist: I think it would be great for you to embrace your anger. If it has been buried underneath your eating, it needs to be embraced and dealt with, before you will be able to fully conquer the need for comfort eating. Perhaps you could use some of your precious free time to journal about your anger. Remember that you are not a bad person for feeling angry, and chances are, it has been accumulating for a very long time.*

> Megan: Today while the kids were out, I "had a go" and was surprised by the results. . . . I used paper and markers to draw/write whatever came to mind. . . . well, I literally found this hard lump of anger and without any time for thinking, modifying, or rationalizing, I wrote "brother" in red, and then the word "protec-

tion" and then this thought emerged: "Why was I not protected from him?" I became angry with the weak people in my life that could not protect me, but simultaneously, I felt angry at myself for being small, for being unable to protect myself. Do you think my mother knew about the abuse? Why else would she tell me that she had to return home to protect me from my brother, after her separation from my father? Why else would I remember that statement when I remember so few other things about my childhood?

E-therapist: I think it is very likely that your mother knew. It is also very significant that you remember this statement so vividly. Perhaps it has remained in your memory because you were attempting to feel protected by her, while simultaneously experiencing the abuse and neglect. How does a five-year-old integrate that much confusion?

Megan: I think my problems with food started around the time I was five. It was all I could get hold of (thankfully . . . it could have been heroin when I was older and for one of my sisters it was) it's almost as if the fatness and immaturity are linked (not in a judgmental way).

One thing I'm feeling about my husband's betrayal is that this particular pain is so severe because it is so familiar. It has cracked open the earlier betrayal, as well as my marriage delusions, that I had suppressed. The feelings were so similar that I went into shock for four days after the affair came out. I suppose that if my husband's purpose in my life was to provide two children and to remind me of childhood incest, so I eventually could deal with my obesity and become the person I was meant to be . . . how can something so awful make so much sense all of a sudden?

I am worried about my health—mainly the obesity. I don't want to go back to school fat . . . but I'm still "using" quite a bit. . . . I wish I could wave a magic wand and be healthy, slim, and fit. . . . do you think I have a co-dependent relationship with my body?

E-therapist: I don't think your relationship with your body is co-dependent. I think that you can attempt to convince yourself that eating well and exercising produce wellness, but there's a voice underneath that one—the voice of deprivation. If you feel deprived about food and dieting, then your mind will continue to rebel against dieting even if your body feels better. You have deprived yourself of love in your life, of supportive relationships, because you were extremely deprived as a child. Not just starved for food, but deprived emotionally. You have been isolated in your marriage. How can you find a way to eat well and exercise without feeling the deprivation from the past?

There is a story called "Fat Lady" in a book entitled Love's Executioner, *by Irvin Yalom. He worked with a client in therapy who was obese. As this woman begins to lose weight, she also revisits each loss in her life. She grieves each individual loss that she experienced at each lower weight. Her grief was never processed because she used food to numb her emo-*

tions. Utilizing food to deal with losses is a very powerful mechanism. Your inner child may actually be mad at you for losing weight—if she has felt protected by it. Somehow, you need to reach her, help her to feel safe, and protect her in other ways, as you lose the weight that you decide to lose. Guided imagery work can help you to access that child inside.

Megan: I have been successful recently in using your guided imagery suggestions to contact the little girl inside of me. I think I need to prove to her that I can protect her now, before she will let go of the safety blanket of flesh.

In some ways, I think that flesh kept me alive through the years. I think I could have been anorexic and disappeared—or even committed suicide—without the zoning out that food gave me. Through food, I was able to leave my body behind, and to drown out my painful feelings. So, it makes sense that as I deal with the pain, and finally allow my terror and devastation to surface, that I will no longer need to binge for the same reasons.

I finally understand why diet programs have seemed so irrelevant to my situation. For now, I am "heavily" OK! I feel solid, fat, and a bit sad. But I also feel hopeful and real. I would like to feel happier and lighter, emotionally and physically. But I trust myself to make this change, now that I understand what I need to do. The lightness will come. . . . I know it will. . . .

In *Mothering Ourselves: Help and Healing for Adult Daughters* (1991), Evelyn Bassoff reminds us:

> The fortunate daughters who, during childhood, receive enough nurture tend to learn, as they grow up, to soothe themselves. For this reason they are less likely to turn to alcohol, compulsive eating, or compulsive sex for comfort. Instead, when they are in crisis—rejected by a lover or friend, overwhelmed by responsibilities at work, suffering the loss of good health or a job—they can turn to their good inner mother for comfort.[3]

Through the course of her e-therapy, Megan is learning to mother herself with love and understanding, despite her neglect history.

For those clients and therapists with neglect histories who are challenging themselves to change their relationship with food, please be patient with yourselves. These complex issues cannot be dealt with overnight. Be compassionate to your inner child, and find out what that child needs from you in order to be successful in eating to live—not living to eat.

Chapter Five

Gone Too Soon: When Death Leads to Neglect

In the book *Mothering Ourselves,* Evelyn Bassoff (1992) describes some of the aftereffects of poor parenting by a neglectful mother:

> One of the most destructive effects of poor mothering can be a child's feelings of disconnection from her self. When the unempathic mother fails to recognize and resonate with the growing child's real feelings, the child herself begins to feel unreal and to mistrust her perceptions. She is not in touch with her inner life—her intuitive sense or instincts—but is rather cut off from it. Instead of trusting her intuitions, the wounded daughter turns to outside sources to tell her how she should feel.[1]

Many women with this neglect history can only experience themselves through the eyes of other people. They see their reflection in people's perceptions of who they are. This lack of consciousness of the self was the most relevant issue for Julie, a former client. Without good parenting, it is a losing battle to search outside the self for acceptance. As adults, the reflections from the outside cannot be easily integrated when we do not feel whole inside. Julie was very familiar with experiencing herself through others, and coping with emptiness.

Working with Julie was very rewarding, primarily because she was able to let go of her sense of herself as a victim. As she began to let go, she could allow herself to select and change those things about her life that she initially thought were beyond her reach.

Julie persevered in therapy until she was able to create the life she wanted, despite her history of neglect.

Julie's Story

My name is Julie. My mother gave birth to me in October of 1969, just fourteen months after she buried my two twin brothers, Stephen and Paul. No one in my family has ever really discussed their deaths, or communicated their grief to me. I knew only that Stephen and Paul were born premature, and that one lived for a day, and the other, two days. They were buried after only a few short days.

I learned very quickly that my mother didn't seem to care about me. As I was growing up, I blamed myself for that. I remember hearing my mother talking about how I was such a "colicky baby," and that I cried all the time. She loves to tell the story about how she would try everything to get me to stop crying, but as soon as my dad would come home from work, he'd take me. Then I would stop crying. I don't know if my mother held me as an infant, but I remember that there wasn't much hugging or nurturing of any kind growing up. Even the words "I love you" were non-existent. I was somewhat closer with my dad, but I remember having very little time with him, and never feeling like it was enough.

I was raised in a small town just outside a small city in Connecticut. As far back as I can remember, my father was very passive and silent. In retrospect, I believe he was depressed. I don't know how much of his depression stemmed from the loss of his sons. I don't know how much of my mother's emotional detachment and inability to connect had to do with Stephen and Paul, either. I don't imagine I'll ever know, because these are not the kind of questions that one asks in my family. Things just are. We just exist. Emotions are "weak," and I was always "too sensitive."

There weren't a lot of other children in the community where I grew up, and I remember feelings of loneliness and isolation. Once I started school, I made some friends—I usually had just one or two friends. I was the good kid who got good grades and did what she was told. When I entered sixth grade I encountered some girls in my class that were your basic bullies. They would do everything to pick on me if for no other reason than that I was the "goody-goody" in class. I was painfully shy, and had already integrated the idea that people didn't like me—because my mother didn't. I felt unworthy of their attention. It got so bad for me that I would physically feel ill every Monday morning. Whenever I built up the courage to tell my mother how I was feeling, she would criticize and blame me. "You shouldn't feel that way" would be her typical response.

I tried not to feel. I tried to function like other people. I tried to read people's moods, and respond to them. I managed to meet a few friends in school. From the very beginning, I remember wanting to hold onto friendships with all my strength. I believed that other people could rescue me from my self-hate, but I wouldn't let them know me. I would think: "If they know who I really am, they'll leave me."

I remember thinking that I needed to be the person they wanted me to be, and I was always generous, cooperative, and considerate. I didn't make any decisions about where to go or what to do, for fear that they would be the wrong decisions. I have always looked for positive feedback outside of my self. But when it was received, I couldn't believe it was true. After all, how could my mother be wrong about me?

I was three years old when my mom had my sister, Jennifer. We didn't live in a neighborhood, so there really wasn't anyone else to play with growing up. We would fight and bicker like normal siblings, but in the end, all we had was each other. Our summers were spent as latch-key kids. We had to stay inside and not answer the phone, unless it was mom's signal—ring once and she would hang up and call back. Then we knew it was her, calling to check in on us. The television was our babysitter.

I enjoyed spending time with my few friends when I could, but they didn't compensate for my detached mother. I would try to do the right thing, always trying to please her. I would not get the feedback I desired, and this would make me try harder. I can remember my mom asking me to smile. Then she would ask what was wrong, and sometimes I would try to tell her, but she never understood. One time I gave in and opened up my vulnerable heart and spelled things out for her. I gave her what she was asking for. It couldn't have been made any simpler. At the end of it all, her only response was "What do you want *me* to do?" Not even a hug or "I love you," or "Don't worry, everything will be alright." As I got older and could handle more responsibilities, I ended up becoming the parent by doing much larger chores for my mom. I took care of ALL of the household responsibilities, inside and out. Sometimes this included taking care of my nana, since she lived with us. Never a "thank you," or "I appreciate all that you do."

I grew to be more and more depressed as a young adult. I didn't know what to name my condition. I did know that I hated being alone, and always felt better when I was around other people. I was always very affected by my perceptions of what others were feeling about me. I would create negative scenarios in my head about what people thought of me. For the longest time, even if someone seemed to like me, I would invent some reason why my perception could not be accurate. In college, I was introduced to a religious retreat program called Emmaus. I was involved for six years, and I eventually took a leadership role with the group. They held four retreat weekends each year, and in six years, I think I only missed working two weekends. It seemed that I had found something to fill the void I had lived with all my life. A void of neglect and feeling unwanted and unloved. During the weekend, everyone received letters called "Kara." These letters were from friends and people who worked at the retreats. This Kara was a combination of cards and letters that expressed people's appreciation for all of my efforts, and thanks for all that I did. They were often an expression of unconditional love combined with kind words of gratitude for being just who I was! I kept all the supportive cards and letters that people wrote to me. But whenever I read them, I would cry. I had trouble taking in any nurturing attention. If I believed them, I would have to ask myself, "If this is true about me, why hasn't my family told me so?" I wasn't ready to ask myself that question for a long time.

My parents gave me material things. Looking back, I can understand that this was the only way my mom knew how to express her love. To this day, when they offer me gifts or money, I tend to feel guilty about accepting them. I would much prefer a kind word or a long hug. My family has never been affectionate, and I don't remember ever hearing "I love you." The only time my mother ever told me she was proud of me was at my college graduation. By that time, I was expected to take care of my mother's emotional needs, while she ignored mine. I would smooth over my mother's anxious edges, and even try to help her with her growing financial debts. So, perhaps I could justify that I had "earned" her compliment.

My initial relationships with men were similarly neglectful. My longest relationship to date lasted less than four years, and I described him to my therapist as "a man with no patience and a Napoleon complex." I had developed a pattern of giving 150 percent in relationships, and getting nothing back. I was aware of giving because I didn't feel worthy, but I didn't have any idea how to change that pattern. I always needed to feel that I had "earned" being liked. I couldn't be myself because I had no idea who that was. I knew only what people needed and expected of me, and I apparently performed to their liking at times.

There were only a few other men I had dated; one was a "drinker," one was a workaholic, and one was simply unavailable emotionally. I had no confidence socially, but I preferred being around people. This was a difficult combination that often kept me feeling lonely, desperate and depressed.

I sought counseling for the first time in 1988, and I have been in therapy off and on for many years. I was very stuck in my depression, and in 1995, I was convinced by two close friends (one was my roommate at the time) to see a new therapist. That was when I was diagnosed with clinical depression. I was told that I needed to be on medication in addition to therapy. This happened only a week before my sister got married. The last thing I was going to do was to let my family know. Yet another example of putting others' needs before my own. When I learned that depression could be exogenous (outside the self/situational), or endogenous (internal/physiological), I thought my version was a combination of both. I did obtain some relief from medication, but I also realized that I was playing a role in keeping myself sad, and therapy helped me to examine that role.

I wanted desperately to be loved, but I would tell myself that I "should be able to handle" my depression alone. I thought it was wrong to want to be in a relationship before I was ready to love myself. I thought I had to resolve my depression totally before someone would love me. My depression was ruling my decision-making process.

I was spending most weekends alone, and staying in my apartment. But staying in my apartment all weekend by myself would trigger past loneliness, and I would have trouble finding the motivation to leave. Sometimes on Saturday afternoons, I would drive to the nearest bookstore, where I would sit and read—simply to get out of the apartment and to be around other people. That is, if I weren't suffering from a migraine all weekend. I suffered with them on a frequent basis for years. I came to find out through the care of a holistic chiropractor that my emotions and memories of the past were being triggered by events in the present, and they would result in a physiological reaction—a migraine. I came to understand that most of these memories and emotions were connected to my mom. After working through these emotions and letting go, I was able to relieve myself of the migraines. It also helped that I was in therapy at the same time.

I told my last therapist: "I house anger." I seldom experienced anger in the world, but I intuited that my awful headaches had something to do with anger. My therapist suggested that I try writing a chronological anger list. I thought this was a good idea, and that it would help me to let go of some of my past, but I could never bring myself to complete it. At this time in my treatment, I had moved away from my family, and had been living in Atlanta for a few years. I had a good job and a few close friends. I wanted to believe that I had left my family problems behind. I wanted to feel better without having to search back in time to all of those feelings of abandonment.

I was living my history, though, in many ways. My one blessing was my cat, Peaches. Whenever I spoke about my cat and his unconditional love for me, I would automatically tear up. He is still with me today, and he is the only one who has seen me through my entire journey toward loving myself.

My last therapist made me conscious of the negative internal voices that I replayed in my head on a daily basis. She had also asked me to make a list of positive traits—things I liked about myself.[2] This was a much more difficult list to make, and it took me much longer than the list of negative thoughts. I actually had to make a list of positive traits from the perspective of what my friends might see as positive traits in me.

I still have that first list of negative thoughts, and the nurturing ones to combat them. An interesting footnote about the lists was that the negative thoughts were written in pen, and the nurturing ones were written in pencil. The list read:

Negative thought: I'm not worthy.
- You are worthy—you can't put a price on friendship.

Negative thought: I'm not important enough.
- You're important because you're you—no one else can be you—everyone's different.

Negative thought: Other people are more fun to be with.
- Everyone's unique—you do your best and that's all that counts.

Negative thought: I can't compare to others.
- Believe in yourself.

Negative thought: I'm scared s/he is mad at me.
- You're not wrong every time—we're only human.

Negative thought: I can never do anything right.
- Any mistake (if it is one) can be learned from—we all make mistakes.

Negative thought: You're so stupid—you should have known better. I don't see what they see in me.
- If they didn't see something in you they wouldn't be your friend.

Negative thought: I'm so dull and boring.
- Be happy with who you are—you can do whatever you want.

Negative thought: I'm always upstaged by others.
- Trust your abilities inside. We all have our own ideas.

Negative thought: I'm never going to amount to anything.
- A step is a step, no matter how big or small—it's one step closer than before.

I started becoming more conscious of nurturing myself. I wrote affirmations and created artistic backgrounds for the words, hanging small plaques around my apartment. I started going to yoga classes and eventually befriended the teacher. She had also been dealing with her own neglect history, and we connected on a deeper level than anyone I had ever met. I think I was also more ready to speak about who I was, and to open my heart to trust friends differently. I wasn't feeling so empty anymore. I still had my old habits though, and tried to tell myself she didn't really like me. Nikki stuck with me, and she remains my good friend years later. Yoga helped me immensely.

Another friend had suggested on several occasions that she could introduce me to something called the Landmark Forum. It was a three-day event that she had participated in a few years earlier and she truly thought that I would get a lot out of what it had to offer. She talked about how it could improve the quality of my relationships with people, how I could gain confidence in myself and experience the joy in life that I was longing for but couldn't seem to attain. Eventually I decided it was time for me to give Landmark a try, and I went in July of 2004. At the time, I was still living in Atlanta, so there really wasn't a need to inform my family that I was participating in such an event. It was hard for them to understand my involvement in Emmaus, so this seemed like something better kept to myself. There was a lot packed into that three-day weekend, and after all that, people were invited back two days later. They were asked to bring family and friends so they could also learn about Landmark. At one point, we were asked to reflect on a negative relationship from our past. One that we still carry in our present. We were given the opportunity during the weekend to contact that person and simply express to them a possibility that you are inventing for yourself and your life in a way that leaves them touched, moved or inspired. I chose to contact my mom. I briefly explained to her the weekend and, without resurfacing the past, that I found acceptance of her and how she expresses her love. That I knew she loved me and that by expressing my understanding, I wanted to create the possibility of us having a better relationship going forward. Late that night I got a message from my mom that she had spent all afternoon searching the internet for a flight to come to Atlanta and be there for me on Tuesday evening. My first reaction was panic and anxiety, mixed with anger because I knew she couldn't afford the trip. Then I realized something and it made me cry. . . . She was doing this because she loves me, and even though the only way she can express her love is through buying things (in this case a plane ticket), the simple fact was that she was doing it out of love. It gave me a whole new perspective on my mom, and helped me better accept her for how she can love me rather than yearning, as I have my whole life, for her to love me in a way she just isn't capable of loving. This was a very pivotal moment for me.

I started nurturing friendships differently, and slowly started thinking of myself as a good person. I decided to make a career change and study computer graphic design, a goal I had for many years but never pursued. I tried chiropractic care for my migraines, and kinesiology and bodywork for my moods. I started releasing accumulated negative emotion in those sessions, and the intuitive nature of the work was quite surprising to me. Part of my chiropractic care included emotional release techniques that were most successful in helping me to overcome my migraines. Most of the emotional releases were related to past experiences with my mom. They were intense feelings with deep emotion that left me very fatigued after a session. I came to understand that the mind-body connection is very strong, and that my body was holding onto emotional memories that became triggered when a similar situation in my present would surface the emotion in a physical sense—as a migraine. At the same time, I was in therapy on a weekly basis, and this was a huge help in letting go of negative emotions. In only a few months, I began to eliminate my migraines, and at the same time, I found feelings of emotional strength, stability, enhanced self-esteem, and happiness. I started actively reducing my anti-depressant medications, with the goal of eventually living without them. I was taking many supplements and herbal remedies for depression and anxiety. I started trying to integrate the positive feedback I received at work, and from friendships.

But letting the positive in meant grieving my past. I had to stop trying to replace the mother I didn't have, and to grieve the fact that she couldn't be what I needed her to be. The Landmark Forum was the start of helping me to do this. There would be times that I would have bouts of seemingly baseless, uncontrollable crying. I would try to reserve those crying spells to the times I was alone. These bouts of crying were most intense while taking my morning shower. But often, they would ooze out into my workdays, and certainly into my lonely weekends.

For the longest time, I would cry in therapy whenever I spoke about positive people in my life. I would often try to distract myself with television, especially with the characters from the TV show *Friends,* since that was my favorite show. I would imagine myself involved in positive friendships with those television characters. This was easier than attempting to allow the positive inside during the reality of my days. Maybe I was practicing for a more positive future.

In order to shield myself from my negative perceptions, my therapist suggested that whenever I thought of a negative scenario, I create three other positive things that might also be true about the same situation. So, for example, when I would tell myself *he didn't call today because he doesn't like me, and he doesn't want to see me again*, I would force myself to think:

1. Maybe he's busy at work.
2. Maybe he'll call later.
3. Even if he doesn't want to see me again, I'll be okay.

Of course, I didn't believe what I told myself at first. It felt counterintuitive, and not genuine. It took a long time to say something like *it's his loss*, and actually believe it.

Most importantly, over time, I began to believe that my neglect history was not my fault. I stopped personalizing it. I started exploring my spirituality, and I started forming a relationship with my two twin brothers. I started perceiving that they were like my guardian angels, surrounding me all of the time with their love and support. I remembered my mother telling me that after the twins died, the doctor told her to try to get pregnant again right away. His intent was to help her to forget. My mother listened to her doctor, but she wasn't ready for me when I came along. Perhaps she couldn't let herself like me. Perhaps a new daughter could never replace two lost sons. Whatever my mother's mindset was, it wasn't about me! I believe that we all come into this world in one of two ways: love or fear. I came into this world in fear. It is this fear that I needed to replace with love.

I started having dreams of the twins, Stephen and Paul. I thought of them as the male versions of my sister and me, and always thought that one would be like me, and the other, more like my sister. I developed a tremendous desire to visit Connecticut, perhaps to return there. I wanted to live close to my family again. I missed my sister, and I wanted to be able to develop some type of relationship with my mother that did not include the loss of my new self. I wanted her criticism and pressure to have less influence over me. My father had divorced her long ago, and he only visited Connecticut occasionally from his home in Virginia. He still maintains his distance from me, even today.

I pondered the decision to return to Connecticut for months and months. Finally, my lease was up, my employer was closing its doors, and I decided to relocate. It was a good time to leave, and I tried to see it as an opportunity. But even losing jobs over my adult lifetime has been very difficult for me. It seems that there is always more grief to deal with. I believed in my friendships, though, and I knew that my friends in Atlanta would keep in touch. I trusted myself to do the same. One thing was certain—the handful of close friends I made in Atlanta would be my friends for life, no matter how many miles separated us. Most people are fortunate to have one or two really close friends in their lives. I was blessed to find four friends in Atlanta. These friends would become my new family.

I moved into the basement of my sister's house when I returned to Connecticut. In retrospect, this was a mistake that sent me into a regression. My sister's husband is a man whom I thought neglected her, but I didn't feel it was my place to address that with her. I started backsliding, and focusing on the facts that I had no job and not very much money. My low self-esteem returned with a vengeance, and I started telling myself "I have no life—what man would want me?"

I tried to keep up with telephone sessions with my former therapist, but it wasn't the same for me as in-person therapy. The hour always felt like fifteen minutes. I did notice that I was experiencing much more anger at my family than usual, though. I wasn't confronting anyone directly, but just the act of focusing the anger outside of my self was beneficial to me. I would get involved with their dynamics, drama and struggles much too often. I was trying to hold onto myself, but I realized that I needed to get out of that situation in order to do better. After suffering through temporary jobs for months, I landed a good permanent position, and moved to my own apartment again. I am still with this company today.

I was able to save enough money to decorate my apartment with some new furnishings, and struggled with spending a small fortune on a new mattress. I had to tell myself that it was fine to nurture myself in this way. I was used to being extremely thrifty on my own, sometimes to the point of ridiculousness. I would often avoid purchasing English muffins, for example, even though I enjoyed eating them a great deal for breakfast. I'd tell myself: *Why do I need English muffins? I have bread, and toast is good enough.*

I wanted to turn over a new leaf in this new space. I actually went out and bought flowers to put around my apartment! My cat Peaches was adjusting well to his new environment, and we settled into a routine together. I saw my family less frequently. My sister gave birth to a son about a year after I moved out of her house. It felt nice to be a part of my nephew's life.

I started meeting people at work, and eventually began socializing with them. I started reconnecting with some old friends from high school, and catching up on the twists and turns in their lives. I even started dating an old boyfriend from those years, and we attended our twenty-year high school reunion together.

I noticed an immediate change in my relationship with this boyfriend. Even though I felt neglected by him, I did not let that feeling influence my behavior. I was able to create those different scenarios in my mind than the ones I was initially thinking about. And, lo and behold, I started believing that I deserved better from someone.

I could also see that there was no intent on this man's part to neglect me. He worked so many hours in a week that he got pneumonia twice within one year. He had no room for a relationship in his life. He was a business owner with a passion for his work. I held onto the knowledge that this neglect was also *not about me*. We drifted apart because of the distance between our homes and our priorities. I had trouble letting go, but I had communicated differently with him, so the grief was easier to process than it had been in past relationships. Like I said, I knew I deserved more, and I knew I wanted a mutual relationship with equal amounts of give and take.

During this time, I started a search for my brothers' graves. I researched, and tracked down a man who helped me locate their gravesite. It strikes me as so sad that I felt I had to do this without my family's knowledge. Once the gravesite was located, I was told there was no headstone. There were no names. My brothers were buried together in the same small coffin amongst other coffins without headstones. There had been no money for a funeral when they died.

But I was thrilled to have found their location, and I could visit with them for the first time. I wanted to start saving some money for a headstone with their names on it. I wanted them to know that I was thinking of them. I wanted to honor both of them. Stephen and Paul. They were born on August 19th.

Within the year, I would learn that they were thinking of me as well. I was talking with friends about feeling ready to date again. I had a friend at work whose husband had a friend who was having trouble meeting the right partner. It was decided that both he and I were open to getting together, so our friends set us up on a blind date. Jeff and I exchanged phone numbers, and met for lunch one Sunday afternoon. Our blind date must have gone well—it lasted four hours! We were developing a wonderful friendship, and the attraction was definitely there for both of us, on many levels. My biggest problem was allowing myself to feel my happiness, and to stop playing the worst-case-scenario game.

My other problem became obsessing about how I would ever introduce Jeff to my family of origin. Initially, this obsession distracted me from my ability to feel my joy and gratitude about this new beginning.

I am proud to say that I have resolved both problems, and I have been with Jeff for five months now. I am enjoying life in the present without dragging any of my past into this wonderful relationship. I am happier than I ever thought possible. I am in my late thirties. I have been single for the vast majority of my adult life, and now I'm part of a healthy couple. I often observe myself interacting with Jeff differently than I ever have before. I can (sometimes) give myself credit for the changes I've made. It was worth all the struggles that I had in my life to find love on the other side.

Jeff has two best friends—their names are Stephen and Paul. And his birthday? August 19th.

Coincidence? I don't think so.

We are not born with good self-esteem. It needs to develop, over time, from feeling special and valued in the world. Initially, we integrate our feelings about ourselves from the caretakers of our childhoods. In the beginning, our nurturing is supposed to come from outside the self. If we didn't get that initial nurturing, some of us tend to try to overcompensate for that loss in childhood—by caring a bit too much about what other people think of us. We measure ourselves by others' opinions instead of our own. This measurement cannot compensate for the loss of nurturing in childhood, and it is a very difficult pattern to let go of. It keeps us in a vicious cycle of reaching out, managing high expectations, being rejected or disappointed in others, isolating ourselves, becoming excessively lonely, and then reaching out again.

If the patterns in Julie's life are familiar, imagine one way to change them for yourself, or for your clients. Maybe you have realized that a particular pattern is no longer working for you. Any change that you can integrate into this pattern of behavior and belief will affect the entire cycle.

Mothering ourselves is hard work, especially if we continue to feel unworthy and undeserving of love. It feels very counterintuitive to nurture ourselves when it has not been a part of our repertoire.

Julie utilized some cognitive behavioral techniques to help her to cope with changing her patterns. For those of us with repetitive, strong, negative maternal messages, attempts to mother ourselves may be met with failure for a long time—before we start to see some substantial progress. Don't give up on yourself, or your clients; you deserve to feel worthy of love, and loving yourself without restraint or conditions will get you there.

Chapter Six

At Home with Incest: The Paved Road from Neglect to Abuse

Unfortunately, when maternal neglect occurs in the life of a child, there is frequently no safe place. There is no feeling of being protected. There is little or no guidance. The child raised with neglect is seldom taught about good and bad touch. Under these circumstances, a child can learn to trust indiscriminately or not at all, to please adults in order to access some soothing attention, or to shut down emotionally to minimize her hurt and pain. The stage is set for boundary violation. Too often, the door is open for sexual abuse to occur.

Healing simultaneously from abuse and neglect is a daunting proposition. It is imperative that women feel safe and supported in their lives in order to recover fully. In my experience working with sexual abuse survivors, the internal voices discussed in later chapters are sometimes louder, and often harder to overcome. The abuse of substances of all kinds is usually present in order to achieve some temporary relief from the voices. The evil inside oneself may feel overpowering. Women often feel helpless to resolve their inner conflicts. There is often more damage to trust, and certainly to the expression of sexuality and intimacy.

Sexual abuse is a trauma that has been described as the *killing of the spirit*. Although survivors of sexual abuse and incest have many strengths, the aftereffects of sexual abuse, like neglect, can often affect every aspect of life. Because sexual abuse is extreme trauma, people respond in extreme ways. There are five basic areas of women's lives that are usually deeply affected.[1]

Trust

Survivors of sexual abuse either trust everyone with no discretion, or trust no one at all. Both extremes stem from the betrayal of trust that is inherent in sexual abuse. Some women fluctuate between both extremes. They trust until they are betrayed, and then they stop trusting altogether. Betrayal in one's present life is usually a trigger to past trauma.

In chapter 2, Jasmin Cori reminds us that: "When you contract, you're a smaller target."[2] Incest survivors have a contracted ability to trust.

Control

Survivors of sexual abuse either believe they have no control at all over their life circumstances, or are "control freaks." Both extremes stem from the helplessness and hopelessness inherent in being out of control of the sexual abuse.

Boundaries

Survivors of sexual abuse have either no boundaries around themselves, or giant stone walls around themselves. Due to the violation of boundaries inherent in both physical and sexual abuse, these extreme responses often occur. It is difficult for some survivors to let themselves be known. Women may feel exposed, transparent, vulnerable, or invisible in the world.

Sexuality

Survivors of sexual abuse can be either asexual or promiscuous. Some people fluctuate between these two extremes as well. If a survivor allows herself to be sexual, she may need to self-medicate with alcohol or drugs, she may re-experience the abuse, or she may not be able to feel pleasure. To some women, touch is painful. To some, the sexual behaviors that are expressed in loving relationships may replicate the abusive environment. Still others may have flashbacks during or following sex. Some may even be able to leave their bodies and not be present while lovemaking occurs.

Passive Suicidal Thoughts

Often, women who have survived sexual abuse find comfort in thoughts of passive suicide. They have no plan to kill themselves, but they may have thoughts of driving off a cliff, or getting hit by a truck. Or, "if I don't wake up tomorrow, that would be okay with me." These types of fantasies are not necessarily about wanting to die. In many women, these fantasies end the inner turmoil that is left in the wake of their abuse histories. Women want to end the life they are living, but they don't necessarily want to die. Therapy with a professional trained in trauma recovery is the best option for women who want a new life, but don't yet have the tools to create one.

In therapy, it is not imperative to bring painful, devastating, detailed memories to the surface in order to heal. Whatever memories that are accessed will assist in healing. But overcoming aftereffects of abuse, one by one, will produce a similar effect. In accessing memory, it is important to help your clients to embrace compassion for that hurt child inside. That child may not want to re-experience all of her trauma. The adult self must respect those defenses learned long ago, in order to survive, while simultaneously holding onto hope that change is possible.

Visual images are not the only forms of memory. If a woman was abused by being grabbed from behind, she may never be sure who abused her. She is certain that she was attacked, however. There are tools for remembering that are trapped in your clients' reactions to people, their sensitivity and intense feelings, in their bodies and where they hold stress, and in their assumptions about people and the world around them.

Healing does not happen in a straight line. It is a jagged line, moving slightly backward and then, perhaps, leaping forward. There is no map to healing. Each journey will be both very similar and very different.

Danielle has successfully taken her first cautious healing steps, and although she is traveling uphill, I am sure that she will not turn back. She has begun the process, but she is unsure about allowing her memories to surface at this time in her life. After I asked Danielle to participate in telling her story, she sent me the following email:

> After you wrote to me about your book, I began working on a piece for you. I was only able to write for about a week (managing half a typed page) before it became clear to me that I am nowhere near where I would like to be in feeling healed. I began having nightmares again, insomnia, bouts of hysterical crying, and then waking in the night hearing my mother's voice in the alley behind our brownstone in Brooklyn (it was just a homeless woman, but at 3 am I could have sworn it was my mother looking for me). . . . I had to stop writing. I had to stop even thinking about writing and I knew that when, in order to fall asleep, I started imagining your couch as a safe space to rest. And I thought: "you're going crazy!" so, I stopped. But this is something I very much want to eventually be able to write through and I think it has everything to do with what I want to be researching and creating while getting my Ph.D. I'm very sorry that I didn't write sooner to let you know how I was processing this. I think a part of me thought that I would eventually be able to return to the piece I began and write it because I know that your book will be so very important to so many women and I very much wanted to be a part of that with you and with the other women you invited.

With Danielle's permission, I have included her beginning:

> *Half a Typed Page*
>
> It has taken me twenty-six years to meet you here. In the space of this page. In the place of this page. It could be a room, as it has four walls, and there could

be a couch, as I am sitting on one now. You could be sitting here with me. It is 4:35 am here. I am writing to you from Brooklyn, New York. I am here. And I am writing to you.

I have some stories I would like to share with you. Most are small dislocations. Memories that suck their way to the surface for a moment and then are buckled back to the other side of remembering. Remembering, in this way, feels like looking through a wall of dark water. At times, it is as if I have the edges of a memory, like the edges of a bright cloth, pulled from me. In this body this is how I've learned to remember.

You are probably sleeping as I write this; at least, I hope so. I was sleeping not more than fifteen minutes ago; there was a woman outside around Dean Street and 4th Avenue. She was yelling. She was cursing someone. And in the liquidness of sleep, her voice doubled over in its anger and I believed, for a moment, that it was my mother looking for me.

The first time my mother's voice woke me.

I await Danielle's return to therapy. She is moving back to Denver and plans to visit my couch again regularly. Danielle was not only neglected by her mother. She was physically and sexually abused as well. She initially sought counseling after being stalked by a strange man who sexually assaulted her. Coping with the aftermath of the assault, Danielle discovered that the feelings she had about her attacker—anger, fear, confusion, helplessness, guilt, shame, compassion—were very familiar.

We block memory for very good reasons. We defend ourselves against our pain and grief. If you are attempting to access early memory with your clients, be patient and compassionate. Help them to determine whether they want to retrieve more memory or not. Respect their defenses, give them permission to remember when they are ready, and trust in the process.

Kathy sought therapy while studying for her Masters degree. She was a very intelligent overachiever, overcompensating for a childhood of emotional neglect and devastating incest. Kathy's mother had a severe, untreated mental health condition. Kathy raised herself and her siblings, and although she suffered through frequent incestuous attacks by her father, she was successful at shutting down her emotions. She could also leave her body at will. Kathy actually recalled memories of sexual abuse from the time she wore diapers. Although she never totally blocked her memories, she blocked the feelings connected to the memories. After about a year of talk therapy in my office, Kathy was able to access those feelings, combine them with her memories, and grieve.

Kathy's Story

I received a package in the mail from my mother; a folded piece of paper placed on top reads "Happy Birthday, Your Loving Mother." It's the day before my forty-third birthday. I never open her gift the day of my birthday. I don't like the way it feels. I hate most of my Birthdays, not so much for the getting older part; it's one of my grief anniversaries. I don't have many, just my birthday and Christmas. It's a reminder of all the loss and pain. The loving mother who signs the card doesn't really exist, but I have no illusions that she does. When I was little my birthday marked the first day of the three weeks my father took off from work each year. For three weeks every summer I was trapped with him all day, every day. I was always trapped with him at night, but at least I could escape and be safe in the day—except for those first three weeks of August every single year.

I open the birthday gift, bracing myself for something like last year. She sent a doll I had when I was a child—a pretty bride doll I was never allowed to play with—in case I ruined it. I remember not caring really; I thought the doll and her intricate dress with stockings and shoes was beautiful but I knew I would never be beautiful and I certainly had no little girl wedding fantasy of my night in shining armor falling in love with me and living happily ever after. In fact, I was hoping I'd be dead before I was twenty-five and would rather be dead than have to be married and be like my mother. I was about eight.

Well, it's not a doll this year; it's a few pieces of fine china from a set she picked up somewhere like a garage sale. I actually like fine china; it makes me feel elegant. The design is pretty, pink and blue flowers, I could get lost in the irony of this since the pink and blue flowers remind me of beautiful children and perhaps dishes you might use for a baby shower. But I don't get lost in the irony. Instead, I call my mother to thank her. I don't need to brace myself for our hollow shell of a relationship or our empty conversation. I've been doing this for years now. It's all that I've been able to salvage, and as long as she follows my rules, she gets to talk to me once every month or so. My rules are very clear: she must remain present when she talks to me with appropriate reality testing, no bizarre behavior or thoughts. This is difficult for her. She's in her seventies and has been surviving in and out of reality forever. She's never psychotic, never suicidal, doesn't drink or use drugs, has worked all her life, doesn't experience depression that immobilizes her. She dissociates, and sometimes she has bizarre changes in her facial expressions and voice . . . and when that starts it's time to end the phone conversation. But I can't save her and she didn't save me. She wasn't born crazy; she used it to survive all the years of sexual abuse by her own father. She's actually the only female child to survive; a younger sister died of a pill overdose at age twenty-five and an older sister died of an alcohol overdose in her forties. Of course no one would ever talk about that. I think the story I heard about her younger sister is that she washed her car when it was cold out, got pneumonia, and died.

When I was about three years old, I would often wake up in my parents' bed, and my mother would be sleeping in my bed. I would wake up next to my father, his penis between my thighs, humping between my legs and he would get me all wet with something that smelled bad and was sticky. Then he would grab my hand and make me hold his penis and move my hand up and down and make my hand go faster and faster and my hand would hurt. I was terrified, and where was my mother? I didn't know what this was and I wanted my pajama bottoms back on, and to wash whatever that white yucky stuff is that was running down my legs. And I was so tired . . . and what were those noises he was making. . . . I can't breathe, now he is holding me, telling me he loves me. . . . I can't breathe. . . . I want to be let go but I'm afraid to speak.

The next night I have a nightmare; my mother hears me and tells me to come to her. I get into bed on her side and want to be snuggled by her. She rolls me over her and puts me in the middle, tells me to go to my father; she turns over with her back to me and goes to sleep. . . . It happens again. . . . She's right there; how can she not hear or feel the movements? . . . What do I do. . . . I'm terrified. . . . I can't move. . . . Why is this happening to me? I'm so tired. . . . It's morning. . . . and I forget.

I'm about five; I'm sitting in the dark bathroom in the middle of the night, cleaning the gross stuff off of me and thinking, "what is this called? . . ." I decide I must give off some kind of signal that makes this happen . . . something not right about me. . . . I already know intuitively that I can't tell my mother or anyone. . . . I block it out in the morning. I get to go to school now. I love school; I wish I could live at school. One night I woke up and I was outside; my mother heard the door unlock and found me outside; I was sleep-walking. When I remember this later as an adult, and learn to love that little girl who was me instead of hate her . . . I high five my little self. . . . She was trying to be safe . . . to get out of that house.

As a child, no matter what you try, there is no escape, especially at night. As I got older I would try to lock my door but he would break the locks. One time at age ten I took the kitchen butcher knife and put it between my mattress to protect myself, but when he entered my room and got in my bed I was so scared I couldn't move. It was sometime around age ten that he raped me completely. To this day I only have bits and pieces of the memory. My mother went to spend the night at her parents' house and made me stay with him at the house so he wouldn't be lonely. It was a few days before Christmas. This time he took all my clothes off; I hit my head against the headboard as he moved on top on me. . . . I have no feeling; I don't know if it hurt; that's the blank part. When he was done, I had to lie on his chest and he told me he hoped I liked my Christmas presents. It wouldn't be until I was twenty-eight years old and met my husband that I could stand to be held close and feel safe.

I was seventeen when the abuse stopped. I fought back, no words, still too scared for words, but I thrashed around violently. He left and never broke into my room again. By this time I had no feelings, an expert at suppressing memories, and felt like I couldn't really remember years of my life, especially younger years. I always knew I was abused but it happened so much, and I would have to forget in the morning so I could function. Acting as if everything was OK was very important. I remember the daytime, going to school. I even had some friends, some best friends where I would stay over at their houses as much as possible to keep safe.

I started drinking alcohol at age twelve on weekends; sometimes I would smoke pot before school, especially if it had been a rough night. . . . I was having sex with my high school boyfriend at age fourteen. I didn't want to but he tried one night and saying no wasn't an option I ever had so I never considered it. I didn't feel anything, physically, sexually, or emotionally. My defenses were strong . . . repression, suppression, dissociation, intellectualization, and minimization. I was smart, a master with the survival strategies but with no conscious control over them. I told myself I was strong and I could never tell my mother because it would kill her. It was my job to protect my mother at all costs. I mostly felt like I didn't exist, or I wasn't real, or I would feel like I was shrinking when others were around and I just knew they all saw that I was different and damaged in some way. I would check my reflection over and over to see if I was really there or if I looked as ugly and disgusting as I felt. The alcohol helped me feel more normal, numb in a different way, a better way than my usual; my friends drank with me and I guess they did it for fun. . . . I needed it to feel something, to forget and to not feel empty, to forget I hated myself for a while. . . . The hangovers helped too. . . . I would have to sleep all day Saturday and Sunday and not get out of bed until it was time to go out again, drink, pretend to be wild and fun and happy.

At about age twenty that behavior stopped working. Alcohol made me feel depressed and I just wanted to disappear. My defenses are starting to fail . . . not completely. . . . I'm still going to college on track to graduate in a year or so and work my college jobs to pay for everything . . . but inside I don't exist and I don't want to. I hide this from others, but I'm having trouble hiding it from myself anymore. I don't know what to do.

I have a boyfriend now. My friends are relieved. They said they were worried about me because I never have any relationships. After three weeks he tells me he loves me. I don't believe him but I tell him I love him back. . . . I don't but I guessed it's what I'm supposed to say. I wished I could feel love—but I can't. In fact as he holds me I just want to run because I can't breathe. I run, I push him away, but he stays. . . . I don't know why. He doesn't hurt me or do anything bad to me. . . .I don't trust him. I want to die. . . . Why can't I feel anything? . . . I'm empty all the time, lonely no matter what. I don't feel real. I'm shrinking again. I'm never good enough. I'm ugly, disgusting, worthless, and a whore.

I'm preparing to leave Buffalo. I am going to graduate school on Long Island and I'm never coming back. It's a summer day in August and I'm feeling so empty. I can't go on living with no feelings; it's torture and I'd rather be dead and I can't keep this to myself anymore. I tell this boyfriend. I'm scared, but I tell him about the abuse and wishing I could just die. He helps me. I made a plan. When I moved in a few weeks, I would find someone who could help me, a therapist who knew about these things. I put my defenses back in place, packed my things, prepared to play the role of a bright, intelligent, graduate student. Then I found Lori.

I sat at my kitchen table staring at Lori's name and number; the paper said she worked with incest survivors. I was terrified to call and didn't know what to say. I don't really remember but I was probably very matter of fact and told her I was an incest survivor . . . a term I had just learned from that paper with her number on it . . . and wanted to make an appointment. With my heart beating rapidly, I planned to see her the following week. I thought about it all week long. The day of the appointment I quit my pack-and-a-half-per-day smoking habit and went to her office.

I don't really know what I said to Lori in our first session but I remember she was kind, understanding, and she thought what happened to me was terrible and she didn't think I was bad or disgusting . . . although it would take many years before I would believe that about myself. I felt some hope for myself.

I went back to see Lori for the next four and a half years. I planned my weeks around therapy, allowing myself time to attend classes, internships, work, complete assignments, and then do the hard work of therapy and healing. I wasn't alone, I had an expert guide on my journey and I kept her with me in spirit always. That's the gift that Lori gave me; she showed me how to internalize her, take her with me so I was never alone with this abuse nightmare again. She's still with me today and I know that words cannot do justice to this special kind of relationship. In fact many therapists aren't capable of it. . . . It can't be learned in school, as I said, it's a gift. Lori has it and she shared it with me to help me.

I spent the first year in therapy trying to have feelings, trying even to cry for myself, for the little girl inside of me who got hurt, but you can't cry for someone you hate. Lori taught me so much about how it wasn't this little girl's fault. . . . It wasn't my fault and I needed to love and take care of this little girl because she is precious and needs me. This was hard. I hated me; I was sure that what happened was all my fault. After all, my childhood belief was that I gave off some sort of sex symbol that made him do this to me; when I was four I wore yellow babydoll pajamas that made him do this to me. As a teenager my body had orgasms when he touched me and it felt good, proof I'm a whore, and it was all my fault. But Lori didn't believe that to be true. One session she asked me to take a look at how little a three-year-old is, a five-year-old, a ten-year-old girl is compared to a grown man. I started to look around places and notice this, how beautiful and small and totally dependent children are on their parents. The crack in my distorted beliefs was beginning. But no feelings. And without feelings you can't really be alive. I would often concentrate very hard trying to make memories come back to me and find the feelings attached. But nothing. My survival skills that had saved me . . . dissociation, suppression, repression, intellectualization, and minimization, now had me trapped inside of myself.

I took a trip back to Buffalo, to disclose the abuse to my mother. I wasn't going to keep the secret anymore. . . . I couldn't. I told her, and that day I lost her, or realized I never really had her. I had created a fantasy of a mother who loved me dearly and would protect me to the ends of the earth if she knew what was happening to me on any level and because I loved her I would instead protect her from the truth. That day I found out that my mother and her sisters had been sexually abused by her father and that this abuse transcended many generations . . . and she told me she didn't know . . . that she thought if anyone would be abused it would be my sister because she was meek and quiet but not me since I was mouthy all the time at home. Her voice changed, her demeanor, her facial expression and she said, "I was seven when it first happened to me." Did she want me to take care of her at that point? . . . I didn't know but I told the secret and that's what I needed to do. She went home, asked my father what he had done to me, and he denied it. I didn't talk much to my mother for the next two years. A few months after this my sister became engaged; she asked me to be her maid of honor. I said yes but eventually had to tell her I couldn't be at her wedding if our father was there and go back to keeping the secret. She said, "Well I'm having him there," and I said I was sorry to hear that and she found a new maid of honor. I sent a card. My mother divorced my father two years later and in the divorce document it stated among the reasons, "for the acts against Kathleen," or so she said. I never saw the document.

It may sound like I was doing lots of hard work, and I was, but it was all in my head . . . the thinking work . . . cognitive restructuring . . . but I still couldn't get to the feelings. At Lori's suggestion I went to a performance, sort of like a playback theater technique for incest survivors, and the visual performance made its way to the back door of my defenses and I started to cry for myself. When I finally opened the floodgates I didn't know if they would ever close. How long can someone cry before there are no more tears? How much can this hurt? Will the pain ever stop? The sharp emotional knives keep stabbing me over and over, deeper and deeper. Pain needs a witness, someone to help hold the pain, because it is too much for one person to bear. Lori witnessed my pain and helped me hold it when it was too much.

For the next three years I continued seeing Lori every week; it was the most important thing in my life; everything came second. . . . I put my life first. I survived and someday I was going to live a normal life and feel something good. I can't find words to describe the pain and feelings of loss of a mother, a father, a childhood, a family. The pain has to be expressed, in a primitive sense and at home (my allotted time to feel because I still had to function at school and work), and I would start to cry; it would turn to screams and deep guttural sounds as if a helpless animal were trapped, hurt and dying. . . . It needed to come out that way. I hated this place, this deep, dark place that I didn't know if there was really a way out of. Lori walked this dark place with me and she was never afraid; she knew I could do it. I wish that I knew how to tell this better; words are so inept. I know I never want to be in that dark place again but without having gone through it, following the tunnel to the end, true healing for me wasn't possible. So I honor the tunnel, the darkness, my pain. I honor myself and everything I did to survive and to heal and to live. I honor my anger, my rage, and the work I did so it wouldn't destroy me and prevent me from being loved. I honor the past generations of women in my family who could not be saved, had no help to break the cycle.

I'm twenty-seven and I walk into Lori's office for our final session, a celebration to say goodbye, to honor our bond. To humbly say thank you. I didn't leave her though; she's a part of my soul. I left her office that day without the gut-wrenching pain that I'd become so accustomed to, no more nightmares, no emptiness or wishes to die. I was no longer a victim; I was beyond being a survivor but the journey was far from over. It was time for me to experience being alive like a normal person. I was hollowed out, but not empty inside, not sure who I was, but sure of who I wasn't, scared again but it was no longer dark.

As I stated at the beginning, I am turning forty-three tomorrow. I have been evolving for many years now as everything is a process and you can't just go from trauma to healing to living in a nice linear fashion. But you do get there.

Today I live with my loving husband, Jon. We have been together for fourteen years. We have a beautiful thirteen-year-old daughter named Lauren and a beautiful eight-year-old son named JD. (Jon David Jr.) Our life is good and it's real and it's all mine.

Kathy was one of the most resilient clients I have ever worked with. Her fighting spirit kept her glued to the process of integrating her feelings. She would come to a therapy session after having a flashback, and she would begin her session by explaining the details of the flashback to me. Then, she would slowly allow herself to cry. During these sessions, my sole purpose was to witness Kathy's pain. She asked nothing else of me. Since Kathy could not talk while she cried, the majority of these *integration sessions* passed without words. But there was plenty of non-verbal communication. Plenty of connection, honesty, nurturing.

Initially, as a therapist who was relatively new to the field, Kathy's presentation was a bit perplexing for me. I would think to myself, "I'm not helping her—I need to fix this," knowing all the while that I couldn't do that for Kathy. The way around Kathy's pain was through it. Eventually, I came to realize that crying in my office for nearly an hour per week *was* Kathy's way of fixing it. All I needed to do was trust in her process and get out of her way. Still, in the beginning, I would consistently ask her "Are you getting what you need here? Is there anything we could be doing differently?" And she would consistently respond "yes" to the first question, and "no" to the second. (My clients will tell you that I have an annoying habit of asking several questions at once.)

Slowly, I began to embrace the role of witness. I was able to enhance my therapeutic ability to separate from my questioning ego, and just sit with Kathy through her pain. I started to witness Kathy becoming softer, more open, more true to herself. More grounded in herself. Our time together became a ritual of compassion. We sat together in this way for years.

It has been more than twenty years since Kathy sought therapy. She has continued to keep in touch with me, sending proud photographs after giving birth to her two beautiful children. Kathy has overcome all of her aftereffects, and has recently noticed an increased ability to access joy and gratitude.[3]

Kathy has come full circle. The following is from an email she wrote me about telling her story:

> I remember reading every book I could find, hoping and needing to find a survivor story that didn't end at the survivor stage, so I would have something tangible to hold on to from another survivor who was living and feeling normal. I desperately needed that hope because of all the too-frequent dark days when it didn't seem possible.

Now, Kathy has become the woman she was searching for.

Working with Kathy was a healing experience for both of us. Kathy taught me how pure, profoundly simple, and sacred a bond between therapist and client could be.

Chapter Seven

The Broken Promise of Love: Addicted Parents and Neglect

Tatum O'Neal

Tatum O'Neal's autobiography, *A Paper Life,* is a tragic depiction of neglect, abuse, and despair. Tatum's mother, actress Joanna Moore, was an alcoholic who remained emotionally unavailable to her daughter. Joanna Moore was orphaned at the age of six. Perhaps a lack of resolution about her own childhood facilitated the repetition with her daughter, Tatum. Tatum was emotionally neglected, and later, physically abused by her mother.[1] Tatum's father, actor Ryan O'Neal, was in the news in 2009 because he "accidentally hit on" his daughter Tatum at Farrah Fawcett's funeral.[2] Really?

While growing up, Tatum was sexually abused by friends of both of her parents. Her father used illicit drugs, and exposed her to a very promiscuous lifestyle. Tatum became promiscuous herself by the age of fourteen.

In 1978, Tatum O'Neal was hospitalized after a severe car accident where she was badly injured: She writes: "My mother showed up once. . . . She wasn't capable of comfort or support. As for my father, he too came just once, with his latest female conquest in tow. I passed the time smoking pot . . . wondering whether my parents were coming back. They weren't."

Tatum continues, as she describes her internalized neglectful parent:

> As I sank deeper into depression, though, I stopped wishing that people would visit me. I was ashamed of the accident, internalizing the notion that I'd brought it on myself and deserved what happened. I felt like the bad seed. Voices kept nagging in my head, mixing my father's words—"You suck, Tatum!"—with my own: "You're not worth coming to the hospital to visit. You weren't even worth picking off the highway."

> By then I'd already attempted suicide more than once—the night when I was molested . . . and another time when I'd slit my wrists with a razor, only to have my father tell me: "You cut them the wrong way, Tatum."[3]

After a failed attempt at reconnecting to her mother when Tatum was an adolescent, she writes about the aftereffects of emotional abandonment and neglect:

> What followed for me was a period of drifting and—finally abandoning my vow to stay clean—losing myself in drugs. It started when I got a bit chubby, by Hollywood and Farrah-comparison standards. My dad had encouraged me to diet for years, and now I learned that cocaine was good for weight loss. The person who tipped me off was a new friend . . . (who) also shared another powerful dieting strategy: vomiting.
>
> Between doing coke and throwing up, the pounds started melting off me effortlessly. It didn't take me long to get down to about ninety pounds.
>
> I found that coke made me feel so much better. It was like the panacea I'd always needed to ease my tormented thoughts.[4]

Throughout her autobiography, Tatum O'Neal helps us to connect the devastating dots of neglect, leading to physical and sexual abuse, eating disorders, suicidal ideation, the bad core, intrusive thoughts, and alcohol and drug abuse. It is clear that Tatum O'Neal lacked restorative experiences during childhood. This fact serves to explain the consistently jagged road to Tatum's recovery. Her tenacity and determination are admirable traits.

TARA'S STORY

A former client, Tara, contacted me via email in May of 2006. As my very first e-therapy client, Tara taught me a great deal about the positive impact that e-therapy can have. I was trained in long-term, psychodynamic psychotherapy. I was skeptical, initially, about whether or not e-therapy could be as helpful to clients as individual, face-to-face psychotherapy. I discussed this issue during consultation sessions with Judy, the therapist who manages the largest online counseling service available internationally. Judy would consistently report that many of her therapists had wonderful outcomes—very similar to those attainable in a therapist's office.[6]

Tara proved to me what Judy already knew. Here is her story:

Early Childhood

My primary parental figure growing up was my mother. My parents had divorced quite early in my life, and my grandmother helped to raise me. But before the divorce, in the early years of my infancy, my mother lived under the rule of my father. Pregnant at twenty-two out of wedlock, my mother was regarded as a social disgrace by my grandmother. Concerned with what "the neighbors would think," my grandma was adamant about my mother marrying, even though my father had a track record of intense jealousy, violent fits of rage, and alcohol abuse. In fact, he went to jail for a short time directly after the wedding, when my mother was six months pregnant with me.

The family environment of my infancy was not a secure one. My father's rages continued and seemed to worsen after the marriage. His jealousy and possessiveness increased toward his new wife. When he left for work, for example, he would remove pieces from the engine of my mother's car so that she could not leave the house while he was gone. What started as a "drinking problem" soon became alcoholism. He was physically violent with my mother.

When I was less than two years old, my mother decided to leave the abusive environment and return home to live with her mother. She would not take my father back and besides, my grandmother was a stern and angry woman who would not allow him to set foot in her house. I saw my father twice when I was a little girl, but only for a short period of time and chaperoned by my grandmother. He died when I was eleven.

I don't remember my youngest years. At least, not many specific events beyond the cherished memories of my mother taking me to the beach, or giving a birthday party for my dog in the backyard, replete with gifts and cake. What I remember the most was a generalized feeling of fear—the kind of fear that makes you curl into yourself, to stiffen your whole body as if in preparation for a physical blow. Yet, I was not physically abused by any member of my family. The abuse was more subtle than that—at any moment my mother's or grandmother's mood could turn to rage, and I would be the target of their yelling and threats, or the audience for their slamming about of objects such as hot fryer pans and bedroom doors. Or worse yet, I could be ignored, locked out, pushed away, or physically abandoned. Maybe even my body remembered at the cellular level the violent fights that had occurred between my parents when I was a baby. Perhaps I felt generally unprotected, as my mother will admit even now that she's never liked infants, and prefers not to hold, cuddle, or play with them. She never offered the breast to me or my brother when we were infants. I imagine that I probably did not receive healthy touch as an infant much less an ongoing nurturing closeness with her.

I didn't know the particulars of my family history as a child, but I did know one thing for certain—the world was a chaotic, unsafe place, and adults weren't people you trusted for unconditional love and security.

Middle Childhood

My middle childhood years begin my painful memories; I remember feelings of great shame, anxiety, confusion, and fear. One intense fear involved leaving my home and being among other families. I didn't like public spaces or loud noises. I would have been the little girl who clung to her mother's leg in public if she had been there to cling to. Often enough, I was sent off with other families alone. They rarely knew my mother, or if they did, they were likely to dislike her. I often heard bad things about my mother in the company of others. My aunt once chastised me for folding a towel wrong: "You'd better be careful or you'll turn out like a bag lady, or worse—your mother." My mother's nighttime excursions (she would sneak out of her bedroom window in the middle of the night to party, have sex, do drugs) apparently weren't a secret from other adults, and they did not take to her behavior kindly. But rather than having a supportive, admiring adult in my life beyond the core family as a mentor or role model, I found that I was just as "bad" outside the home as in it.

For I did develop the idea at home that I was a bad girl—surely that explained why I was ignored except for when I was in trouble. It is amazing to me now to think that I was ever in trouble for anything. For all intents and purposes, I was a wonderful little girl. I was quiet, obedient, prone to studiousness, and loved to be by myself. I didn't break the rules or talk back. I did what I was told. Yet my grandmother had a violent temper and scolded often. She would yell if even a single item was misplaced during cleaning (I have an enduring memory of her entering my bedroom, sweat-faced, and picking a piece of lint off the floor. "*What is this!*" she cried, barring her teeth with rage). She didn't like laughter or for other children to be in the house. My grandfather was a quiet man who stayed out of her way and busied himself until late evening in the garage. My mother worked full time until I was eight, so she was not home often, either. When she was around, she could be just as moody and unpredictable as my grandmother.

I might have spent more time away from home in other people's houses if I hadn't been so shy and afraid. When I did get the courage to spend the night at a friend's house, almost inevitably I would wake with a headache so crippling that I would vomit. My grandma would pick me up at two or three in the morning and take me home, putting a cold washcloth to my forehead and rubbing my temples. It was probably the only time that she showed me physical affection. I also used to pee in my pants as a little girl when visiting friends or extended family during the daytime. I was too embarrassed to ask to use the restroom. Now I think how poorly my needs were met during that time that I did not feel able to ask—or allow—something as basic as elimination.

Middle to Late Childhood

I was about eight years old when the dynamics of my core family worsened. My mother lost her job and went on welfare. Since she was home more often she would take me with her to pick up her unemployment checks and visit her friends. These were often scary affairs and I would have preferred staying home—except that I got to spend time with my mom—an unusual event. Her friends were often very poor, living in decrepit neighborhoods of Los Angeles. They lived in dirty alleys and rented rooms in buildings that bloomed with mold. Their apartments stank and were littered with rotting food, discarded clothing, and sometimes animal offal. I believe, now, that these were probably my mother's drug dealers. She was addicted to heroin then; however, I did not realize this at first.

Soon enough my mother was taking me and a friend with her to cheap motels where I am sure she shot up. She'd drop us at the pool for a few hours unattended, and then drop us back home. It was my friend who, needing to use the toilet, first went up to the motel room to relieve herself. When she returned she informed me that my mother was doing drugs. I did not believe her but then she was no innocent to such behavior. Her mother was an addict of some sort and her stepfather sexually molested her and physically abused her. It is horrible to me now, but when I was a child even this seemed "normal"—if not another terribly scary environment to be in.

Eventually my mother stopped taking me out, but she also stopped coming home. Her nights of sneaking out the window would turn into a many-days absence; as time went on days would turn into weeks or sometimes more than a month. I was not offered an explanation to this. My grandparents continued on as if my mother hadn't just disappeared on us. No one asked how I felt or tried to comfort me. Only once did another family member remark on the situation. She pulled me into the bathroom and grabbed me tight by the chin. What she said was, "You know this isn't your fault. Your mother is a terrible woman." *As if that explained everything.*

Pre-teenage Years

I look back at my experience of puberty, and later of my teenage years, and I first think about how it all could have turned out much worse. When I was as young as eleven years old, my life was off track in very serious ways. My same friend who had seen my mother in the motel room doing drugs got into trouble herself. She started hanging out with boys four, five, six years older than she was. Wanting desperately to have any kind of approval or acceptance, I started to hang out with her and these friends. I would spend the night at her house and we would sneak out in the middle of the night, her parents' consciousness at this point obliterated by drugs. At midnight, or sometimes as late as two or three in the morning, we would roam the streets of Orange County—not safe, indeed. We'd walk for miles, to the houses of grown men where parties were dying down after heavy drinking and substance use. I had my first kiss in a dark park after one of these parties, with a boy that barely knew my name and was already seventeen. Fortunately, I was never physically hurt during these nighttime forays in the streets, and the boys did not take advantage of me beyond kissing. My friend would have less luck. The last I heard of her, she had already been in and out of juvenile detention several times, and was put in the hospital because her boyfriend broke her nose and cheekbone.

When I was twelve, my grandparents put their house up for sale—we were moving to Oklahoma, where my grandmother had grown up. By this time, my mother had been to rehab several times; but she always returned to the needle and her old group of friends. The only thing to do was get away from Los Angeles and try to start a new life. We moved when I was on the cusp of my thirteenth birthday. It is a part of my memory that I have at least partially suppressed. I don't remember the physical move to Oklahoma, rather, just living in a two-story house next to the woods in a country town one day. My grandparents must have been there during the initial move, but they left soon thereafter to return to LA to close escrow on the house. That left me and my mother. It didn't take long for her to disappear. I didn't understand it at the time but it is clearer to me now. She was no doubt nosing out a new dealer. I've inferred this because she became pregnant during this time with my brother, whose father lived in the ghetto. He had (has) a drug addiction also. At the present time, this man no longer has contact with my family, and my mother no longer abuses drugs.

Teenage Years

While my grandparents were in LA closing escrow on the house, and my mom had disappeared, I was naturally left alone in the new two-story house. The little country town where we had moved in Oklahoma was populated with many of my grandma's relatives. So on the rural street where I lived (it was a gravel pathway) there were about a half dozen other houses and trailers—all of which were owned by some great-aunt or uncle, or descendant thereof. I'd met these older brothers and sisters of my grandmother's before, during summer trips to Oklahoma. That's where I also met my second cousins, who became my first friends when I moved.

It doesn't make sense to me now, but no adult seemed to have figured out that my mom was gone. Why didn't my grandparents call to check in? I don't know. As for my great-aunts and uncles, many of them were already well into their eighties and nineties by the time I had moved there. Some were suffering from cancer or other serious illness (my grandmother is now the last surviving sibling). Perhaps they just did not know. In any case, two of my cousins stayed with me most the time. The older cousin, a female, would spend the night with me and make sure I had dinner. She never said anything to anyone about what was going on; I would find out years later, while in therapy, that she had been repeatedly physically and sexually abused as a child. Perhaps because of this she was trained in keeping secrets.

My other cousin, a male, was my age. He would make sure I got to school okay and helped me with my homework. He introduced me to his friends at my new school and I felt safe and at home there right away. My mom probably wasn't gone for more than a few days, but when she came back, it was like she wasn't there anyway. I remember her lying on a blanket on the floor in the kitchen reading paperback novels under a single light. She was covered in cuts and bruises. She wouldn't talk about what happened to her; she only said, "I don't want to talk about it. My car broke down, alright? That's all you need to know. I have a headache; let me read." My cousins continued to keep me company, to help me adapt to my new home. After a few weeks, my grandparents returned to the house.

In the midst of all of this, I was molested by my male cousin. I remember it started off as him wanting a single kiss while he was helping me with my homework. The truth is, I wasn't sure that I wanted to, but I didn't know how to say no. It seemed better just to give him what he wanted. After all, didn't I owe it to him after all he'd done for me?

The kisses turned out to be very uncomfortable, and in fact, quite gross. I remember hating the way that he smelled and how he tasted. Yet he pushed me and pushed me to kiss him. If I made excuses—oh what if someone sees?—he would push me into the closet. As time went on, he expected more and more of me. He would remove my shirt and fondle my breasts; he would suck on my nipples and kiss me and put his hand in my pants. One day, the younger brother of my female cousin caught us, looking in through the window from the bushes outside. I was so ashamed that I avoided both my cousins as much as I could. I made every kind of excuse not to be alone with my cousin. Later, I would date one of his best friends, and so I was around him again. But our relationship never had a sexual element again. Nevertheless, I can today still feel that great shame of being seen through the window—half naked, sick to my stomach, not understanding how I felt. Or how to get out of something that felt so terribly wrong.

My later relationships with males were always colored by this experience, and also by what I saw of my mother. She was very obviously sexual—I'd seen her through door slats naked in bed with men—but she never had a good relationship with a man. It seemed that what she got from sex was a bad reputation from other women and some bruises and sores from men. So sex was a dirty thing, and I had no concept of it within a loving relationship (my grandparents, though married, had separate bedrooms). Then, my own first sexual encounter was manipulated and shameful. I felt no desire for my cousin but rather just its opposite—disgust. My mind equates sexual stirrings with queasiness. Dating other boys, having sexual intercourse for the first time at age fifteen, saying yes to my first husband's proposal at twenty-two . . . all of these experiences are marked by this queasiness, by feeling sick but not knowing how to say "no." I didn't know my own feelings. Nor did I know emotional and physical boundaries. I only knew that I wanted to make the other person 1) Love me 2) Pay attention to me and 3) Be happy. So I gave them what they wanted, hoping to get some acknowledgment and acceptance in return. I never got those things: I learned to appreciate and honor myself less and less. It was only through looking at my past and understanding my patterns that I've been able to work through some of these issues and develop healthier self-esteem and self-worth.

Some Other Effects

There were two ways I learned to gain positive attention from adults as a child, both within my core family and outside of it. The first, and most important, was getting good grades and showing high intelligence in all subjects, especially reading. The second was learning how to act cute and funny enough that my grandfather would wish to photograph me. He loved to use his camera, and could easily be prompted to take out his camera to capture what he considered was a good moment to remember. Both of these survival skills—the ways I learned to act or be in order to gain positive attention—worked very well when I was a child, and naturally I carried those behaviors with me into adulthood. Each has its positive benefits for me even now. But as I came to understand later in therapy, how I was accustomed to acting (the key word here being "act," rather than authenticity) also had negative effects on my ability to live peacefully and in harmony with myself.

I am a perfectionist. In some ways, this has helped me to achieve what I have wanted most for myself. I have a long list of accomplishments to be proud of: excellent grades, two collegiate degrees and one post-graduate degree, scholarships and awards, publications, elected seats on committees and boards, thousands of volunteer hours. I had the great fortune to study abroad at Oxford University, and to win a scholarship in order to do so. My professors have generally loved me beyond the student-teacher relationship and many have vied for my application to their doctoral programs, believing that my intellect and compassion were needed in their respective fields. All of those accomplishments are admittedly compliments to myself—but more than anything, the components of a great resume that most people will never care to read.

The truth is I have never truly been happy at my studies. My experience of school was always fraught with anxiety and pressure. While I love to learn, I have never gone to school purely for the satisfaction of the processes, or even to get me ahead in my chosen career. Instead, I worked hard in order to gain approval, and to prove to myself that I had some kind of worth. If I failed at anything, it meant that I was a failed person. That belief took joy out of my learning experience and also made it impossible for me to ever relax, to just enjoy my life.

I remember all the long hours I put into my coursework, and how I would sit on the floor of my shower and cry because I was so exhausted. I was constantly sick and depleted; writing papers was torturous and almost all of the time I denied myself any degree of pleasure in favor of doing something for recognition and praise. I had few friends and rarely went out and did anything fun. Just sitting and relaxing, enjoying myself or a friend or a movie, was out of the question because I needed not only to do good, but also to do better, and to be the best. When I couldn't be the best, I was devastated. Criticism of any sort threw me into a void of self-doubt and self-hatred. Even when my teachers praised me, I felt I was never enough. The loving pleading of my professors to join their ranks only caused me to feel worse about myself. I knew that the persona I had presented to them was a total sham, and that, no matter how much I might impress them, they would never be my mother. It was her approval I was ultimately seeking, and no matter how hard I tried, a good grade or recommendation could not replace the terrible, empty feeling I had of not being good, special, or loved. I hoped that a grade and a handwritten comment would make me feel any one of those things. Instead, it was only more pressure to do more, to be more. All I really wanted was to be content with myself.

As for my grandfather taking pictures of me, it was another way for me to get attention when I felt so neglected and ignored in my life. Posing for the camera taught me how to act, how to behave in a particular way to get attention. I'm not sure that this helped me so much when I was a teenager—I was largely ignored in middle and high school, and was known as "the quiet girl who reads big books." I wasn't popular or unpopular, I was just . . . invisible. But later, when I was in my twenties and began losing some of my babyish looks, and gained a little bit more confidence in public, I started to use my acting to gain attention from others, especially men. I knew what kinds of stories to tell, funny faces to pull, how to hold my body, and how to use my voice to attract a kind of adoring attention. Just like I was in front of my grandpa's camera again! This behavior affected me adversely, however, because 1) I sought attention from the very people I knew were least likely to return my affections and 2) it was a way to deflect true intimacy with my partner, by focusing on getting others to "adore" me. This is very much like my experience with school, except I wasn't acting with my teachers, but with coworkers and friends. I entered into therapy because I had been dating a good man who I wanted to love me for me, and I wanted to be able to love and be myself with him. I didn't want to create drama and chaos anymore, or seek love and attention from outside of myself. I wanted to reconcile my past, work through my depression, and seek a fulfilling life in my future. I wanted to reconnect with *me* and see all the good I had inside.

Living Past the Neglect

Beginnings

I still remember quite clearly my first week of therapy. I was nervous; it was something I'd considered since I was a teenager but wasn't sure that I would "do well" or be comfortable with opening up emotionally to another person. Yet it was the need to open—to explore and accept myself, to have healthy, fulfilling relationships and life experiences—that brought me to therapy in the first place.

I had been dating a man for a couple of years who was affirming and respectful, supportive, and fun. I desired to marry him, but felt great discomfort in intimate experiences. I was also afraid to just be myself with him, believing that I was inadequate and in some way innately awful. I was sure he'd find me out! Having this consciousness, I soon realized that I often felt that way with others, and in fact had great anxiety in my relationships with friends, teachers, coworkers, and family. Around this time I also started to experience high levels of stress, insomnia, daily headaches and weekly migraines, as well as generalized physical pain. I cried a lot, felt worry and despair, and doubted myself all the time. I realized I'd felt that way since I could remember. I was ready to get some help, and hopefully in the process figure out what was "wrong" with me.

So I took a risk and started therapy, even though I was nervous. I had no idea what it would be like. Amazingly, what I felt in the beginning was a huge release. I remember receiving my first reply from Lori and crying from sheer relief. Here was someone who not only understood what I was feeling, but also didn't judge me, either. In fact, I was praised for what I *did* accomplish, for surviving my neglect and abuse, for paying my own way through school and seeking healthy relationships. I'd never considered my life and myself in such a positive light before. Instead, I'd always assumed that every bad experience, every bad relationship or failure, was a reflection of my failure as a person. It was both a bit shocking and completely lovely to suddenly experience a different perception of myself. A perception that I was essentially okay, and that I'd always been okay. I may have even done very well—so well that I had brought myself to a position where I could understand my past and acquire some tools to shape my future.

First Stages on My Road to Recovery

I think in the beginning the most important components of my recovery were 1) understanding my past and how it affected my behavior and perceptions combined with 2) a safe and nurturing environment in which to explore these issues, which was provided in the therapeutic relationship. I learned very quickly that it was okay to explore with my therapist feelings that were confusing, painful, and even shameful and embarrassing. She didn't judge me at all and in fact could give me perfectly clear reasons why I might have those feelings stemming from childhood. For example, if I was constantly searching for love and approval from my teachers and friends, and putting on masks and shows in order to gain this approval, I didn't have to assume that I was flaky, dumb, a liar, and at my core unworthy of experiencing positive reactions from people by being my true self. Instead, I could understand how, through the neglect of my childhood, I had developed coping strategies for getting love and attention from others. I could see that I had learned those behaviors in an effort to survive as a little girl.

Once I started to look at my behavior in another light—as ways to cope with neglect rather than as my fundamental flaws as a human being—I began to question my belief that I was a "bad" and "undeserving" person. Maybe I really could be a good wife and friend. Maybe I could learn to stick up for myself and nurture myself. Maybe I had a lot of positive qualities that I just had never focused on before. Maybe who I thought of as "me" (bad me) was really a compilation of ideas, negative messages, fears, and patterns that I got from my childhood environment, specifically my mother. Being able to examine my experiences, as well as the behavior and words of my family, allowed me to start separating what others said of me and for me from what I thought and felt of and for myself.

Unlearning

Once I began to identify my own negative patterns of thinking and behavior, Lori encouraged me to modify or rewrite them in a way that felt better, more positive and supportive, for me. This has been a long process that, nearly three years later, I still work at consciously as much as I am able. I've found there's a lot of negative self-talk to unlearn! On some days when I'm feeling depressed, I'll record my thoughts in my journal so that I can look at those thoughts in a more objective manner. In a single hour my mind can create a long litany of personal deprecation, like: I'm too fat, lonely, unlovable. I'm overly sensitive, can't stick up for myself, and utterly disposable to others. I'll never be good enough. Nobody cares or notices me unless it's to tease me or to criticize. I'll never be able to do what I want to do. Life is unfair.

Putting my thoughts down on paper helps me because it allows me to examine those thoughts. Where did I get the idea that nobody cares or notices me unless to criticize me? Well, my mother never paid attention to me, and when she did it was usually because she was angry. Likewise with my grandmother, she only yelled at me to criticize some small thing I did. So that's where my belief comes from. But is it true? Is it really true that I can't succeed, that I can't achieve my dreams?

I might write down in my journal all the ways that the negative statements I've made about myself aren't true. Or why it would be important to think about the people who told me such things when I was little. For example, my mother didn't pay attention to me, but was that because I was an unlovable child? Sometimes I'll take out pictures of myself as a little girl and write about her. She has such pretty hair and a pretty little nose. In the picture she's smiling brightly—she glows with happiness and delight. What a beautiful, loveable child! That's me. My mother, who I discovered in the course of therapy had been sexually abused multiple times as a child and teenager, was addicted to heroin. If she neglected me, it wasn't because of anything that I did. She was doing the best she knew how to do. As for what I am capable of now, I can comb through any positive experiences I may have had and record those, too. I want to be a writer—that is my dream. I can list all the ways I've succeeded in creating this reality for myself. For example, I've had the courage to enroll in writing classes. I've sent my poetry away for publication and, even though I've received dozens of rejections, I've also had several poems published in small presses. And I've made friends in my writing classes who seem to enjoy my work. So it seems that I *can* succeed, after all.

As I said before, this working with my thinking is a continual process. And, I admit, it's pretty slow. But I've noticed just in the past few months that it's starting to become a habit of mine to stop and take stock of my moods when they turn very depressed or anxious. If my mind is running away from me, bottoming out in negative self-talk and creating episodes of worst-case scenarios over and over, then I say "Stop!" Out loud if I can. Or, if that seems too harsh, I'll just smile and say, "Now, now dear." Then I'll consciously think of something that makes me happy. A compliment I heard, my black cat playing with his toy, a funny show I watched recently. Barring that (sometimes I can't get my mood to change no matter how hard I try) I'll do something that is nurturing of myself. I found it helpful to make a list in my journal of activities that make me happy that don't cost any money or very little. These include listening to my favorite CDs, playing cards, doing a yoga video, having hot tea with honey, taking out needlework, and walking around the block to the park where there's a swing set. It's amazing what a little swinging can do!

Nurturing Self and Safe Environment

Something that has worked really well for me is a system of rewards. Self-spoiling I guess you could call it, although I try not to think of it in terms of being "spoiled" but just taking care of myself. It's particularly hard since as a child I didn't get many of my needs met, so I don't really know how to take care of myself. When I do something that feels nice, I try to make a note of it, because when I'm depressed I seem to forget anything at all that makes me happy. So in addition to doing small activities to cheer me up (I try to incorporate these daily) I also give myself rewards. For example, if I write in my journal twice a week for five weeks, and in the journal I work to release a negative emotion, dream something positive for myself, or record something good about myself, then I will treat myself to a new book, coffee, and pastry, or will go someplace new. Some cool things I've done in the past year is visit the river five miles from my house for the first time, and a few weeks ago I went to an outdoor concert.

I'm learning how to save and spend on myself without guilt. As a reward, I might buy something I've wanted to wear like earrings or a blouse. I take the catalogues I get in the mail and clip pictures of my favorite outfits and keep them in a file. I'll go through the file happily and pick out the item I want the most and usually wait for it to go on sale (it almost always does). I particularly enjoy saving money for clothes because then I feel beautiful also. This year one of my goals was to clear out my closet of everything that didn't excite me to wear. I've been slowly re-working my wardrobe for about eight months now. I don't have a lot of money, but I have managed a few pieces that I just adore, and people compliment me on them. That reinforces the positive self-image that I am cultivating for myself. Getting a new item is also something to look forward to and that feels nice.

I should say here that I feel lucky to be able to reward myself in these ways because my spouse is very supportive of my healing work. He encourages me in my rewards and in fact he will take me on "celebrations" when I've had a meaningful breakthrough or have accomplished something that's difficult for me. I think one of the most important processes I went through when I started therapy was creating a safe environment for myself. That meant examining my personal relationships to see if I had trustworthy and supportive people around me. Of course I had friends and acquaintances that were critical or dishonest or just downright negative. I slowly put space between myself and these people and pulled closer the people that were respectful and kind. This was perhaps one of the hardest parts of recovery, and it still is. As I grow in self-worth, though, I notice that I tolerate less and less those angry and manipulative people. Or, more specifically, I recognize the manipulations when they begin, and find ways to put a healthy boundary between myself and the other person.

With my husband, we too have had to go through changes in how we interact with one another. I went through a long spell where I needed to push him away from me and say "no!" It was a very difficult time for both of us, but he understood that I was learning to create personal boundaries, and he was the person I felt closest to. Now I am able to just kindly tell him, "I need some personal space now," and there are no hard feelings on either side. It is something I'm proud of—learning to identify my needs and then ask another to respect them. Now I am working to express my needs and boundaries in relationships outside of my relationship with my spouse, like with my employer and my friends. I believe that having relationships that support my recovery, and creating a safe environment to live in, has been integral to the recovery itself.

What My Parents Never Told Me: Taking Care of Personal Health

One aspect of my life that has changed dramatically since I started therapy has been self-care. In fact, I went into therapy in part because of my deteriorating health. I had so many headaches and migraines, stomach pains, muscle aches, and insomnia that I was having a hard time making it through work. I remember right before I went into therapy I had a UTI that was so bad I had to go to the emergency room. I was exhausted and sickly all the time.

When I was a little girl my parents never took me to the doctor or the dentist. I only have one memory of going to the doctor and that was because I had migraines as a child. My mother was worried and sought treatment though I don't remember what the doctor said. But we never went back. Later, when I was in my late teens and right before I went to college, I went to the dentist. My teeth were riddled with cavities. My parents paid for those fillings and for me to get the requisite physical exams for college entrance. After that, though, I was on my own. I didn't have health insurance in college, and, since I was already paying my own tuition and rent, I didn't go to the doctor then, either. I just couldn't afford it, and I'd never gone before, so canned chicken soup was the solution to all illness.

I graduated from undergrad after five years, when I was twenty-three, and started working full-time. To make ends meet, I had two jobs, each twenty hours per week, but one of them was a long commute and required me to take work home on the weekends. This is when I really started to have a lot of health problems. I went to the doctor for the first time in ages (the exception being my emergency room visit). I went to the dentist. It was pretty terrifying—it just felt so unknown and I didn't know how to respond to doctor's questions or the intimacy of them touching me. I needed a root canal and more fillings. All four of my wisdom teeth were impacted, deteriorating the bones around my molars, and needed surgical removal. I'd worked myself to such exhaustion that I was on the verge of adrenal collapse. My neck was misshaped because of a car accident I'd had when I was twenty that I never had looked at. I needed chiropractic care three times weekly and a splint to help correct an open bite that gave me jaw pain and terrible headaches. I discovered that I had fairly severe food allergies—one of which was eggs, a staple of my diet. I drank too much caffeine to keep me going and had no exercise routine. I hadn't exercised in years.

I'm still working to correct my ailments but I am *so much* better. When I first started taking care of the big problems I felt so ashamed. For example, the surgeon who removed my wisdom teeth said, "My, these should have been removed seven years ago. You must have been in pain for a long time!" It was sad to think that I'd been so used to neglecting my body—that was normal or ordinary for me—that I accepted pain as a natural part of my existence. I never thought about asking for or getting help. I just lived through it. I was ashamed that my tooth (that needed the root canal) had festered for so long. I'd been not eating on that side of my mouth for about five years. It was a molar I'd had filled right before I went to college. . . . It had abscessed. My family never taught me good eating habits, how to care for myself or love my body. Now I take very good care of my teeth, and I exercise almost daily, and I eat mostly organic food and I've given up caffeine except for a once-weekly treat. I've implemented a relaxation program into my daily schedule and that helps my anxiety tremendously. I like to do Qi Gong and yoga and guided meditation CDs. I still have chronic pain in my jaw from my open bite and I'm scheduled for surgery this fall. My surgeon says that I've taken great care of my jaw in the meantime with all of my muscle work, so that the joint is still intact. I'm very proud of myself! And, through all of this, I've learned a tremendous lesson: I'll never neglect my body and my health again. It's my choice now, and even if my parents didn't do it for me, I now have the ability to do it for myself.

Sexuality

This is the big one for me. I wish I had some tried-and-proven technique to share, but I don't. My first sexual experience was molestation and manipulation by my cousin. I saw my mom in sexual relationships but they seemed scary and confusing when I was little. I never saw my mom in any kind of mutual or loving relationships. But I knew that she slept with strange men, disappeared all the time, and had abortions. She never explained to me what sex was or how to understand menstruation or any other natural part of growing into womanhood. A woman outside of my family gave me my first bra and when I got my period at age eleven I would hide my soiled underwear so that nobody would know my shameful secret. It was a few months before I finally told my grandma what had happened.

I had several sexual partners before I married my husband, Ben. I can't say that any of those experiences were pleasant. Sex was something I did because the man wanted it. I had no idea about my own desires or even if I should have them. I didn't know what it was like to experience real bodily pleasure outside of hugging and kissing. When I started to date my husband, we took things very slow. In fact, we didn't have sex until we'd already decided to get married. He was the first sexual partner I'd had that I felt very safe with. He paid attention to me and was gentle and loving. It was in this safe environment that I began to have anxieties and panic during sex. I don't think I would have made the connection on my own between my experiences with my cousin and these feelings of panic, shame, and disgust. But therapy has really helped me to explore, and ultimately move beyond, those feelings.

I'm not completely comfortable with sexual pleasure or with my own body, but I am getting there. I went through a period with my husband where we agreed that any time I felt panic or discomfort that I would say "stop!" and he would and we would cuddle instead. I did this for a long time and then gradually moved on to being able to identify 1) whether or not I wanted to have sex in the first place, 2) if I wanted to continue having sex once started, and 3) what kinds of sex I enjoy. This past year I've been working on not feeling guilty for saying "no" to sex and identifying when sex is painful or ceases to be pleasurable and asking to stop (again, without feeling guilty—the hardest part). I'm also working on feeling better about my body, its natural cycles of menstruation, its smells and functions. I'm starting to explore pleasure. Sex no longer seems like an obligation but something fun to do, like getting an ice cream cone or playing in the park. I admit that I may have a long way to go, but I've also come a long way, and it's been very rewarding. I can see in a very real way in the sexual arena how I'm developing and changing.

Where I Am Now: Some Positives

To end this narrative, I'd like to share some positives that I've experienced since I started therapy. I've married a wonderful man and we live in a shabby little apartment but we've fixed it up very nicely into a comfortable and bright home. I no longer have migraines and my body feels a lot better. I still have trouble sleeping but am starting to take naps again. I have a job that has good insurance and is low-stress. I've started my first savings account. It's meager, but it's something! I have three animals that I adore and give me great joy. I've completed a Masters degree with high marks and have taken writing classes consistently for about two years now. I've had two teachers tell me that I'm a wonderful writer and that they have high hopes for my future career. I've had poetry published in five journals. I send packets of my writing off to publishers and contests two to three times per month and handle rejection better. I'm gaining confidence that I'll get published more and more often as my experience and publishing credits grow. I have a better relationship with my family than I've ever had. I have greater self-esteem than I've ever had. Some days, I'm just really happy and grateful to be alive. And that's something I'd never experienced before, so it's one of the most amazing rewards of doing therapeutic work.

Tara initially contacted me at www.find-a-therapist.com, after viewing my professional profile on the website. I wrote about my expertise in working with adult survivors of neglect and abuse. And yet, when Tara began her therapy, she was very guarded about discussing her history of sexual abuse with me. Even via email contact, her defensive structure was evident. She utilized minimization and suppression to cope with the severity of her neglect and trauma. Over time, Tara became more capable of removing the barriers to her truth.

Tara impressed me most with her ability to extend a loving, compassionate hand to her mother throughout her therapeutic work. She was able to integrate the pain and neglect that her mother caused, while simultaneously enhancing the quality of her communication with her mother. It is rare that clients are able to process their childhood experiences with the person who was responsible for much of the trauma. Tara's mother stopped using heroin. She was able to take responsibility for some of Tara's worst memories. Her mother can express love at times, and Tara can feel that love.

Be careful not to advocate for one communication style or another when working with your clients. Many clients want to forgive and forget, without processing their negative feelings first. Even if parents cannot apologize or take responsibility, it may still be beneficial for clients to confront their histories at the source of the pain. And, the opposite may also be true. A confrontation may be totally unproductive for your client. This dynamic needs to be assessed over time, as clients process their emotions about their histories with you.

In *The Source of All* Things,[7] Tracy Ross (2011) confronts her stepfather about his abuse. The confrontation is both productive and overwhelming for her. The complex and confusing results of that confrontation are discussed further, in chapter 12.

Chapter Eight

Adoption and Neglect

Heide's story in chapter 3 introduced us to the concept of magical thinking. Magical thinking can also pervade the minds of adopted children. Unlike those of us who grew up with our biological parents, many adoptees were told of their adoptions at an early age. These children tend to carry with them the inventions of a birth mother who loves them dearly. For children who were neglected or abused by their adoptive parents, these fantasies can take on the flavor and texture of escape, of the hope of a better life in the future. Adopted children can also invent worst-case scenarios about their biological parents, creating stories about rejection that permeate their behaviors, even though these stories may never be verbalized.

During the writing of this book, an esteemed colleague told me the story of her neighbor. This neighbor, Samantha, had a young son, Jared. Jared used to visit my colleague's home regularly, to play with her son Dustin. Jared was shy and reserved, and Dustin would attempt to coax and cajole him in the course of their play. Jared didn't talk very much at all. But my colleague noticed something unusual and consistent about him. Whenever Jared visited, he always carried a photograph in his pocket. It was a worn photo of a young woman. When my colleague asked about the photo, Jared told her, "That's my real Mommy." Then he volunteered, "I always look for her."

Although adoption regulations have relaxed a great deal in recent years, and *The Locator* has aired on television, many adult adoptees still live with the scars of a closed adoption.

What does neglect feel like in relation to the adoption experience? If children are prohibited from knowing that they were adopted, or if it is expected that a child will keep silent about it, this family secret can cause an adoptee to feel emotionally neglected and deprived in many ways.[1]

Joelle and Gary

Joelle initially came to therapy when she was nineteen years old. She was struggling in relationships with men, and she acknowledged a very poor relationship with her adoptive mother. Although Joelle's family was involved in an open adoption, there was no solace in that option for her. In fact, when Joelle confessed that she was adopted to a little four-year-old friend in nursery school, the friend's mother called Joelle's mother to verify the story. Joelle remembers her mother being furious with her about exposing the family secret. It is her first memory of physical abuse.

Joelle's early memories are colored by her adoptive mother's consistent criticisms and blatant rejections of Joelle's efforts at being affectionate. Her adoptive mother physically abused Joelle as she grew older. The abuse was severe, and frequent. Her father was passive when he was present to witness the abuse; he would not make any attempt to stop it. Joelle would try to do all she could to please her mother—she would clean the house, vacuum the carpets, take care of her younger brother, and mow the lawn. It seemed impossible to please her mother, however. Nothing was ever good enough for her. Joelle's adoptive father was often kind and loving, despite his lack of willingness to protect her. Spending quality time with him served as a restorative experience for Joelle, despite his neglect of her emotional needs.

Even when adoptive parents do the best they can to discuss a child's adoption openly, and to create a sense of specialness about the adopted child, that child may still grow to adulthood with unanswered questions. The sense of early rejection can pervade their consciousness. Adopted children often respond to this sense of rejection in extreme ways. They either learn to please to the *n*th degree, to avoid rejection by others, or they learn to act-out, to bring on the rejection. These are similar extremes to the ones seen in biological children of neglect.

In Joelle's case, her sense of being rejected was exacerbated by her mother's abusive treatment. During Joelle's adolescence, she became intimate with a young man who physically abused and orally raped her. He would, on occasion, be affectionate toward Joelle, and she was so starved for affection that she stayed with this young man for several years before he eventually abandoned her for another young woman.

Joelle chose this moment in time to decide to begin psychotherapy. She had survived so much criticism that she had become extremely self-effacing. Joelle's initial task in treatment was to monitor how many times she called herself "stupid" on a daily basis. She began to realize how she had taken on the role of "dumb blonde," so that she could take charge of expected criticism. Joelle was actually very intelligent, and also quite attractive. She had no female friends. She could not trust women at all. Joelle was able to explore her transference responses in the world, and create a new sense of self, with years of hard work in therapy. The young woman who initially told me, "I have no opinions," began to form an identity. She was able to examine her need to please others, and to make choices about setting limits when appropriate.

Because Joelle was told she was adopted when she was four years old, she had an imaginary introject. Here, magical thinking served Joelle very well. Joelle believed that her biological mother was kind and loving, but that she was probably too young to keep Joelle and raise her. In this way, Joelle was able to hold onto the fantasy of a magical mother who would one day want to meet and rescue her. They would share stories and remain in each other's lives forever. Joelle believed in her own capacity to mother because of this introject. She could consistently remind herself, during the abuse by her adoptive mother, that her abuser was not her "real" mother. Joelle wanted to mother her own children more than anything else in the world.

When Joelle met Gary, they were both in their mid-twenties. They met at work, where Joelle excelled as an executive secretary. They didn't date long before Gary proposed marriage, and Joelle accepted without hesitation. Gary wanted children, and he wanted her to stay home to raise them.

The first few years of Joelle's marriage to Gary were as blissful as any time Joelle had ever known before. She became pregnant easily, and had two children within three years. She noticed signs of neglect, when Gary would forget her birthday or their anniversary, but she felt so wonderful about being a mother that she was able to squelch her negative feelings. Gary would occasionally become very stressed out from working long hours, and he began to take Advil in the morning, like other people take vitamins, to help to alleviate his consistent headaches. He became more and more distant from Joelle as the years progressed, and he withdrew from her sexually. He told Joelle he was tired, but of course, Joelle blamed herself for his growing lack of interest in her and the children.

Still, Joelle gave birth to two more children, further apart than the others, and she continued to experience a heaven on earth as a mother. Joelle volunteered at her children's school, became a soccer mom, the neighborhood chauffeur to her children and their friends, and managed a Girl Scout troop. She began scrapbooking, to record all of the stages of growth and activity for her four beautiful children. Her life centered around her children.

Throughout their marriage, Gary had experienced conflict with his family of origin. He had acknowledged a history of sexual abuse by an uncle, but he had not sought help to process the experience of abuse and violation. As a child, Gary told his secret to his mother, but his truth was both neglected and negated. Still, like many male incest survivors, Gary did not define himself as a victim.

Due to the nature of male genitalia, men with incest histories are more likely than women to have experienced physiological pleasure during incidents of sexual abuse. Certainly, pain may have also been present. If the memory of pleasure is intact, however, many men incorporate their abuse as a positive experience, as "starting early." Depending on the age that the same-gender abuse occurred, there may also be a strong fear of homosexuality. Experiencing some physiological pleasure with a male authority figure and family member can play havoc with a young boy's sense of self. Often, the young boy has loving feelings toward his abuser. All of this makes it very difficult, later in life, to combine sex with love in partnership with a woman. As with female incest survivors, sex can feel dirty. It is easier on the psyche to separate sex from love, especially after marriage, when one's partner is associated with "family." Being intimate with a loving partner can be a strong trigger to the memories of incest. If heterosexual men subconsciously fear that they are homosexual because they felt pleasure during the abuse, they may need to prove to themselves with sexual encounters with women that they are indeed heterosexual. This is especially the case if male incest survivors are unable to hold onto the initial attractions they once felt for their spouses or long-term partners. For gay men with incest histories, there can also be intense internalized homophobia, especially if their abusers were male, and if the abuse was also pleasurable on a physiological level. It can be very difficult for a man to separate his need to come out as gay, from his history of abuse, and there may be many questions about gender identity in the course of therapeutic treatment.

Due to his unresolved sexual abuse history, the stage was set for Gary to begin an extramarital affair. When Joelle turned forty, she began therapy again. She had recently single-handedly conducted an exhaustive search for her birth mother. With her heart in her throat, Joelle had found and contacted her biological mother, and arranged to meet her for lunch. Joelle's birth mother had remarried, and had a son, Joelle's stepbrother. Although this meeting was pivotal for Joelle, her birth mother showed no interest in continuing a relationship with Joelle, or with her own biological grandchildren. Joelle left the restaurant, defeated and alone. When she returned home from this meeting, Gary met her at the door, anxious and scared. He admitted to the fact that he had been involved in a twelve-year affair during the course of their eighteen-year marriage. He had also begun individual treatment on his own. Gary confessed his love for Joelle, did not want to divorce her, and told Joelle that he had ended the affair. He had started to make the connections necessary to resolve his abuse history, but it was too late for Joelle. Too many fights where he blamed her for his withdrawal, too many years of feeling unattractive to her husband, too many hours of single parenting, too many forgotten birthdays, and finally, a total lack of trust in people, due to too many maternal rejections. Gary started individual therapy to resolve his history and save his marriage; Joelle started individual therapy to gather the strength she would need to cope with her divorce, and the dissolution of her fantasy of having a mother and a husband to love her.[2]

The good news is that despite her continued traumatic experiences in life, Joelle never questioned her ability to provide wonderful mothering to her four children. She learned "what not to do" very well, and she is there for her children in every way that she ever wished that a mother could be there for her.

Both Gary and Joelle experienced abuse and neglect as children. Under different circumstances, and if the timing were different, perhaps they could have healed together.

The breaking up of families through divorce and infidelity can be one of the most tragic aftereffects of an unresolved neglect and sexual abuse history.

Dorothy

I met Dorothy when she was in undergraduate college in Boston, over thirty years ago. Dorothy was adopted when she was an infant. She lived for seventeen years with her adopted family, believing that they were her biological parents. There were curiosities in everyday life as Dorothy grew older, however. There were very few photographs taken of her. She resembled no one in her family. When she would try to bring this topic up in conversation, there would be silence. She would feel the tension within the household that a secret carries. Certain things were taboo to discuss, and Dorothy's sense was that if she discussed them, she would be betraying her family in some way. I have met with many adopted adults who felt this way as children, regardless of the age when they were told of their adoption. The tension of carrying a secret can lead to stifling one's emotions, dissociation, and the feeling of being neglected and unloved. Even adoptees in the best of all possible circumstances will tell me that they do not want to search for their biological families, because they feel it will "hurt my parents." Should this weight need to be carried by an adoptee?

At seventeen, Dorothy was told that she was adopted. She was finishing her last year in high school and beginning to date. Dorothy integrated the fact of her adoption with fear and panic. She would obsess about her dates with young men, wondering if any of them could be her biological brother. She was given no information about her biological family, and had no support in conducting an adoption search. Dorothy had no idea whether or not she had any biological siblings. As a young woman, it became very difficult for Dorothy to be intimate in relationships with men, due to her fear that she could be unknowingly participating in incest. She began using alcohol to block her fears and panic about relationships with men. Alcohol quickly became the friend that she needed to support her in dealing with her fears and panic in relation to adoption and intimacy.[3]

When adoptive parents neglect the adoptee's emotional wellbeing in order to create the image of a well-adjusted family with no secrets, there is always damage done to the adopted child. All children need to feel a true sense of belonging, and all children are entitled to know their roots.

Part II

WORKING WITH NEGLECT

Chapter Nine

"It Wasn't That Bad!": Working with Defensive Structure

As you may know, Freud (1962) had heard his female patients disclose numerous stories of sexual abuse from their histories during the time he practiced psychotherapy.[1] When he presented his theory of the prevalence of sexual abuse, however, he was ridiculed by his fellow analysts. Many feminists believe that Sigmund Freud may have abandoned his research on incest as a response to the opposition of his male colleagues. In Masson's (2003) book *The Assault on Truth,* Freud is described as reinterpreting his patients' reports of childhood sexual molestation as fantasies. He dismissed them as untrue, and reframed the molestation as "seduction theory."[2] This is perhaps where our culture developed the notion that women want to be raped, as well as the habit of "blaming the victim" in abuse cases.

Although Freud did not do us any favors as women in this regard, he was also responsible for the explanation of defense mechanisms and theories of defensive structure in individuals. Many psychotherapists continue to utilize their knowledge of defensive structure in helping clients in treatment today. Not unlike Heide's father in chapter 3, Freud was clearly capable of empathy and understanding, but also, of unintended abuse and trauma in service to his own ego.

Our defensive structure tells us a great deal about ourselves. Neglect and abuse survivors develop defenses as survival skills. Defenses need to be respected as well as challenged during the process of therapy.

The most important aspect of understanding defenses is the fact that they are developmental in nature. We develop specific defenses at different phases of life.[3] For example, a young child would not be able to utilize the defenses of intellectualization and rationalization, but an adolescent might find those defenses particularly soothing to the ego. Some defenses are quite strong, even obstinate, and difficult to manage. Your clients' defenses can be used as tools in detecting the approximate age that they felt the most traumatized. Many of your clients may have been traumatized enough to develop and rely on their defenses in order to cope more effectively with their circumstances.

Although these defenses serve as survival skills when we are children, they become less productive in terms of our mental health as adults. They may keep us from connecting to others, or from knowing our true selves. If you are working with a woman, for example, who utilizes denial—our earliest developmental defense—in order to cope with a history of neglect by her biological mother, you might hear: "My mother was my best friend. She did everything for me."

In this chapter, I will review the defenses that are most commonly seen in abuse and neglect survivors. I will juxtapose the defense of denial against the phases of grief[4] established by Elisabeth Kubler-Ross (1969). In this way, I hope to assist you to enhance your understanding of how your clients coped with grief and loss, and to develop more compassion for the little children they once were.

Denial

Denial is associated with very early childhood trauma.[5] Denial is a defense that can be formed as early as we can say "no"—during the phase of rapprochement,[6] described best by theorist Margaret Mahler (1975). Mahler discusses a phase of separation-individuation in childhood, between approximately fifteen to twenty-four months, when toddlers typically begin to walk more steadily, and test their parents' limits. In college at Boston University, I learned about rapprochement as the process of "holding on and letting go." A young girl from a normal family background can safely begin to walk away from her mother, but she will walk a certain distance, and look back to be sure her mother is still there. It is the safety of the knowledge that her mother is watching that allows the child to separate, and to walk a bit farther. What happens to her steps if she teaches herself to walk? What happens if she walks away, and nobody cares? What happens if she looks back, and no one is there?

Denial is defined as "a defense that is formed when a person is faced with a fact that is too uncomfortable or painful to accept and rejects it instead, insisting that it is not true despite what may be overwhelming evidence."[7] Children faced with the need to deny reality from an early age will grow into adults who are more likely to deny their problems, especially in relation to addiction. But keep in mind that denial is also a healthy mechanism that assists us to cope with grief and loss. It is the first stage of Kubler-Ross's phases of grief. Following the death of a loved one, we initially rely on denial to cope with the awful pain and longing for that person. Denial can manifest itself in the process of coping with anticipatory grief as well. Parents of children who are terminally ill are the last to give up on their children—they often continue to deny the reality of their child's impending death, long after the child has come to accept it.

Avoidance

Avoidance is another defense that is usually formed as a result of early childhood abuse and trauma. It occurs when individuals must retreat from their reality. Like denial, avoidance protects us from unbearable pain. Later in life, the retreat may be exacerbated by low self-esteem, fear of failure, embarrassment, or insecurity in a relationship. Conflict avoidance is a form of this defense, with an obvious source of having witnessed conflict that was emotionally or physically violent, with no resolution.

Avoidance is also a natural by-product of immediate trauma, as well as a characteristic of post-traumatic stress. Women who have been raped outdoors at night, for example, may avoid going outside after the sun sets, immediately following the rape. We avoid those places or people who may remind us of the trauma that we are attempting to deny. Denial and avoidance often come in the same package. What good is denial, after all, if we don't avoid? How might avoidance behaviors exhibit themselves in your therapy office? People might change the subject when you begin asking questions about their histories. They might make a joke when the subject matter is not at all funny. They might talk so much that you have no room to respond or comment. Your job as their therapist is to notice, and reflect back to your client, in a gentle way, what you observe. Try not to avoid avoidance!

Psychological withdrawal occurs when we feel uncomfortable in a particular situation, but feel forced to be physically present. Incest survivors are skilled at psychological withdrawal. They may be able to leave their bodies while remaining in the room. They become virtuosos at finding internal escape routes.

Minimization

Minimization is a bit like denial, but its cloak is lighter to carry. It occurs when we are able to admit that something happened to us, but we need to deny the seriousness of the hurt, betrayal, or loss. Coming out of minimization can reproduce symptoms of post-traumatic stress. Once we realize the extent of our neglect or abuse, it is natural that nightmares could increase, exposure issues and old ways of coping could resurface, and survivors may feel "raw" or "inside out." It is important to help survivors to create enough support in their lives to facilitate the process of letting go of this defense.

A current e-therapy client described the pain of letting go of minimization in the following email to me:

> I hid the courage to heal in my attic for twenty years.[8] When I finally found my old copy of the book the other day, I had to write to you and confess. When I had first started the book twenty years ago, I was drawn to the stories of other survivors, but their abuse histories always felt much more traumatic than my own. Now, when I read a few paragraphs here and there, I am feeling much more scared and raw.
>
> I've spent the whole weekend asking myself the "Do you want to be happy?" thing. Or maybe it should be "Are you willing to do what it takes to be happy?" I do think I want to be happy and I know how to be happy, but with all the negativity in my mind it is really hard to get there. I am so afraid that if I allow myself to feel happy, it will quickly be taken away from me.
>
> There is so much that went on that caused all this, and now I realize that. There is much reprogramming I have to do of my brain. I think what would make me happy is if my mind was quiet. I'm tired of all the noise, and once in a while, when things are right with the world, I get a glimpse of sleeping well, and can deal with things so much better.
>
> But recently, I have been having horrible dreams. Last night, there was a line of stories—lots of stories and it was like they were being shown to me one after another and I woke up in so much pain. Every part of my body hurt like I had gone through it all over again. Then all the yelling in my mind started—trying to get me to realize that this stuff happened to me. And then, it all goes away. Like this morning, all the memories are gone, but the pain stays—which allows the doubt to resurface. I feel like there is a long line of truths waiting for me inside. The truths don't fit into my life so I think I can wish them away as in a fairytale. I've gotten extremely good at pushing all the stuff away—making it disappear or lessen, and for the most part, it has served me well. Except now, I think it's festering inside, growing stronger and stronger and taking more and more room inside—wanting attention like never before.
>
> When I see my girls growing up into young women, especially my oldest, I know what she has not had to go through, compared to myself. I know she did not have to experience all of the trauma I had to cope with at that point in my life. She didn't have to experience one world and then go experience the other like each exists only for its own purpose. By the time I was her age, I had to be such a slave to the world I couldn't think of my future. I never expected to graduate high school; I thought for sure I would be dead. I am starting to remember horrible things that I don't have explanations for, and I wonder if they really happened.
>
> I wish I could be angry but I'm scared of that anger and it is easier for me to accept it as my fault—then it becomes easier to understand. You want to believe that there is a certain amount of justice in the world, but it seems to me that it's all upside down. Between what I'm actually responsible for and what I

have taken responsibility for—the world is a pretty burdensome place from my standpoint.

When you hear clients minimize their history, you can do some didactic work with them regarding their defensive structure. No one would need to tell themselves that "it wasn't so bad," if it were actually true that it wasn't so bad! The fact that a client uses this defense is actually proof that things were bad.

Rationalization and Intellectualization

Rationalization and intellectualization entail the ability to think logically, and to form intellectual concepts. Rationalization occurs when something happens to us that we find difficult to accept, so we make up a logical reason why it happened. This is a more mature version of magical thinking. The need to rationalize is more likely to form in early adolescence and throughout early adulthood.

Rationalization can be utilized to soothe one's ego. How many of us heard from a parent after being physically abused, for example, that it was "for our own good"? Rationalization is another way that incest victims can blame themselves for the abuse as well. Thinking that they deserved what they got, or that they are generally unlovable, is a rationalization. Self-blame can be a very pervasive by-product of neglect. Whether that self-blame takes a tangible form ("I was a rebellious brat, and I deserved to be ignored") or a generalized form ("I never do anything right"), your client is using rationalization to avoid identifying the source of the pain.

Intellectualization also allows us to distance from our painful emotions. It is considered the flight into reason, whereby clients can focus solely on their intellectual explanations for occurrences, rather than the emotions attached to those uncomfortable circumstances. Intellectualization allows us to ignore our emotions, as if they are irrelevant.

I used to believe that the authors of the Diagnostic and Statistical Manual for Mental Disorders, the text most frequently consulted in the field of mental health to diagnose and treat patients, was written by people who needed to intellectualize, and distance from their emotions. If we can label people, then we can, as professionals, distance from the connections we may have felt when we read the criteria for those diagnoses. I have, over time, learned to see the value in establishing criteria for diagnosis and treatment, and in retrospect, I can define my initial belief as an intellectualization, based in my own fear.[9]

Sublimation

In describing sublimation, a current client comes to mind immediately. This client has felt disconnected from her neglectful mother for most of her life.

She has repressed memories from birth to eight years old, when her mother stopped drinking. Recently, her mother visited, and told a "funny" story. Her mother spoke of an incident in my client's childhood, when my client was about four years old. Her mother was yelling at her to "move—why are you just standing there?" to which my client responded: "But Mommy, you're stepping on my feet!" Her mother continued: "And when I looked down, I was standing on your feet, preventing you from moving, and I just laughed and laughed!"

My client has no conscious memory of this incident. However, she does have feeling memory of being trapped, unprotected, and abandoned. As an adolescent, my client started running. She enjoyed the escape it offered, and the runner's high. As an adult, she runs for endurance, not speed, and she has reached an Olympic skill level. She continues to train for marathons on a very frequent basis. My client is not sure that she ever wants to access more memory from those repressed years. But it doesn't matter. No one will ever step on her feet or keep her trapped again.

In sports, we sublimate our anger, aggressive urges, and the desire to fight into the ritualized activity of formal competition. In creating art or poetry, we often take suffering and create beauty from it. In comedy, we can create healing laughter from discomfort.

Sublimation is often the creative person's defense. When faced with the conflicts associated with uncomfortable thoughts, we create psychic energy. This energy has to go somewhere. Sublimation channels this energy away from destructive acts into something socially acceptable or creatively effective.

The sublimation is apparent in the incest survivor's sculpture pictured on the cover of this text. The sculpture was created by Darlene Warren Doerr, and entitled "Breaking Free." Before Darlene allowed memories to surface about neglect and abuse in her childhood, she was speaking through her art. An article published by the *Augusta Chronicle* in November of 2002 described Darlene's artwork:

> Bits of metal, pieces of stone and figures of body parts found their way into her artwork. When admirers suggested the sculpture was about child sexual abuse, she would disagree—that was not what she meant—but people read the meaning anyway, she said.
>
> "My art told my story before my voice was able to," said Mrs. Doerr, a survivor of abuse.[10]

Repression and Suppression

Repression is sometimes referred to as *motivated forgetting*. It is a primary defense mechanism that usually occurs early in life. Repression is unconscious. Many abuse survivors have repressed memory. Although there may be no conscious memory of abuse, there are aftereffects in a woman's present life that point to trauma in the past.

When we deliberately and consciously try to push away thoughts or memories of abuse, we are using a defense called *suppression*. The memory comes up, and we attempt to bury it again, with varying degrees of success.

For the most thorough list of aftereffects for sexual abuse survivors, see the Incest Survivors Aftereffects Checklist in E. Sue Blume's (1990) groundbreaking book *Secret Survivors*.

When I suggested to a former client, Danielle, that she check out the Incest Survivors Aftereffects Checklist,[11] she did not stop at reading the list. She began to write down some vulnerable thoughts in the form of poetry, following each item on the checklist. When it became too overwhelming, Danielle stopped writing at the fourth item on the list. Here is another beginning:

From Danielle:

I had almost completely forgotten that I began this piece. . . . I began it after you gave me the checklist for incest survivors. It was my attempt to begin answering all of the questions on that list. I only answered four.

They are creative responses to the questions. . . . The breathing in them is staggered. . . . It was my interpretation of how my body was responding to the questions asked. I'm attaching it here in case it might be of help.

fear of being alone in the dark, of sleeping alone,
nightmares, night terrors (especially pursuit, threat,
entrapment)
the net a net in the dark a net it follows me
the net i cover me in the dark
i see shadows translucent shadows they
skin them selves tell me to come to come
with them them that they can help me help me
i can't ask them how are you are you coming

swallowing and gagging sensitivity; repugnance to
water on one's face when bathing or swimming
(suffocation feelings)
no
there is the way light rhymes with its selves
here how they tumble upon themselves
this is holding a cradle
i liked it there between the lips of water
upon water upon my miniature self

by the ankle i was drug out
they thought i was crying crying because i
had been towed towed under but i was crying
because they had drug me
out

gastrointestinal problems; gynecological disorders
(including spontaneous vaginal infections); headaches;
arthritis or joint pain
i don't i don't see what these these have to do with
each other
but yes the head aches it aches into nothing sometimes
there is nothing there for a moment and then then
i remember my self my body and it scares me
my body i don't want it these hands the skin i want it
all off
and then then there is the pink my second mouth
here i remember i remember there was a boy once
i remember wishing wishing he was he was a
girl but he but he was not she there was a she once
before the boy this is the color a color like purple i
am i am not supposed to to speak to speak from this
mouth

wearing a lot of clothing, even in summer; baggy clothes;
failure to remove clothing even when appropriate to do so
(while swimming, bathing, sleeping); extreme requirement
for privacy when using bathroom
"when are you going to start wearing color again?"
i've swallowed i've swallowed them all
"all?"
yes the colors all up
"i've never heard of no eight year old wearing all black,
these bag-like clothes. it's just not right . . ."
i wanted to be like wednesday at eight
have a severed hand a doll head a butcher's knife
i used to press it press it against against the thigh

When you work with clients who have repressed memory, or use suppression to help them to cope, you will find that memory resurfaces in many different ways. Memory can resurface as a result of a sound, a smell, or a deep feeling. It can resurface as an emotional overreaction to a present circumstance that is a trigger to the past. It can also resurface from the outside-in—in other words, from the circumference of the memory (the least painful) to the center of the memory (the most traumatic event). Here is an example: A former client of mine remembered being selected to go for a ride in her father's new car. She was from a large family, with eight siblings, and felt starved for attention a good deal of the time. No one asked her about school, her siblings shunned her, and she had few friends. The family relocated their home almost every year. This client remembers being thrilled to get into the car with her father. She remembers observing the scenery from the passenger window. Then, the memory fades. The next recollection is of getting out of the car, feeling very disappointed and lonely. This particular client has no interest in accessing the center of the memory. She has other memories of sexual inappropriateness perpetuated by her father, but they occurred when she was older, and less vulnerable. This is an example of successful repression in service to the ego. There would be no reason to decide to explore this type of early memory further, unless your client told you that she wanted to know more. This client felt that she retrieved what she needed in order to heal.

Identification with the Aggressor

In my work with men, I often find that this defense is used as protection from pain, as well as a negative introject. As in Gary's story in chapter 8, it is more difficult for men with abuse and neglect histories to identify themselves as victims. Men tend to externalize their anger, while women are more likely to internalize ours, and turn it against ourselves. This may explain why men may be more likely to repeat the cycle of abuse and neglect than women. Men are still discouraged in our culture from feeling the extent of their feelings. Often, men disguise all of their other difficult emotions—pain, betrayal, grief, sadness—and meld them together into rage.

Many men with same-gender neglect and abuse histories will learn to integrate a powerful identity, as described in more detail in chapter 11, "Working with the Introject." This defense is easier on the male psyche than to acknowledge that they were weak and helpless victims of a father who abused his power. Yet, it is this very acknowledgment that allows men to heal. If they can modify or let go of this defense, and define themselves as victims, they can often stop repeating their abuse histories with their wives and children. The need to master their experience by repetition often fades when their victim identity becomes conscious. When men learn to define themselves as victims, there is much more room to identify with other victims, and to feel compassion toward them. In this way, they learn to love themselves, despite the feeling of being unloved during childhood, and unlovable as adults.

When men's anger becomes abusive, it is easy to see how they continue to set themselves up to be isolated in relationships. Often, men are angry when they are feeling scared or sad underneath. The anger is the emotion that surfaces first and foremost. When men express anger toward their partners, they are often feeling abandoned, disconnected, and alone. The anger, in turn, continues to push their partners away, reinforcing the notion that they deserve to remain unloved. This is the pattern that occurred numerous times for Joey, mentioned in more detail in chapter 11. Joey's initial identification with his father, the aggressor, ultimately cost him his marriage and custody of his children.

The defense of identification with the aggressor is not limited to men, however. I have worked with some women with neglect histories who have later been sexually abused. One woman chose to work in a topless bar, and later, as a prostitute. She used the money that she earned to pay her entire tuition at a very expensive university. She did not define herself as a victim. She did not have repressed memory. She remembered the details of her abuse and neglect history clearly, but she had integrated the negative attention from the incest as positive. She had also dissociated from her painful feelings. This client was paid for her "services" to her older brother and his friends. She told me in one session that "I'm getting men back" for all the abuse. This rationalization made sense to her. It was more than a year later, after consistent weekly sessions, that I was able to help this client to grapple with her tangled list of defenses: identification with the aggressor, denial, avoidance, suppression, minimization, and dissociation, and to start to claim her victim status by "owning" her pain.

If a woman tells you that she "enjoys" her work as a prostitute, she is most likely employing the same defenses as my client.

Dissociation

The psychiatric definition of *dissociation* is "a defense mechanism in which specific, anxiety-provoking thoughts, emotions, or physical sensations are separated from the rest of the psyche."[12] Dissociation comes in many forms. Incest survivors who remember detailed abuse histories can dissociate from their feelings. Infant victims of neglect can dissociate enough to avoid the pain of being ignored. We all dissociate to some degree. Have you ever been driving along the highway, when you suddenly realize you missed your exit? This is a mild form of dissociation. You disappear from yourself for a while. In cases of severe neglect and abuse, dissociation occurs 24/7. It is another subconscious tool that we utilize when our pain is too much to bear. There is one very unfortunate thing about dissociation, though. When we use dissociation to distance from our negative feelings, we are not conscious enough of the technique to pick and choose. We also dissociate from all positive feelings. In your therapy office, this could sound like the following:

"I don't know what I'm feeling."

"I feel numb all the time."

You could respond: "Do you know what you might be feeling, if you could allow yourself to feel?"

If the answer is still "no," try to reflect on what you have heard the client talk about, and use the technique of "lending an ego."[13] Be careful to utilize feeling words that are the least toxic to hear. For example, you might say "If my mother had neglected me as much as yours neglected you, I might feel frustrated or upset." Use more generic terms like *upset* instead of *angry*, or *resentful*. This use of feeling words opens a door without making it too scary to walk through it.

Also, let your clients know that there is always some good reason for them to be utilizing dissociation. Help them to see how it has served them, what the benefits are of holding onto the defense, and what the rewards might be of letting it go. This psycho-educational work can be done with each of the defenses described above.

There is good news for clients who dissociate. Once you gently help your clients to feel their emotions, you will open them up to a wide range of feelings. I often tell clients that "if you don't allow the full extent of your pain, you will never experience the full extent of your joy." This can turn fear to hope in the hearts of some survivors. Clients who have been dissociated for many years can become very fearful of the process of allowing their true feelings to unfold. It is important to assist clients to know that the pain has accumulated over years. The pain of the abuse and neglect is not happening now, and the feelings just need to be expressed, to come up and out. I also tell clients that "no one will feel the pain of that little child if you don't." It's a gift that your clients can give to themselves. As long as they are safe and supported, they can let go of the need for this defense, become more present in their daily lives, and more compassionate and genuine in their choices in relationships.

Allowing ourselves to experience the full range of emotion enables us to feel more whole. To move past trauma and to discover peace. Therapy is about finding balance.

There are some survivors of neglect and abuse who did not employ the defenses above. They were not able to dissociate, or forget, or block their pain easily at all. If you do not see your client's defensive structure in this chapter, and you have clients that are extremely sensitive or in acute pain about their histories, you may need to help them build defenses rather than gently tear them down. They may need to learn to nurture, self-soothe, and re-parent themselves with your help. You can assist them in negotiating and managing the intensity of their memories and their grief. This can be achieved with the help of techniques like EMDR, brainspotting, relaxation, guided imagery, CBT, and meditation. Much of this work with clients' defensive structures is about helping them to find balance.

Margaret, a former client and survivor of severe neglect and abuse, began her therapy with very few defenses. Margaret was victimized throughout her childhood by every adult in her life, as well as her older siblings. She had a clear memory of her parents' alcoholism, as well as her own physical abuse, sexual abuse, and trauma due to physical and emotional neglect. Margaret began inner-child work with the hope of closing her wounds. She began this work by hiding beneath a knitted afghan that I kept on the back of the couch in my office. She would allow herself to be vulnerable from beneath this afghan. She could see out; I could not see in. This protective coating allowed Margaret to feel less like a target. She could permit herself the relief of releasing her deep emotions, as long as she felt invisible and guarded. The afghan served as a tangible defense against pain, exposure, and vulnerability.

Margaret and I worked together for many years. We still remain in contact via email. Today, she is the administrator of a hospital; her areas of expertise include alcoholism and drug abuse. One of the Chinese characters in the word *crisis* is the same symbol used in the word *opportunity*. Margaret discovered the opportunity to help others by exploring the crisis of her neglect history.

Chapter Ten

The Integration of Deprivation: Intrusive Thoughts and Hypervigilance

Wisdom consists in being able to distinguish among dangers and make a choice of the least harmful.

—Niccolo Machiavelli[1]

Neglected women learned as children to paint worst-case scenarios on every wall of their minds. They also learned observational techniques as children that often serve as a sixth sense in adulthood. Sometimes, however, there is extreme difficulty in deciphering clear intuition about others from intrusive thoughts about the self.

Intrusive thoughts are developed during the time we are being abused or neglected. Because it is too difficult to experience anger toward our caretakers, we internalize that anger, and turn it against ourselves. We believe that we are at fault instead, and we come up with numerous negative internal voices to explain to ourselves why we are unlovable. At the same time, we develop the ability to observe our surroundings, the emotions expressed around us, the tone of people's voices, the sound of their footsteps, the details of a ceiling that we monitor when we can't sleep. Our observational ability evolves into hypervigilance, and our intuitions evolve as well. We trust our observations and intuitions, as well as our negative beliefs about ourselves. Often, it is very hard to distinguish between the two.

The greatest distinction I have seen between intuition and intrusive thought, is that intrusive thoughts about the self are always negative, and rarely accurate. Good intuition about others can be clouded by assumptions about them. These assumptions are inaccurate because they stem from intrusive thoughts about the self. The intrusive thoughts stem from the post-traumatic stress response to living without love. They are our beliefs that helped us to survive neglect, and they are sometimes our worst enemies as adults.

In Sue Bender's (1995) book *Everyday Sacred,* she addresses some simple concepts about negativity that make profound sense. During a talk for the Women's Press Association, Bender was educated by one of her attendees:

> "Sue, I don't think it's wise for you to be so hard on yourself," she began. "Each time you say something critical about yourself you are making that message to yourself more real." This wise young woman, supposedly in need of my assistance, told me something very true. How we speak to ourselves can have a powerful effect on what happens in our lives.
>
> I might never have even recognized that I had a harsh judge, or understood her power to demolish my spirit, if friends had not shown their concern. "Why are you so hard on yourself?" they kept asking. The judge was even more powerful before I was consciously aware of her. Not only did I listen, but I believed what she was saying.
>
> When I finally realized the price I was paying for this deep-seated habit, I decided to get rid of her.
>
> So much for wishing.
>
> Her voice got louder and more insistent. Nothing I did made a dent in her fierce persistence. On a sunny weekend in June I spent two days indoors, in a rather stuffy room, taking a workshop given by Yvonne, called THE JUDGE.
>
> "The first step is to *notice,"* Yvonne began. "Don't try to change your behavior."
>
> "Get to really *know* the judge. Notice the subtle ways she undermines your sincere efforts. Notice without blaming.
>
> We can't heal what we don't know."
>
> "Treat her with a light touch," she suggested. "Oh, you're here again. Start with a five-pound weight, not five hundred pounds! Show kindness to that critical voice," Yvonne concluded. "See how the judge serves you."[2]

In discussions with my clients, I often refer to the fact that we can't make substantial changes within ourselves unless we understand what we are about to give up. We batter ourselves for good reasons. The reasons may be outdated, but they once served an important purpose. We blamed ourselves when we felt the most helpless and unprotected. Blaming ourselves may have helped us to feel that we had some control over a situation that was totally out of our control. It may have helped us to cope. This ingrained habit is so hard to break that at first, we need to understand how the demeaning words of our inner judges benefitted us in the past.

In the criteria for PTSD from the *DSM IV-R*, the diagnostic manual that practitioners use to diagnose and treat our clients, intrusive thoughts are mentioned as one criterion:

Recurrent and *intrusive* distressing recollections of the event, including images, *thoughts*, or perceptions. Note: in young children, repetitive play may occur in which themes or aspects of the trauma are expressed.[3]

Some women who have intrusive thoughts experience symptoms of PTSD without meeting full criteria. Neglect can take many intangible forms. It may be more subtle than physical abuse and sexual abuse, but it often lays the foundation for a lack of safety in the world. This foundation leads to children keeping painful and toxic secrets, which can later evolve into PTSD. The aftereffects of neglect are pervasive. They invade every aspect of our lives, every layer of our being. Of all of the aftereffects of abuse and neglect, intrusive thoughts are often the most difficult to change.

A neglected woman will take a compliment, for example, and twist it around in her mind until the person who gave her the compliment becomes wrong. If someone is kind to her, she may develop a theory about that person's agenda. Although positive feedback is very difficult to take at face value, without a negative spin or interpretation, negative feedback is usually seen as accurate. If a neglected woman gives a presentation at work, and receives ten compliments and one criticism, she might focus totally on that criticism, negating all positive feedback.

Elizabeth, a current client, copes with an excessive amount of intrusive thought. She is also extremely intuitive. It is easy to imagine how this combination of characteristics creates a great deal of confusion in Elizabeth's daily life.

Elizabeth learned to be self-conscious and negative from a critical father, and a mother who ignored her emotional needs. Elizabeth has obtained a Ph.D., but has lived her first thirty years without ever hearing that she was intelligent. Instead, her mother told her that she was "needy," and her father told her that she was "fat." At stressful times in Elizabeth's life, she feels boring, needy, and overweight. Stress exacerbates the negative aspects of the parenting she received. Elizabeth's own intrusive monologue includes her internalized parents' voices. She has had difficulty connecting with others, fears that once they know her they will abandon her, and blames herself for her loneliness. She judges her interactions with others without mercy, and reports, "I can put a negative spin on anything."

For Elizabeth, positive feedback and occurrences are merely "dumb luck." As Elizabeth learns to see herself in a more positive light, she must reject her mother's perception of her. She must, perhaps, betray her mother by succeeding in relationships. It is safer in some ways for Elizabeth to continue her negative internal monologue if she wants to continue to have some respect and belief in her mother.

Elizabeth's inner child is still hopeful that her mother will be able to love her in the way that she needs to be loved. This is a hope that dies a very long and painful death. On a daily basis, Elizabeth hopes for the best and is consistently disappointed. Because of this strategy, especially in relation to her mother, Elizabeth feels that she continues to live her neglect history.

Perhaps the most difficult part of all of this for Elizabeth is coping with her very complicated introject, or internalized parent. Her mother projected onto Elizabeth her own neediness at an age when Elizabeth was forming an identity. Like most neglected children, Elizabeth internalized the negative messages received. Under stress, Elizabeth truly believes that she is needy and boring. She is neither, but no one can convince her of that. At the same time that she fears being like her mother, Elizabeth experiences her mother as both needy and boring. How confusing is that?

Elizabeth's last two visits with her mother are described in the following pages, printed here in order to further explore and validate her experience of neglect.

From an email in August of 2008:

> I've had kind of a tough week and have struggled to put my finger on the problem. I was feeling almost paralyzed by life again. I know that part of it is that I had a really hard time with my mom's visit—we couldn't seem to get along at all. AT ALL. She made snide comments about doing or not doing things so that she "wouldn't get yelled at" by me. But then, the morning she was leaving, she told me what a nice time she'd had. I said, "Really? I didn't think we got along very well." To which she replied, "Oh, you were just stressed." My fault. All my fault. It's true; I was stressed, but my mother was really in prime form too. The concepts of competition and sabotage from our Saturday meeting really resonated. With every conversation, I felt like she was trying to one-up me. My friend Jeanne came to dinner with us on Monday night and my mom just wouldn't shut up. It's hard to explain, but she did what she always does, which was to dominate the conversation so that nobody else could talk. And what she did say was exaggerated. Or just plain painful and hurtful. She talked about how wonderful the dogs were and how her loving dog died of cancer. No mention of me trying to finish my Ph.D., or the fact that she didn't attend my graduation because of her dog being ill. When I tried to change the subject, she suggested that I just didn't like dogs. Kind of ironic, given that my ex-partner Chris faulted me for liking dogs too much. I've often wondered how my mom could have any friends, given her behavior, but it has more recently occurred to me that maybe she only acts this way when I'm around. I feel so conflicted because I felt like I was being really mean to my mom, but also like it was a defense mechanism against her being mean and critical to me.

Elizabeth's mother has clear traits of Narcissistic Personality Disorder, and Elizabeth was able to acknowledge that her mother met most criteria listed in Karyl McBride's book *Will I Ever Be Good Enough?* (2008).[4] Elizabeth's mother was also severely neglected by both parents, and Elizabeth barely knew her maternal grandparents at all. Elizabeth's mother was very isolated as a child. She taught herself to read at a young age and began a lifelong escape into books. The homes her mother visits are often judged by the number of books each home contains. Elizabeth's mother barely learned to socialize with others. She is an intellectual who teaches college, but she knows only her area of expertise; she has a very difficult time functioning at all, outside of academia. This is where Elizabeth comes in. Elizabeth acts as her mother's eyes, ears, and her cushion against the world. From an early age, Elizabeth wrote the checks to pay her mother's bills. She was recently asked to negotiate a deal on a new car for her mother, and she was the one who assisted her stepfather in negotiating his recent hospital stay. During a visit to Whole Foods Market, Elizabeth's mother could not manage to fill a paper bag with the cashews she wanted to purchase. They were in a bulk container, and Elizabeth's mother could not figure out how to maneuver the release handle and cover the container's opening with the bag. As Elizabeth watched in awe, her mother continued to try to maneuver the handle, dropping cashews each time on the floor. After observing her mother's difficulty for what felt like forever, Elizabeth took the bag from her and filled it with the nuts.

At home that same night, Elizabeth's mother cooked dinner. As they finished their meal, her mother wiped her mouth with the potholder. Although this behavior can be seen as somewhat eccentric and absent-minded, Elizabeth has difficulty accepting her mother's obvious limitations. When she fights with her mother, either to ask her to do things differently or to tell her something that is blatantly obvious to Elizabeth, her mother cowers and takes a victim stance. She refers to Elizabeth as a "bully". Elizabeth does not believe that her mother intends to hurt or embarrass her. But Elizabeth's forcefulness in attempting to change her mother is the voice of her own grief. If Elizabeth's mother could take care of herself, then she could take care of Elizabeth. Elizabeth's anger is expressed about more petty concerns, but the bottom line is that she continues to have to face the accumulated grief related to her mother's incapacity to care for her. That's what the fighting is about.

This past spring, there was another difficult visit. Elizabeth made some important realizations along the way. Although Elizabeth was responsible for making many decisions for her mother throughout their lives together, she has been hesitant, if not emotionally paralyzed, to make decisions for herself. She still has difficulty with job selection, and with the selection of a mate. Elizabeth would appear to go with the flow, accepting the jobs and partners who showed interest in her, without selecting anything or anyone for herself. Sometimes, Elizabeth still has no idea what she needs. Underneath this paralysis lives a little girl who is still waiting for her mother's guidance.

There is much ambivalence for Elizabeth in taking on the maternal role with her mother. She felt mixed emotions about hearing the one compliment her mother gave her, aloud to Elizabeth's housemate, Michael. "The thing that makes me the most proud of Elizabeth is her competence—she is SO competent!"

While Elizabeth can acknowledge her competence, she does not benefit any longer from continuing the role reversal with her mother. During this visit, Elizabeth noticed just how neglectful she was of herself. She spent the vast majority of her time taking care of her mother, attempting to predict her every need and "swoop in" to help her. Often, Elizabeth would forget to eat, and at times, she would even postpone taking care of other basic physical needs in order to be there for her mother. Her bladder would have to be hurting before she would take a minute to use the bathroom. Most significantly, Elizabeth, who is a wonderful conversationalist with strong opinions about politics, health, and the environment, noticed that she could not find her voice during this visit. While her mother was being loquacious, Elizabeth became silent. Self-expression seemed almost impossible around her mother. She spoke in whispers occasionally, to Michael, when there was a break between her mother's sentences.

Michael had heard stories about Elizabeth's mother, and was supportive during this visit. He offered to accompany Elizabeth, and spent time with her mother. He served as Elizabeth's "buffer" during walks, shopping, and dinner at area restaurants. Here is an excerpt from an email I received from Elizabeth regarding this visit:

> Tonight, Michael, my mom and I walked to a restaurant for dinner. My mom talked non-stop from the time we left the house, all through dinner, and until Michael retreated to his room after our return home. I was looking for the "off" button, but couldn't find one. She would not shut up. It was all of this inane stuff. At one point, she turned to me and said that she was "trying to describe to Michael the layout of her house." I asked why. She didn't really answer. While my mom was in the restroom, Michael told me that I'm not anything like my mom and he can't figure out how I came out the way I did. And then, after Michael was gone, my mom whispered to me that Michael's family sounded a little "odd" (because his mom is vegan).
>
> Anyway, I do find that her version of reality is very different than mine. She told a friend of mine last night that I grew up surrounded by people who thought I was smart. Perhaps they did, but no one told me. Another example: when we walk together and my mom always walks in front of me—she says she's just trying to keep up with me. I can't think of other examples right now, but I think there are many more. She acts like she's scared or intimidated by me, which I can't figure out. She thinks I'm bullying her, but I'm only trying to connect with her. I wish things could be "normal."

Michael validated Elizabeth's experience of her mother. Elizabeth had experienced this validation in the past as well, during her long-term relationship with her partner, Chris. Michael uses humor to validate, while Chris would embrace Elizabeth's deep hurt and pain, helping her to recover. Elizabeth contacted Chris during this visit, in order to feel connected about the dynamic with her mother. As usual, Chris was able to offer support and confirmation that Elizabeth is not minimizing the extent of her neglect history. And later, Elizabeth's housemate Michael helped with the comments noted toward the end of Elizabeth's latest email:

> He actually agrees with me that I was raised by a pack of wolves now. Here are some clips of what he's said about my mother:
>
> - "I honestly just don't know how to act around her. I feel like I'm being a little too pushy and overbearing, partly because I'm mirroring her and dishing it back. But I feel like I'm being terribly rude to do that."
> - "I don't know how she managed to dedicate enough time to squeeze you out of her body!"
> - "I don't think I've ever met someone I've grown so quickly to dislike, with such little experience. It's really quite amazing; she has a power. I mean it's not a true dislike—she hasn't insulted me or done anything intentional—she's just . . . difficult."
> - "I feel binary around her. Either I'm overbearing and rude, or I'm completely walked on and ignored. No middle."
> - "And I've had what . . . barely five days? You've had thirty-five years. You should be sainted. Or knighted. Or given a Kevorkian waiver!"

Perhaps partly due to Michael's validation, Elizabeth decided to try to stop arguing with her mother during the remainder of this visit, and to make a conscious effort to accept her mother's limitations. Her mother brought photographs of Elizabeth's early years. Out of dozens of photos, Elizabeth appeared with another adult or child only a handful of times. Even during her birthday parties, she was alone with her cake and candles. Elizabeth often wished for a sibling to grow up with, to accompany her through life's adventures. She learned to occupy herself on her own. She never learned to play. Elizabeth's mother gave her clear messages about being "needy," if she simply wanted some attention, or to spend some time with her. In fact, during this visit, Elizabeth's mother called her cats "needy," for wanting to be petted and loved, and for wanting to be fed.

Elizabeth's mother and stepfather brought Elizabeth's old dollhouse with them on this visit. Her father had begun to build it with Elizabeth before her parents divorced. It had never been finished. No furniture or dolls had ever lived inside. It was tilted to one side, without much of a foundation to speak of. Part of the dollhouse was painted and part of it was not. Elizabeth plans to finish building this dollhouse, making it sturdy and filling it with a miniature family. The symbolism of the dollhouse is not lost on Elizabeth. Despite being single, she is hopeful about a future with a loving partner and at least one daughter—a daughter that she can bestow with the love and attention that they both deserve.

Perhaps you have offered to work cognitively with your clients and they are unresponsive to making lists, like Julie did in chapter 5. If your client is not interested in recording the negative voices that she hears, or in finding nurturing replacement voices, there is another alternative technique called *psychodrama* that can assist her.

Psychodrama is depicted on the American Society of Group Psychotherapy and Psychodrama (ASGPP) website:

> Conceived and developed by Jacob L. Moreno, MD, psychodrama employs guided dramatic action to examine problems or issues raised by an individual (psychodrama) or a group (sociodrama). Using experiential methods, sociometry, role theory, and group dynamics, psychodrama facilitates insight, personal growth, and integration on cognitive, affective, and behavioral levels. It clarifies issues, increases physical and emotional well being, enhances learning and develops new skills.[5]

I have found that psychodrama is a very effective tool to utilize in treatment of clients who are coping with powerful intrusive thoughts and negative voices. There is often a kind of war going on internally for clients, between their hearts and their minds. When intrusive thoughts and negative voices are externalized through psychodrama, therapists can assist their clients to reframe the internal fighting and to discover a path toward peace.

Although psychodrama is often effective in group treatment, individual sessions can also be conducted. A client can be asked to speak from her adult self, for example, when she is seated on the left side of the couch. She can begin a dialogue with her child self, who is currently invisible, on the right side of the couch. When a question is asked of the child, the adult self switches seats, and answers the question from the view of the inner child. When the inner child has a question, the client again switches seats. Often, a drama unfolds that includes a very critical adult self, and a very vulnerable child self. The therapist can offer suggestions by joining the psychodrama, and making statements that relate to the externalized conversation. The client may accept the statement and repeat it, or ignore it altogether. I usually limit psychodrama to ten or fifteen minutes of a session. This leaves time to process the experience, and any feelings that might have surfaced during the course of the exercise.

I have had clients realize that they are criticizing their internal child in the same manner that their parents criticized them. I have had clients ask their inner children what those children need, toward the end of the exercise. Some inner children are aware that they need a hug, or they need to be told that everything will be alright, or they need to hear a genuine "I love you". Adult children can make pacts with their inner selves during psychodrama. If the inner child is demanding airtime to feel her neglected emotions, the adult self can offer to write a daily journal entry, or to spend some quiet time listening to that child without criticism or judgment. This technique also serves as a wonderful tool to help people to re-parent themselves.

A former client, Gracie, utilized psychodrama to tell her neglectful mother what she could never say to her during their visits. I asked Gracie to look around the room, and find an object to place on a chair, to represent her mother. Gracie chose the trash can! This choice added some comic relief to what might have been an awkward moment at the onset of the exercise. Gracie was able to express herself, her anger and hurt, at her mother's treatment of her. She spoke loudly and found her voice in ways that she hadn't experienced in talk therapy. Gracie told her mother what she needed, and never received. Soon, her tears were flowing. But after the tears subsided, Gracie was able to tell me how relieved she felt. Finally, Gracie had said what had never been said aloud. But the dialogue was very familiar, having existed in the corners of her heart and mind for decades.

Chapter Eleven

Working with the *Introject*

The psychoanalytic definition of the word *introject* is as follows:

- noun: parental figures (and their values) that you integrated as a child; the voice of conscience is usually a parent's voice internalized
- verb: to incorporate (attitudes or ideas) into one's personality unconsciously[1]

Introjection was considered by Freud as "one of the important defensive mechanisms employed by the ego."[2]

Although things have changed in recent years, there is still some unwillingness to acknowledge that women can be neglectful parents. It is sometimes the nature of neglect, however, that forces the repetition of it. Rarely, if women become mothers prior to resolving their own histories of abuse or neglect, there is a possibility that patterns from their own childhoods might be repeated. More often, women learn "what not to do" in their families of origin, and can heal from their own upbringings while raising their children. The process of parenting can be healing in itself. The variables that determine the repetition of a pattern of neglect are numerous. Especially in cases of same-gender neglect, the "introject," or "internalized neglectful parent," must be explored as one of the most relevant factors in resolution and healing. It is the unconscious introject that often contributes to the repetition of neglect in families.

If a female child is introduced to her world by a woman who respects herself and her daughter, that child will have no concerns about an *introject* as an adult. The concerns come about as a result of neglect, abandonment, and abuse. Women may begin to fear as young adults that they are fated to transform into their neglectful mothers. They often hear the very beliefs in their own heads that their mothers described to them years ago.

Although these women may make valiant attempts at ignoring these beliefs, the voices in their heads are persistent, and the beliefs often seem to interfere in their daily lives nonetheless. When women are neglected as children, they sometimes do not trust that they exist at all. As detailed in chapter 4, many women suffer with eating disorders, or carrying extra weight, simply to prove to themselves that they are here. Neglected young adults tend to abuse themselves in order to relieve the emptiness of their lives. Some cut themselves, some use drugs or alcohol to numb the pain, and some enter into relationships with partners who continue to treat them in neglectful ways.

The pain of neglect is often obscured. Sometimes, women are not abused, but merely forgotten. It is difficult to measure how damage occurs, but in listening to dozens of women describe their histories, I have learned that neglect may have an even more insidious effect than abuse. The pain of feeling abandoned by those who are supposed to love us is often unmatched by physical wounds that can heal.

Being ignored can cause an intelligent child to look for reasons that her life is the way it is. We are not born with good self-esteem. It is developed over time, with the integration of positive feedback from the nurturing people around us. If there is a lack of nurturing in a child's environment, the child does not learn to nurture herself. She begins, instead, to blame herself for the neglect. She may develop specific reasons why the neglect is occurring, or she may have a generalized feeling of being bad in some way. The little girl cannot become angry with her family for the neglect. She has too much hope that they will love her someday. So, she turns that anger inward, against herself.

Internalized anger becomes a means of self-expression and self-hate. It becomes a survival skill that allows this child to make some sense of a world that is too chaotic and painful to conceptualize in any other way.

Some young girls overcompensate for feeling evil inside. They become *parentified,* or *pseudo-mature,* and begin to provide nurturing and care to their own parents, or to their siblings. This is done in the hope that the nurturing will become mutual, but it usually backfires. This particular way of coping may lead to a future selection of partners that are needy and dependent. In this way, the pattern of neglect continues to repeat itself.

Eventually, if young women seek therapy to examine these patterns, they may discover that the process of treatment will need to include an *un-learning* of what they taught themselves, and a learning of new behaviors. The process of un-learning and re-learning can take a lot longer than simply integrating a new lesson, and women need to be patient with themselves as a result. As therapists, we need to be especially patient with this process.

Women also need to learn to separate themselves from their introjects. They need to be able to define who they are as separate from their neglectful parent(s). The best example I have read about this concept is from the "Breaking Silence" chapter of *The Courage to Heal:*

> For a while I didn't know where my mother left off and I began. I thought she had a psychic hold on me. I was convinced she knew every thought I had. It was like she was in my body, and she was evil. I felt I was possessed, that I was going to be taken over. I've had a real fear that if I look at all that stuff that I don't like about myself, it would be my mother inside of me. And I've had to do a lot of growing over the last few years to know that she's not inside me anymore.[3]

The process of separating oneself from one's internal, neglectful mother can be quite a challenging one. Sarah, from chapter 1, is at this crossroads in her treatment. She is unable to move forward without questioning and reevaluating every step she takes, every word she utters, every choice she makes. She is attempting to distinguish her post-traumatic stress responses in her daily life, from the reality of her current situation. She is learning that an emotional overreaction to something or someone is a tool to help her distinguish another trigger to her past. She is becoming proactive in her approach to relationships, and after careful and compassionate evaluation of her reactions, she is choosing to express her needs differently.

As far back as elementary school, Sarah remembers wishing that she could escape her home life. Both of Sarah's parents were alcoholics who communicated with each other via criticism and arguments. Sarah was the victim of her mother's rage on a regular basis. She remembers sneaking out of her bedroom, for example, to watch a favorite television show. Although she did this as quietly as possible, Sarah was discovered by her mother. Sarah frequently wore her hair back behind her neck in a ponytail. On this evening, like on many others, Sarah's mother dragged her back to her bedroom by her hair. Because this abuse was very painful, Sarah cleverly chose to cut off her ponytail, to protect herself from her mother. To this day, however, Sarah sometimes awakens to shooting pains and spasms in the back of her neck as she relives her abuse.

Sarah would often look out her bedroom window and dream of living on her own, in a beautiful, cozy house nearby. She would pass this house on her walk home from school, and imagine herself living there, free of her mother. In an effort to escape one day, Sarah jumped from the deck on the second floor of her house. She was very young, and she misjudged her ability to grasp a nearby tree limb in order to lower herself to safety. She held on to the wooden deck as long as she could, before falling to the ground and injuring her ankle. During the fall, Sarah actually remembers looking through the window of her mother's study. She remembers that her mother looked up briefly from her work, to watch her daughter fall to the ground. Sarah sat on the ground in the back of her house until her father came home and found her there. Her mother had locked the doors.

A locked door is still a trigger for Sarah, now in her mid-thirties. Her ankles still swell, but for the most part, Sarah has been numb to pain throughout her childhood and adult life. She has ridden, trained, and shown horses with severe back spasms and sciatica. She pushes herself past her pain. When Sarah first started sharing the story of her failed escape, she told the story with humor. Today, she has begun to integrate her many levels of pain.

Sarah came upon an early childhood memory recently, in the morning hours, while pouring dry cat food into a container. The smell of the cat food provoked the awareness that Sarah had tasted it; in fact, in the moment of memory recovery, she could still taste it.

Children are resilient. They attempt to find guidance in unusual places, if it is not offered to them. Even in her neglectful environment, Sarah attempted to learn from observation.

Sarah had seen her father eating peanuts, one by one, from his hand. She knew that the peanuts were kept on the third shelf of the pantry. Sarah tried to climb to the third shelf, but she needed both hands to open the peanut jar, which left her unable to hold onto the shelf. Her efforts to feed herself by imitating her father initially failed. Then, Sarah noticed that the dry cat food was within reach. She could use a kitchen chair to climb close enough to the counter, lift the lid, and pour a few morsels into her hand. They looked a bit like peanuts, and Sarah found that she could tolerate them, especially when she was very hungry. It was very rare that there was food in the family's refrigerator, but there was always money for alcohol.

Sarah also learned to neglect her needs and her pain as a result of being neglected. Ignoring her pain became a badge of courage. As a young adult, Sarah was both physically abused and emotionally neglected by her male partners. Recently, Sarah has become involved with a man who is capable of nurturing her. Although her "relationship picker" (from *Will I Ever Be Good Enough?* by Karyl McBride, 2008)[4] has evolved, Sarah continues to struggle with intimacy, in the form of her internalized mother's voice. Sarah challenges herself to censor her initial words, evaluate them in relation to her history prior to speaking, and create a new history for herself. She empowers herself to argue differently than she was taught. She empowers herself to stop pushing people away with her words, as she learned to do in childhood when she was feeling abandoned. She empowers herself to attempt to create safety in relationships, to feel loved for who she is, and to allow herself to trust.

Although it feels tentative, Sarah is beginning to find her own style of communication, one that leaves the criticism, emotional abuse, and neglect behind. A style that includes respect and integrity. She speaks out of love, instead of speaking from the heart of her abandoned, hurt, and betrayed inner child. Sarah is clearly able to utilize the therapeutic relationship to heal. She has a witness to her pain. She has consistent, nurturing communication and feedback. She has discovered that it is possible to re-parent herself, and she is becoming more capable of overcoming her introject.

Sarah is coping well with her concerns about "morphing" into her mother. She notices how frequently she judges herself by comparing herself to her mother. Finally, she is noticing how unfair those comparisons are. For example, Sarah's mother has become agoraphobic, and unable to work outside of the home. At the same time, Sarah is questioning her choice of career, after becoming extremely successful at a career that she no longer wishes to pursue. Sarah is working several part-time jobs, but is not sure of the direction she wishes to take in the future. Although there is no comparison, Sarah is fearful of becoming her mother in regard to work.

Sarah is also attempting to access her anger toward her mother. But because Sarah remembers her mother mumbling to herself on a regular basis, Sarah's healing cannot include talking with herself aloud. She is very deeply afraid of becoming like her mother by imitating that behavior, despite the fact that the behaviors have nothing in common. Psychodrama would be contraindicated in Sarah's treatment.

Here are some additional memories of Sarah's upbringing:

New Shoes

I really wanted a pair of black and white saddle shoes when I was in kindergarten. I wanted to be able to take the walk to my new school in my new shoes, so my dad and I went out and got the shoes. I'm not sure exactly what time of year it was, but it was hot and my ankle started to hurt on the walk back and forth to school, and then during school. I told my parents of the pain and my mom's response was cool at best. I can't remember exactly what she said but it was clear to me that the problem was the shoes that I "just had to have." She told me that I needed to break them in. A day or so later I developed a really high fever and had to be taken to the hospital. My mom stayed home with my brother Charles, and our neighbor Jane wrapped me up in a blanket and held me while my dad drove me to the hospital. It felt strange to be held. I started crying and she just whispered that everything was going to be okay. I loved that ride to the hospital; I still think about how nice it was to have an extended hug like that. It turns out that I had osteomyelitis, a bacterial infection in the bone of my ankle. I was in the hospital for several weeks and my memory of it is pretty foggy. I overheard a conversation about amputation and I remember my grandma (my mom's mom) being there. My dad told me that my mom couldn't visit much because she had to take care of Charles at home. That was fine with me because Jane came to visit me every day and she was really fun. I was shy at first and totally overwhelmed with joy when she would smile at me or ask me questions about school. When I did get to go home from the hospital my mom was very critical about how I looked. She said that I looked pale, gray, and too thin. I was still on very large doses of antibiotics and she seemed totally exasperated by the fact that she had to keep track of what pills I had to take and when. I remember her saying, "Thank god you didn't lose your foot." I also remember asking her if she missed me while I was in the hospital and her response was that she was busy taking care of Charles. I guess she wasn't too worried.

Seventh Grade

My mom is an alcoholic. She liked to drink and she didn't like to drink alone, so I started drinking with her at a pretty young age. She explained to me that if I "learned how to drink" at home, then I wouldn't have problems with alcohol later in life. Yes, she seriously said that. She would have me drink this concoction she called wine-water; a half glass of wine watered down. She was in the mood to celebrate the night before my first day in seventh grade so she had some wine and so did I. I have no idea where my dad and brother were, but they weren't in the dining room with us. I went to school the next day feeling sick, nervous, and stupid. I didn't know why I felt so completely awful and I thought something was wrong with me. I had a hard time finding my classrooms and I had to walk in late to a few of my classes, which was bad given the fact that I was very shy to begin with. The last thing I wanted to do was to have to walk in front of all of my classmates and then try to find a seat. It was awful. That was the point at which school became a game of survival. I became excellent at flying under the radar, just like at home. I never did anything wrong or tried to stand out in any way. I just had to get through a day at a time. I maintained a B average throughout school, right in the middle, not great but not bad. My mom rarely asked about my grades or what I was interested in. She seemed more interested in whether I was popular or not (I was not) and who the "cool kids" were. She would get drunk at night and sing Beatles songs and want me to sing with her. I still can't stand "Yellow Submarine." I love the Beatles though; it's not their fault that my mom is a drunk.

For Sarah, accessing her anger about her past will stop her from needing to "fly under the radar." She will be able to make career choices that she values for herself, without considering her difficulty with exposing her true self to the world. Individuating from her mother and rejecting her internal voice will lead to Sarah's discovery of inner peace and contentment with her life choices.

April's story

It is rare to work with someone who was abused in infancy, with no conscious memory of it, but whose introject tells her early childhood story. April described herself as capable of evil. She felt like a bad person. She came to therapy to explore her need to steal. April had been stealing from childhood through her first year in college, and wanted to stop. She was embarrassed by her behavior. During the course of therapy, April remembered being taught to steal by her mother, when she was about eight years old. She had very few memories of her mother prior to that age. Being taught to steal in a department store, April felt special, and valued by her mother. Her mother was proud to show her daughter this new skill, and April wanted to please. So she stole without questioning it, until it became more uncomfortable. I believe that April was able to examine this behavior in more detail because of having moved away from home to attend college. She was no longer accountable to her intrusive, yet neglectful mother, on a daily basis. Despite stealing to please her mother, April knew it was wrong. It was very difficult to grapple with her intuitive knowledge and her need to please her mother. She was at war with herself internally, attempting to be the young woman her mother wanted her to be, while developing the need to explode the mold that she had been trapped in for so many years.

April could not trust her own intuitions, because in order to trust herself, she would need to betray her mother. When April talked about her feelings with her mother, the feedback would be very negative. April was told that she was not feeling what she thought she was feeling. This feedback caused April to withdraw further into herself. She was not in charge of her own reality.

April remembers doing well in school, despite criticism from her peers. She felt the same need to please her teachers as she did her mother, so her grades were good. But she was very isolated and alone. Her mother told her that her friends would never care about her as much as she did. Each friend was judged and criticized by April's mother. April longed to experience love, and began looking for it—through sex—as a young adolescent. She began a phase of promiscuity that would last more than ten years. She kept this lifestyle a secret from her mother. She also began cutting herself with a razor blade. Just to break the skin, and to feel some pain. She was so shut down emotionally that the cutting actually helped her to feel alive.

Throughout this time, April felt evil inside. She loved watching little puppies and kittens at play, but she would never allow herself to lift one into her arms and hold it. Her internal voice shouted at her, "Don't pick her up. You could hurt her. You could kill her." With infants, the voice was similar, "Don't pick her up. You will drop her."

April was asked in therapy to identify any memories of touch in childhood. She had none. But April visited her grandmother's home soon after this session, and asked her grandmother about her infancy. Her grandmother immediately started to cry. Her grandmother shared stories about witnessing April's mother abusing her as an infant. She was lifted onto her bassinette when the abuse occurred. *April had integrated lifing as a behavior that could hurt and kill,* with no conscious memory of the abuse. Her grandmother had tried to stop the abuse, and April's mother kicked her out of the house during the confrontation. April learned that she had had an ally as a result of this visit. Within a few months of that conversation, her grandmother died.

Although April had no visual memories of her abuse, she had body memory. She had feeling memory. And she had incorporated an evil introject with evidence of the abuse intact. After listening to her grandmother's version of her infancy, April began to make sense of her life. She began to understand on a conscious level that she had meshed her mother's behavior with her perception of herself. She was carrying her mother's shame, and she was relieved to be able to let it go. For April, knowing what happened to her catapulted her into healing, and into forming a new positive self-image. April has never turned back. She no longer grapples with a negative internal monologue. She no longer steals, and her days of promiscuity are over. She is grateful to her years in therapy, and to her grandmother, for setting her free. And she holds kittens, puppies, and infants whenever she can.

Belle's story

Belle contacted me online to begin the process of e-therapy in 2007. She was involved with a narcissistic, passive-aggressive partner, but she blamed herself for the problems in her marriage. We worked together to help Belle to separate her identity from that of her alcoholic mother, and to divorce her husband without guilt. She has been successful on both fronts.

Here is a passage from Belle's email in July of 2008, with a clear description of her emotional neglect history: I've not been to NYC since I was ten years old. We drove around the country in a van James customized by cutting a hole in the top and constructing a storage area which, at ten, I could actually fit into. We took my six-month-old kitten, Butterscotch. This is a story I tell about my father occasionally—how they stopped for gas somewhere and Butterscotch slipped out of the van. A search ensued and James enlisted three boys with the promise of five dollars if they found the cat. "That cat over there?" they asked, pointing to Butterscotch, who was lounging in the shade of a vehicle my parents had overlooked. So James gave the biggest boy the 5 dollars, because, he always said (he liked to tell the story) he figured the biggest boy would get the money eventually and this was safer for the smaller two.

Except for in New York we stayed in campgrounds, and Butterscotch got lost regularly. I got upset regularly. James threatened to leave without the cat regularly. I more or less believed he would do it. It hadn't really been my idea to take the kitten, though I was thrilled when it was suggested. Butterscotch was a replacement for a cat that died: Hershey, who had been mine and Gail's cat, but mainly mine. Hershey hadn't been feeling well and I'd been keeping him in, but my mother said she thought he was doing better and let him out, and when he was at last found, he'd been hit by a car. His hind end was paralyzed. There was a surgery that would have cost four hundred dollars, which my parents, reasonably enough, wouldn't spend, but for some reason the vet said there was a possibility of a spontaneous recovery. James built an open topped, high-sided wood box to confine him in, as, I suppose, must have been the vet's instructions, and a period of my nursing the cat which could have been days, or weeks, or even a month—I don't remember—followed. My parent's involvement stopped with the vet, the decision, the box. I am nine years old taking care of a paralyzed cat who is not getting better. I'm a kind, sensitive kid—my mother was given to pointing this out, how she could see that in me from the beginning. An illustration of how some temperament is innate.

I want my mother to be kind and sensitive, too. I think she is—it's not a matter of wanting. I'm sure she's sorry she let him out. I know she cares about me because when James, drunk, flies into a rage about the animals—a dog made a mess in their room—and he yells upstairs, "If this happens again we'll get rid of all of them, and that includes that cat up there if he gets better, Belle," my mother says, "James, James," the way she does, to calm him down. She's defending me.

Surely she understands. Cares. James goes storming off into the night saying he needs to take a walk to cool down and I'm crying but it doesn't occur to me that my mother might come upstairs and see how I am doing—it does not occur to me, as it does now, that if I can hear what's going on down there, she can hear what's going on upstairs. I have the cat in my lap and then I try to lay him down in the bottom of the box on the bed I made him but it's awkward, and I drop him and he definitely looks a lot worse and there's not a damn thing I can do and I start sobbing and someone does come: Arthur, seventeen years old or so, and he keeps asking, What's wrong? What's wrong? . . . Even if I've mixed up two different nights—which I may have—his question seems strange to me—there's a cat dying in a box, and there's a little kid crying—why does nobody connect the dots? I have remembered this moment with Arthur, though, and thought well of his caring. He really did care.

Somehow my mother does know the cat is in dire straits the next day, and in the last part of this episode, I do reproach her a little in my heart. I've been at school all day and I rush in and ask her how Hershey is. She is sitting in the living room reading. She says she doesn't know. She hasn't been up there. I run upstairs; the cat can barely breathe. My mother does go into action; I don't have to go to the vet to have him put down. I learn later he dies on the way. My mother draws me to her, sounds comforting, wants to know if I want ice cream. Maybe she really does care, then, but how will I ever know? I can't feel it; I pretend to be comforted.

All right. So my mother was either so sensitive that she couldn't deal with this, or so cold that she wouldn't. Or something, because the two excuses I have always given her don't really excuse her. If she was afraid of James, she could've come upstairs after he left. He wasn't even around the day she sat downstairs, ignoring the cat even though she must have known what it meant to me. Neither were the other four kids around; I don't think Gail was even living at home. So much for excuse number 2: that she must have been overwhelmed caring for the five of us. But the truth is, especially by that time, her chief responsibility was dinner and stocking the shelves with food we fixed ourselves for other meals. By then, or shortly thereafter, she abdicated herself from doing laundry, saying we were always bugging her about if something was in the dirty clothes was washed and we could do it ourselves. She was never up when we got ready for school. She never helped with homework. She didn't go to parent-teacher conferences much, and was not involved in the school. She seldom drove us anywhere; I was made to feel quite ridiculous for being anxious about making a transfer downtown to get to the orthodontist—I might have been eleven, by then. I remember a fuss over a Halloween costume she'd sent me with money to buy. I was sent with money to buy my own clothes. I remember being sent to buy a birthday present for myself—a sizable farm set and, having a friend of my mother's happen by and drive me home—it was this sort of occasion that would cause me to be slightly embarrassed, but slightly proud of the independence and self-sufficiency expected of us. Once, my mother decided she would read *The Once and Future King*[5] to us, but she didn't get very far. I mention this, because, if she had used all the time she saved not doing some of the traditional things by dedicating herself in less traditional ways, or if, say, she'd been working, I wouldn't have to conclude that she was avoiding being there for us. Avoiding being a parent. Actually, though I can't say how I know this, she was proud of not being a typical mother. Certainly of our independence.

And she was encouraged in this by James. It wouldn't surprise me if they discussed the strategy and congratulated themselves as having managed a feat which so clearly overwhelmed so many other parents. They used, after we were grown, to congratulate themselves on a job well done. Well, James did, and mother didn't contradict him. Neither did we. Well trained.

And, Belle continues, in September of the same year: What happened to the little kid with the cat? My mother was holding me, at the end, but I felt nothing, not even, I think, by then, sadness, although I was crying. There was way, way too much to feel: sadness, anger, grief over what had been taken from me, what had been expected of me, what had been withheld. And I was revisiting old ground—certainly this was not the first time such things had happened or I would have been surprised—but I was old enough to process things at a semi-conscious level. Maybe I didn't really care about the cat, after all; maybe I was just trying to get the ice cream my mother eventually offered me. It did sound good, though I managed to refuse it. Later, I would feel better doubting myself than having to even touch the morass of cognitive dissonance in so many family interactions. And that is a kind of control—inside me, I can make it make sense, howsoever distorted.

And the independence serves as a control, and an insulation. I can actually be in a relationship and remain somewhat protected.

And later that year: I made another dip into recognizing my mother's limitations as a mother. . . . If nothing else, my mother colluded with my father in the "look, no hands" parenting scheme which left us getting up on our own, nursing our wounds on our own, planning our lives on our own, dealing with crises on our own, dealing with sibling conflict on our own, and learning to tie our shoes on our own. One thing I have puzzled about over the years is that the few times my mother stepped in, with reasonable advice or admonitions, I remember shrinking from her overture, feeling trapped or pressured. In my own parenting I offered this sort of guidance every day, or nearly so, and only occasionally got reactions from my kids indicating feeling overcontrolled, which could usually be diffused with humor or even, where I was compulsive (e.g., their driving), apologies.

Perhaps Belle learned to shrink from her mother's occasional overture as a result of this example: Intrusiveness. One thing I could usually count on was that my mother wasn't intrusive. She kept her distance. I could do as I liked. But there was one glaringly peculiar episode from my childhood. When I was ten or eleven, my mother said she'd read somewhere that a good way to control weight in a child was to keep them at the weight they are and they will grow out of "it." So, she offered me five dollars a month to remain at ninety-four pounds. Yes, I remember the exact weight; this went on for a year or longer. I suppose I might have had a prepubescent pudge, there are not enough photographs to be sure. I think my sisters' weight "problems" were held up as something I could avoid in this way. Arthur was there, and offered to chip in two dollars a month. At eighteen he surely didn't care how much I weighed. Neither, to my knowledge, did I—yet. But I was hot after the money and not opposed to the idea at all. I never got a dime from Arthur, but I remember, vaguely, the mature air he had during the initial deal-making.

My mother showed me how to use her dial-a-diet calorie counter, but if I tried to stay under 1500 calories or whatever it said would fuel a woman for a day (it didn't have a calorie figure for a ten year old, of course), I wound up—surprise, surprise—starving and binging in secret. Not, at that point, really disgusting myself, just worrying about how I was going to make the mark at the end of the month and get the money. Naturally, I figured out that by not eating the day before, I could weigh in close enough for government work. It was an honor system, and towards the end I just lied. Then, my conscience working on me, I began admitting to ninety-five or ninety-six pounds, and my mother would pay up, anyway, saying that was close enough, so I started lying when I crept up above those markers. By then, the money was no longer my chief motive. Were one plotting a method to make a child devious, dishonest, and ashamed of herself, one couldn't come up with a better one. Nor for developing an eating disorder, though it is not as bad as it might be.

My mother was so hands-off about so many things—as in virtually everything else—that this controlling obsession puzzled me, later, sorting things out. Somewhere, I read that it is not uncommon for alcoholic mothers to compensate for their out-of-control consumption by controlling their daughter's food consumption. Another more compelling conclusion is that my mother didn't want me to grow up, especially sexually. Fortunately, I happened upon *Fat Is a Feminist Issue*[6] and swore off dieting in my early twenties. Howsoever, I never have come to terms with my body image. Going through the pictures I took away from the house, I felt a heartbreaking sense of loss looking at that beautiful younger self, remembering looking at those same pictures at the time and seeing—but I can't figure out how—someone who was overweight. There are pictures where I look positively gangly—I never, in a million years, ever felt that way. Never mind that I should have been able to accept whatever package I came in; I couldn't see the package clearly.

The 94-pound diet ended, somehow, but not the issue. The summer I was fifteen, I was bicycling nearly twenty miles a day commuting to a racetrack where I cleaned stalls, then coming home and swimming, riding, and hiking all afternoon. I eat a lot—aside from occasional eating-disorder binging and garden variety emotional overeating—I like food—but even I couldn't keep up with such an energy drain. I was soon as trim and fit as I will ever be. My father and mother were commenting on this, but then my father took a pinch of my side and said, "There's a little more that could come off there," or words to that effect.

And I can be angry at all of it. But I don't really seem angry at my mother. I can work myself up to a beseeching questioning of her ghost, but not a simple "How dare you!"

And finally, in November of 2008, acknowledging the impact of her internalized mother:

What I'm thinking is that for years, my mother's pain has been wrapped up with my pain in my mind. And it has only been in the last ten years, probably, that I have really begun to see how I'd confused our identities. Since this didn't look like dependency on her, but an adult role of wanting the best for my mother, I didn't think of it as an effort not to feel abandoned. I am only managing to think this now intellectually: whatever way I managed to intertwine us protected me. I know the dark, howling feeling of abandonment, but as an adult only the two times in my life which I fell completely in love did I attach the feeling to a specific relationship. The rest of the time, it arrived unannounced, or at least seemingly so. Currently, just the thought of seeking out a relationship can bring it on. First, but briefly, the notion of how sweet it would be to have someone in my life, then reality check and the bottom falling out. And certainly, if I had to assign this feeling to something between myself and a parent, it would be my mother. And certainly, during this relationship hiatus would be a good time to figure out if I am looking for a mother in a man.

I wonder if sometimes when I held up ideals for my mother—what I always pictured she would be if she weren't an alcoholic under James's thumb—I was really matching my personal ideals for myself to her, because to realize them in myself would be to outstrip her in some way. This most obviously in my writing, but also child-rearing, reading selections, or even, God help me, taking a walk. I would think to myself, roughly: If only Mother hadn't been worrying about making money (because of her dependency on James), her writing would have been better; if only she hadn't had five of us, she wouldn't have been so exasperated; if her mind hadn't gone to mud with the alcohol, she would have been more literary; if she hadn't been traumatized by the move to the Midwest, she might have enjoyed the incredible green world here.

My mother would have been offended if she'd ever known I was excusing her in this fashion. Highly offended, and perhaps rightly so. Maybe my mother wasn't particularly literary—maybe my wanting more out of her was due to my need to look up to her. To respect her, so that I could respect myself.

So, my mother wasn't me, and I am not my mother. This should be easy to handle, given her fate. But I don't seem to be completely individuated. I still can't grasp, let alone feel, the sense of fear of abandonment. It was always guilt over abandoning her.

Obviously, the tables got turned when I was young. No, I don't remember specifically anything from being two, or three, or four, but I do remember being left in the car when my mother went to the bank and panicking, getting lost in the grocery and panicking, being left with a babysitter and feeling deeply alone (although a friend was there—she wasn't happy either, though). But my mother did come back; she did find me. She did, indeed, seem exasperated by my tears, and embarrassed by the strangers who rescued me. Years later, I'm eleven or twelve, I suppose, and she leaves me off at the orthodontist and then doesn't come back for a long time. How long? Long enough that the office closes, but then, it could have been the end of the day. By the time she shows up I am weepy, and somebody from another office has taken pity on me. And yes, I guess she seemed sympathetic in front of the strangers, but wasn't really apologetic to me. "I wasn't gone that long," something like that. And I wasn't mad. I was embarrassed, too, but mostly just glad she'd gotten back. I could have found my way home—at least I think I've got the right age; maybe I was younger. But already it wasn't my survival that concerned me. It was the darkening day; the very fact that the strangers were fussing made it worse. Where was she? Even now I puzzle. Not going to a bar—so far as I know, she never did. I suppose she may have just gone on an errand that took too long, but then, wouldn't she have explained?

Well, no, I didn't get explanations, and I didn't ask questions. And to some degree, all my life, I have been that waif child, biting her lip, depending on the kindness of strangers, who are almost always kind, almost never judgmental, but will always remain strangers. Anyone can see I am a motherless child, standing on the cold, dark sidewalk, waiting.

In Sarah's story as well as Belle's, both parents were neglectful. There was no restorative experience. There were no clear role models—and if there was a kind grandmother, a good teacher, or a caring neighbor, not enough time was spent with that person to combat the negative sense of self, or the feeling of being unlovable. For some more fortunate albeit neglected children, the parents of a friend or the consistent presence of a loving grandparent can restore some positive self-worth. Restorative experience can help a child's natural resilience to blossom.

If a child is neglected or abused by only one parent, and the other is loving and protective, the child is able to process emotions with one safe parent, and to evolve into an adult who does not place blame on the self. When feelings are processed early, and the perpetrator is acknowledged as such, there is no need to shut down one's emotions, and less need to utilize the defenses discussed in chapter 9. The abuse can be dealt with, and a child can feel protected and loved once again. Even if the abuse continues, the child has already learned that s/he is not at fault. There is an understanding that the abuser is the one who needs help. Because of this understanding and the presence of one's true feelings, there is less likelihood of developing post-traumatic stress disorder later in life. PTSD forms when a child has been given no permission to feel, when a child is forced to shut down emotionally and dissociate from the reality of feeling unprotected and unsafe, as well as abandoned and unloved.

When one parent is protective and loving, that parent is called the "non-offending spouse." Non-offending spouses often seek help for their children when they are young, and showing symptoms of withdrawal, depression, anxiety, or acting-out behaviors. Non-offending spouses who can prioritize their children over their relationships with their abusive partners can frequently save their children from an adulthood filled with grief and isolation. Although there may still be memories of abuse and neglect by one parent, these memories also include feeling protected, safe, and loved by the non-offending spouse. There are many subtle forms of neglect—but these more subtle forms are usually accompanied by restorative experiences of comfort and love. They are therefore much less devastating to us as adults.

The most relevant example that comes to mind to explain this dynamic is that of President Barack Obama. Prior to his election, Obama reported in a television advertisement: "I learned more from my father's absence than I learned from his presence."[7] Obama only met his father a handful of times in his life. In his book *Dreams from My Father,* Obama discusses his difficulty in integrating an identity as a result of his father's absence from his life.[8] He relied on other role models, and had many restorative experiences. His grandparents played a major role in teaching Obama his values, his work ethic, and his openness. His mother, despite her work schedule, spent time in the very early mornings assisting little Barack with his studies. She instilled in him a sense of empowerment, a sense of self-worth, and guided him with the knowledge that he was capable of accomplishing anything he wanted. He talks of her criticism of him when he judged others, and he integrated a non-judgmental core personality as a result. In his short time as president, we have seen numerous examples of Obama's openness to political, racial, gender, cultural, and ethnic differences, as well as his ability to listen to each side of an argument with respect. Despite his fatherless childhood, he grew to become a confident leader who is able to experience compassion for others. Perhaps because Obama felt abandoned by his father, he has become a strong advocate for the importance of fathering, and has clearly integrated that role in his own life. It is clear that Obama is proud of himself for breaking the cycle of neglect in fathering. He demands involvement and participation of fathers everywhere. In *Dreams from My Father,* Obama discusses the fact that some of his father's traits were similar to his own. He does this with language that is colored with coincidental observation. He does not identify with his father's neglect. There is no negative introject. This is partly a result of Obama's own introspective work in establishing an identity as separate from his father, and partly a result of his mother's unconditional love. Although Obama's neglect history had a strong effect on his sense of self, his mother's love had a much more profound influence on his identity.

The Male Introject

As with women, when men are neglected or abused by the same-gender parent, the introject can be very difficult to integrate. One's identity can be starved for other male role models. If there are no restorative experiences, or if there is an early childhood loss of love, men can sometimes form a superficial identity of arrogance and power, with a very insecure foundation underneath. This insecure foundation can include unresolved feelings of being abandoned and unloved. The insecurity is frequently cloaked in an expression of anger and rage. Often, this rage is directed at a partner when that partner threatens to abandon them. This pattern of repeating neglect and abuse in order to re-experience abandonment is at the foundation of many battering relationships. For some men, the pattern surfaces and they are able to change it. A group formed in the Boston area, called EMERGE (www.emergedv.com),[9] was created by former batterers in 1977 to eliminate violence in intimate relationships. This group provides a crucial service to men who batter. It would have been a tremendous asset to one of my former clients.

More than twenty years ago, I received a call from Joey. I learned that he was mandated by a judge to seek counseling. He had tried to strangle his wife three times. The third time, she prosecuted him, and he served some time in jail. Joey's release was contingent on his seeking therapy for his aggression and rage. The court would be monitoring his sessions. We scheduled our first appointment, despite my hesitancy to work with him. Initially, I arranged our appointments after checking with my colleagues in the same suite, to be sure that another professional would be in the building with me.

Despite my feminist concerns that I would have trouble remaining impartial with Joey, I saw him for the first time. I relied on the words of a former professor in social work school once again. "If you find something you like about a person, you can connect with that person, and engage that person in treatment." I was determined to find something I liked about Joey. Fortunately for me, this was not a difficult goal to achieve.

Joey was a very congenial gentleman, with a sense of humor and a willingness to trust, upon first meeting. He had no idea why he had tried to strangle his wife. He experienced some enlightenment in our very first session, however. Joey was able to explore the three attempts at strangling his wife in more detail. He was able to tell me what, in his mind, had led up to the abusive incidents. Each time, his wife had threatened to divorce him because of his cocaine use. The couple had three small children.

Here was the threat of abandonment. Here was a man who crumbled at the thought of being left. He could not reach that pain and fear, and instead, he became rageful. He attempted to master the experience of his earlier childhood losses by repeating them. His attempts to kill his wife were expressions of profound, complicated grief. He had been victimized, and it was my job to connect the dots for him.

Now I could relate to him. I could imagine him as a small child, and I could engage his interest in discussing his childhood with me. His wife had left him, and he had only supervised visitation with his own children. Joey was anxious to find some answers, some understanding. He had stopped using alcohol and cocaine to cope. He was ready for some introspective exploration of his life.

Joey's mother was killed by a drunk driver when he was nine years old. She was struck head-on by the driver, racing at 90 mph in a quiet suburban subdivision. Joey was not permitted to attend her funeral. He had two older brothers who were allowed to say goodbye to their mother; Joey stayed at home with a babysitter. He had to gather information from eavesdropping on conversations with bereaved family members. No one spoke with him about his mother's death. It was as if he was supposed to forget about her. He felt ignored and invisible.

Joey loved his mother dearly. She was not only a nurturing parent, but also a cushion for Joey, protecting him from his stern, emotionally unavailable father. Soon after the death of his spouse, Joey's father began to drink heavily. His father could not cope with his grief, and he began physically abusing his sons for random offenses. Joey had not only lost his mother—but also lost his safety and protection. He was left to fend for himself in a new world, without the opportunity to grieve his terrible loss. His neglectful parent became his abusive primary caregiver. He was living a nightmare.

Joey began fighting in school. He would act out and hurt his friends. He was suspended several times. He was approaching puberty, and he was beginning to identify with his father—the aggressor. The defense of this identification took hold, and Joey stopped defining himself as a victim. He became a powerful abuser in his mind. He was able to tolerate this image of himself much easier than that of victim, and although he could still express a soft side on occasion, he became a rageful adult.

Joey discussed his road rage in session one day, and made an important connection for himself. He carried a baseball bat in his truck at all times. When another driver cut Joey off in traffic, he would pull ahead of the driver, cut him off, stop his vehicle, and get out of his car with the baseball bat. He threatened many people in this way. Always men, always with the trigger of being cut off. On this day, while discussing his road rage, Joey actually started to sob. He realized that he was indirectly getting back at the man who killed his mother by cutting off her life with a speeding vehicle. His road rage subsided after this session, and his acute grief was finally expressed. He was finally able to cry about the loss of his mother.

This session began a series of sessions of bereavement counseling for Joey. He would remember his mother fondly, and even express anger at her for not wearing her seat belt. He blamed her for his loss, despite knowing that it was extremely unlikely that she would have survived the impact of the crash, with or without a seat belt. But, in realizing that he blamed his mother for abandoning him, he was also able to connect his rage about his wife's threats to leave. His irrational thoughts in regard to his wife actually belonged with his unresolved grief about his mother. He was transferring his unspoken anger at his mother to his wife.

In later weeks, I began to see profound changes in Joey. He seemed more confident, more able to experience the range of his emotions, and more capable of taking responsibility for his actions. He grieved not only his mother's death, but also the loss of his wife and his children. He grieved the fact that he did not access help for himself before it was too late for his marriage. He tried to reconcile with his wife, but she was convinced that he was incapable of changing, and she moved on. There was too much damage to her trust level for reconciliation. She did, however, help him to remove the requirement of supervised visitation for his children, and he was able to spend quality time with them once again.

Joey had scheduled his last session with me in the spring of 1987. It was a sunny Tuesday afternoon. He walked into my office with a big smile on his face. His new girlfriend was waiting for him in the waiting room. He was holding his baseball bat. He handed it to me. Joey said: "Do you work with any kids you can give this to? I don't need it anymore."

Joey was able to return to the sense of self that his mother instilled in him. He had only one neglectful parent. He was a loving, sensitive child with a gentle nature, before his mother died. Joey's successful recovery from neglect sheds additional light on the fact that it is much easier to return to a loved but forgotten self, than to create self-love where no love existed.

When emotional neglect by both parents is severe enough in the life of a male child, that child may have trouble with attachment and connection to others for the duration of his life. Emotional neglect in itself can sometimes lead to criminal activity. If a child is not provided with the opportunity to bond with others during infancy, that child can develop *failure to thrive.*[10] A pervasive pattern of neglect along with a lack of a sense of belonging in the world can actually be fatal. If children live through this level of neglect, they often exhibit symptoms of Attachment Disorder and, later, Conduct Disorder.

Children who abuse animals are often exhibiting an early symptom of Conduct Disorder. They abuse creatures that are more vulnerable than they are, perhaps to gain a sense of power and control over their worlds. When I worked in the field of foster care, I often served children with this aftereffect of neglect. One child who had been severely ignored by both parents was given the opportunity to live with a very loving foster family. The foster family had a small dog with a great deal of fur around its neck. Upon moving to his new foster home, this child hid a rubber band around the dog's neck, under its collar. I doubt that he had any idea of the harm that rubber band could do. Eventually, the dog's trachea was affected, and it stopped barking. The rubber band had imbedded itself under the dog's fur, in the nape of its neck. The dog required surgery, which our foster agency paid for, but he lost his ability to bark. By the time of this discovery, the foster parents had grown attached enough to this child to help him to take responsibility for his actions, and they chose to continue to open their home to him. Each time this young boy witnessed the dog attempting to bark, he was able to face his own victimization by neglect. His repetition of neglect played a pivotal role in his recovery.

Emotional neglect by both parents is a topic of discussion in Dr. Justin Frank's book *Bush on the Couch.* He assimilates from several biographies of George W. Bush's parents, and by varied accounts of Bush's childhood, just how much Bush's neglect history affected him and, in turn, all of us, while he held the office of the presidency.

By her own account, Barbara Bush was a stern, critical mother. She was less stern than her own mother, perhaps, but she was very emotionally unavailable to her son. So was her husband, who was still studying at Yale when George was born. George W. Bush was the oldest of three children. His sister, with whom he was very close, died when she was three years old. Dr. Frank writes:

> George W. was six years old at the beginning of the tragic episode that he has said yielded his first vivid childhood memories—the illness and death of his sister. In the spring of 1953, young Robin was diagnosed with leukemia, which set into motion a series of extended East Coast trips by parents and child in the

> ultimately fruitless pursuit of treatment. Critically, however, young George W. was never informed of the reason for the sudden absences; unaware that his sister was ill, he was simply told not to play with the girl, to whom he had grown quite close, on her occasional visits home. Robin died in New York in October 1953; her parents spent the next day golfing in Rye, attending a small memorial service the following day before flying back to Texas. George learned of his sister's illness only after her death, when his parents returned to Texas, where the family remained while the child's body was buried in a Connecticut family plot. There was no funeral. [11]

We can easily speculate on the lessons that George W. learned from this experience. He learned that those he loved could disappear in an instant, while his parents kept secrets from him. Perhaps he felt that he was not worthy of inclusion, and he most likely felt abandoned from an early age when he was prohibited from playing with his sister. He learned no ritual regarding death, and he was forced to deal with this loss on his own. We do not know how George W. integrated this loss, but we do know that he prohibited the caskets of fallen soldiers to be shown on television. Could this be a repetition of neglect?

George W. is also known to have maimed and killed animals. "According to childhood friends, Bush used to blow up frogs with firecrackers and shoot them with BB guns."[12] Even more devastating is the fact that Bush did not grow out of his childhood acting-out behaviors. "He was embroiled in a scandal at Yale when it was discovered that he branded pledges at his fraternity with red-hot wires."[13] Once again, we learn that unresolved emotional neglect in childhood, with no restorative experience, can be a dangerous and pervasive phenomenon.

Chapter Twelve

Neglect in the News

Scott Brown

In January of 2010 in the state of Massachusetts, Scott Brown was elected to fill Ted Kennedy's Senate seat. In 2011, he published an autobiographical memoir entitled *Against All Odds: My Life of Hardship, Fast Breaks, and Second Chances*. In this memoir, Senator Brown discloses that his upbringing was filled with alcoholism and violence, as well as physical and sexual abuse. He does not name the issue of emotional neglect in relation to his parents, but he discusses it thoroughly throughout his autobiography.

It is this neglect-without-a-name that colors Senator Brown's decisions to maintain silence throughout his childhood, regarding his molestation and abuse within the household and outside of it. As with most survivors of neglect, abuse and trauma, his trust had been severely damaged. Senator Brown's mother worked several jobs to support her children, but there were many times when her son went hungry, and resorted to stealing meat from area supermarkets in order to maintain energy for his first love, basketball. When Senator Brown shared a home with his stepfathers, he often witnessed violent arguments, augmented by alcohol use. His biological father left when Senator Brown was an infant, and early in the book, he remarks about his father's visits: "When he did come, it was on his own time . . . I don't remember what we did; I just remember the waiting."[1]

Senator Brown developed a survival skill called *personification* as a young boy. He speaks very openly about how he attributed human attributes and traits to one inanimate object in particular. Although he remained emotionally isolated with his parents, coaches, and friends, Senator Brown did have one thing he trusted.

"That night, as I did on most nights, I took my basketball to bed. I would trace my fingers over the black ribs and talk to the ball. It smelled of sweat and dirt and whatever had dropped from the sky or trees onto the court. And it listened companionably in the darkness. I slept with my hand resting alongside its worn pebblelike surface."[2]

Senator Brown "almost believed" his mother when she apologized about what they were all going through, but "then nothing would change".[3] He used the defenses of sublimation and dissociation to cope with his circumstances.

"I took it out on the court. . . . I had found a way to burn off some of the anger; for me, the path to inner peace was through sheer physical exhaustion. By shutting down my body, I could also shut down my mind."[4] Children with histories of physical abuse often learn to push their bodies past their limits. It is one way that we continue to violate ourselves while attempting to obtain mastery over the abuse. It is as if we are enforcing our beliefs that our bodies can handle just about anything. Scott Brown played basketball in the frigid cold winters in Massachusetts, without gloves, until his fingers were nearly frostbitten. He cleared the outside courts after it snowed, and the freezing temperatures were never enough of an obstacle to his need to shoot those hoops.

Senator Brown bravely discusses how he had to fight off oral rape on two separate occasions—once with a camp counselor, and once with a teenage "friend". He was less than eight years old the first time, and a pre-teen the second time. He feared for his life during both times he was molested. When he was asked to participate, he managed to scream loud enough at the camp counselor to attract attention. With the "friend", he was able to grab a rock and overcome his terror to use it.

The aftermath of the first incident was described this way: "I didn't know exactly what happened, and I told no one. I was too sick to eat dinner."[5] After the second incident: "I did try to tell someone, my mother or my grandparents, but whatever I said, however I said it, I couldn't get the whole truth out or they didn't believe me."[6] Senator Brown might agree that this memory is not crystal clear in his mind. The Senator may have suppressed this memory for obvious reasons. Which do you think is more likely—that he couldn't tell his story, or that he wasn't believed? The self-blame, the inability to find one's voice, and the abandonment involved in not being believed are classic aftereffects of emotional neglect. It is clear once again from Senator Brown's courageous account of his childhood, that it is the neglect that came first. It set the foundation for his abuse to occur.

Later in the book, Senator Brown revisits the issue of the personification of his basketball:

> Most nights, I would take my basketball to bed with me. I would lie in the dark, sometimes crying, sometimes thinking, but most of the time just talking to my

> basketball, and I would fall asleep with it in the crook of my arm. It was nothing more than a nylon carcass and a butyl rubber bladder pumped full of air, but it seemed to be nodding or occasionally whispering back to me, a sage sphere listening in the darkness, absorbing my secrets and my despair.[7]

Senator Brown found a nurturing parent throughout a bleak, confusing, neglectful childhood, in the form of his "sage sphere."

Tracy Ross

Tracy Ross is an award-winning journalist and editor. In 2011, she published her own memoir, entitled *The Source of All Things*. Tracy Ross utilized her love of nature to survive her childhood in the same way that Senator Brown survived through basketball. She was able to sleep through the night most soundly while camping in mountains where bears and coyotes resided. . . . Being amongst wild animals felt safer to Tracy than being in her bedroom, behind a locked door, after her sexual abuse had occurred.

Tracy expresses more hostility toward her emotionally neglectful mother than Senator Brown does. We learn early in the prologue of the memoir that "in the creases of her mouth, a white paste had congealed, proof that she was taking anti-depressants again."[8] There are attempts at understanding her mother's pain and depression from the time that Tracy was a very small child:

> So when my mom offhandedly mentioned how alone she felt on that blustery February afternoon, confusion swirled like a cloud of mosquitoes. Even then, a part of me knew that my mom's sadness was more powerful than any love anyone could give her, and that her life before me had been too difficult for her to ever be truly happy. I knew she'd grown up in a place where love was doled out in slaps and insults, and that, more than once, she'd received actual coal in her stocking. This knowledge made me feel both lucky and guilty. I'd sit with her on the couch looking at pictures of my real dad and hold her hand as sobs wracked her body. But I was young and full of energy. I bounced up and down on the sofa and said "But I love you, Mommy. *I* do." "Oh, I know you do sweetpea," she answered. "That's not what I mean."[9]

Later in the memoir, the neglect becomes more obvious for Tracy, and she chooses to remain emotionally guarded with her mother as a result:

> "*Tracy?* What's the *matter?* Talk to me. You're acting crazy." But I couldn't talk to her, because I knew the second I opened my mouth I'd have to take on her feelings too. And I'd spent too many years making sure that she was okay at the expense of myself.[10]

Tracy speaks clearly to us about her use of defenses throughout her recovery from sexual abuse and neglect. Her stepfather began abusing Tracy sexually when she was very young, during a camping trip to Redfish Lake. In Tracy's eyes, however, her stepfather had also rescued her mother from her grief after Tracy's father's death. Tracy's father died when Tracy was an infant. When her stepfather came along, she was hopeful that her search for a father figure was over. For many incest survivors, the road to recovery may be rockier, because their abusers are capable of evil as well as love. Because children see the world as black and white, they cannot conceptualize ambivalence. Having loving feelings for the same person who abuses you can become a nightmare of confusion, terror, and doubt. Defenses are developed as a way of surviving the nightmare.

Tracy discusses minimization, suppression, and dissociation:

> I'd convinced myself that my own memories were overblown; the truth couldn't possibly have been as terrible as I remembered it. . . . It was probably better if I stopped thinking about it. It took work, but I had managed to bury the past deep inside of me, especially when I was around my family. What else could excuse the feigned "forgiveness" I had shown my dad at the wedding? How else could I have spent more than ten minutes with my mom without trying to kill her?

And finally, Tracy addresses the negative ramifications of maintaining her defensive structure: "What emotional amnesia could allow me to let my parents babysit my precious little boys?"[11]

She addresses her suppression as she recalls not being believed:

> Deep down, I knew that my dad had done something bad to me. But if my parents were so sure that I'd been mistaken, I must have made myself believe them. Who was I to question the people who fed, clothed and protected me from things like Bigfoot and monsters under my bed? If there was a God, to me, they were It. I had no business refuting their version of reality[12]

Later in the memoir, Tracy recognizes her transference patterns in love relationships after a fight with her boyfriend: "I should have known that was my cue to leave. Not just the dance, but Colin. But at twenty-four, I still inhabited a long, dark tunnel. I repeated my cycle of love and despair, my most familiar emotional rhythm."[13]

As an adult with her own family, Tracy decides that her healing from neglect and abuse must include a confrontation with her stepfather. She had already learned that her stepfather had had a sexual abuse history of his own. The way that her stepfather integrated this history was by identifying with the aggressor, without defining himself as a victim. This defense allowed her stepfather to repeat his own abuse as an adult.

"An older cousin sodomized him at a family gathering when my dad was five. It went on for years, said my dad, but he didn't think he was scarred by it. 'It taught me that sex wasn't something to be ashamed of,' he said. 'It was how you showed your love.'"[14]

This is a very telling example of the confusion that occurs for children when abuse happens. If there is no trustworthy adult in the child's life, the child can integrate a very warped sense of reality because of the trauma. Tracy's stepfather repeated his own abuse on or near the anniversary of its occurrence. He used sleeping pills to drug Tracy, and told her that the abuse was her fault. Yet, he believed internally that the abuse was a demonstration of love. There are massive contradictions inherent in this repetition. This is also an example of how magical thinking can go very awry, and how people can repeat the cycle of abuse and trauma without conscious knowledge of affecting harm. Because they did not see themselves as victimized, perpetrators do not assume that the abuse will be damaging to their vulnerable prey. Unresolved trauma is repeated partly because of a lack of compassion for the self. Without compassionate parents, those of us with introspective ability are forced to learn to love ourselves despite our histories. It is an uphill battle worth fighting. Therapy can be a great milieu to fight that battle, but therapists must integrate skill in the following areas:

- Help your clients to alleviate negative self-talk.
- Once negative beliefs are alleviated, help your clients to notice their defensive structures, with more compassion and understanding for the neglected child.
- Help your clients to notice and to change their transference patterns.
- Help your clients to grapple with and to embrace the elusive introject.
- And if you are a therapist with your own history of neglect, help yourself to deal with countertransference issues in your work with neglected clients.

From decades ago, there are more stories:

Cheryl Pierson and Sean Pica

In her book *A Deadly Silence: The Ordeal of Cheryl Pierson,* Dena Kleiman tells us about a sixteen-year-old girl who pays her friend, Sean Pica, $400 to murder her father, in February, 1986. Cheryl had suffered through the death of her mother, as well as sexual abuse by her father for years, prior to asking her friend for help. She had also spoken to a classmate, who told her guidance counselor, who did nothing.[15] In 1988, Betty Rollin of NBC News wrote,

> Ms. Kleiman hammers away at the point of Cheryl's normality, as well she should. Every adult knows that surfaces deceive, but we forget how extreme the

> deception can be, especially when—consciously or unconsciously—we want to be deceived. No fewer than 14 people testified that they suspected something was going on between Cheryl and her father; yet no one except a classmate acted on that suspicion. Most of the 14 simply did not want to believe their own eyes and ears.[16]

Cheryl learned to live with the incest. In her mind, she had no choice. It was only when she realized that her younger sister was at risk that she acted against her father. Cheryl talked with Sean in class, and told him of the abuse. Sean, also sixteen, was the son of a policeman and a Sunday school teacher. He did not want his friend to be abused. He did what he thought was right in the moment, served his time, attended school in prison, was actively involved in his rehabilitation, and now, he counsels other people in similar situations. The judge took pity on Cheryl. She served only a few months in prison. Her family turned their backs on her. There were candlelight vigils during her nights in jail. Hundreds of women, many incest survivors among them, prayed for Cheryl, from outside her prison walls.

Susan Smith

Andrea Peyser's biography of Susan Smith, *Mother Love, Deadly Love: The Susan Smith Murders*, is a difficult book to read. Susan Smith was convicted of murdering her two small sons, Michael and Alexander Smith, in October of 1994. She drove them while they slept, into a nearby lake, and watched as the car sank, and her children disappeared from view. After reading about Susan Smith's history of abuse and neglect, it is difficult to imagine why she chose to leave that car, instead of committing suicide, her original intent.

Susan Smith was the youngest of three siblings. Her parents divorced when she was seven years old. Five weeks after the divorce, her father committed suicide. The marriage of Susan's parents had been volatile, and her father's suicide, devastating. Susan withdrew.

Soon after the death of her first husband, Susan's mother married again. Susan's stepfather was a successful businessman, respected in the community. Susan developed a cheerful disposition to hide her internal pain. The sexual abuse by her stepfather was said to have started when Susan was sixteen. Susan reported the behavior; her stepfather was removed from the home temporarily, and upon his return, Susan was criticized and ridiculed for speaking her truth. Since her stepfather faced no ramifications for his actions, he continued to abuse Susan. Once again, in her senior year of high school, Susan turned to a school counselor, and the Department of Social Services was notified.[17] Again, there were no ramifications for her stepfather. How does a young woman integrate this betrayal by her family and her community, without serious consequences? More than once? How does a young woman understand that her own mother chose to stay with her abuser, without protecting her? How many people are responsible for the deaths of those innocent boys?

Like many incest survivors, Susan became promiscuous. She was dating and becoming intimate with men while her abuse was still occurring with her stepfather. She had an abortion, and the married man she was dating broke up with her. This event preceded Susan's second suicide attempt. The first attempt was at thirteen, three years before her sexual abuse started, so we are told.

Susan married David Smith in 1991. Both partners were adulterous during the marriage and the subsequent separations. Both parents were reportedly nurturing to their two boys, despite the difficulties with intimacy that they shared.

One of Susan's extramarital partners, Tom Findlay, ended their relationship just prior to the divorce papers with David being finalized. He confronted Susan about kissing a friend's husband at a party. Tom wrote: "If you want to catch a nice guy like me one day, you have to act like a nice girl. And you know, nice girls don't sleep with married men."[18]

In an ideal world, adultery would not exist. Incest would not exist. Nice young girls would not be made to "sleep with" their stepfathers, and they would not get penalized for speaking their truths. When Susan read that nice girls don't sleep with married men, her first thought may have been one of self-blame and deprecation regarding "sleeping" with her stepfather. In this same Dear John letter, Tom Findlay stated that "the fact is, I just don't want children." The day that she read this "Dear John" letter was the same day that she drowned her boys.

National media coverage of the couple's missing boys led to discrepancies in Susan's story about abduction, and her eventual admission of guilt. How is it possible for a loving mother to murder her own innocent children? There is no more informed individual to answer this question than psychiatrist and author, Alice Miller.

In a lecture given at the New York City YWCA in October of 1998, Alice Miller spoke her truth:

> Since adolescence I have wondered why so many people take pleasure in humiliating others. Clearly the fact that some are sensitive to the suffering of others proves that the destructive urge to hurt is not a universal aspect of human nature. So why do some tend to solve their problems by violence while others don't?
>
> . . . How is it that so many turn-of-the-century German children were born . . . (to) become Hitler's willing executioners? It has always been inconceivable to

> me that a child who comes into the world among attentive, loving and protective caregivers could become a monster. Then, by closely examining the childhood histories of murderers . . . I began to comprehend the roots of good and evil: not in the genes, as commonly believed, but in the earliest days of life. Today, neurobiological research seems to fully corroborate what I discovered almost twenty years ago.
>
> Repeatedly I was told, "I, too, was a battered child, but that didn't make me a criminal." When I asked these people for details about their childhood, I was always told of a person who made the difference, a sibling, a teacher, a neighbor . . . who liked or even loved them . . . (giving) the child a notion of trust and love. . . . The criminal outcome seems to be connected with a childhood that didn't provide any helping witnesses, that was a place of constant threat and fear.
>
> Anyone addressing the problem of child abuse is likely to be faced with a very strange finding: it has been observed again and again that parents who tend to maltreat and neglect their children do it in ways that resemble the treatment they endured in their own childhood, without any conscious memory of their early experiences. Fathers who sexually abuse their children are usually unaware of the fact that they had themselves suffered the same abuse. It is . . . in therapy . . . that they can discover, sometimes stupefied, their own history. And realize thereby that for years they have attempted to act out their own scenario, just to get rid of it.[19]

Neglect and abuse from childhood remains stored in the brain, in the body, and in the spirit. Some people repeat it without remembering, some people kill themselves instead of killing others, and some people batter themselves internally for their entire lives. Death may be the only silence for some; prison may be the only safety for others.

Neglect in childhood breeds neglect of ourselves as adults. We must take every opportunity to continue to break this cycle of neglect. We must stop cutting preventive programs, and fund more non-profit organizations with prevention as the goal. We must establish more far-reaching consequences for those who cannot see the cycle, and provide more opportunities for healing and recovery.

Protecting our children from neglect is tantamount to protecting our society from nearly every societal ailment: war, torture, physical abuse, sexual abuse, rape, robbery, adultery, prostitution, murder, incest, suicide, domestic violence, pornography, eating disorders, and addiction.

Why do some people seek help while others remain stuck? Denial is a powerful defense. Early childhood cruelty may be the hardest to remember, and therefore, the hardest to resolve. As discussed in chapter 9, denial is also the first phase of grief. People often get stuck in their grief. Denial is a vicious competitor in our culture's race against neglect. We awaken society, one person, one cycle, at a time. Change is slow but steady. Breaking a cycle of neglect is nothing short of a major life accomplishment. If it is all that you accomplish in your lifetime, you have done enough.

Together, we also continue to make a home for neglect and incest in our culture. Tatum O'Neal's parents, whose stories are detailed in chapter 7, have paid no consequences for neglect, except perhaps for an embarrassing book that they can ridicule.

Woody Allen

We continue to flock to Woody Allen's movies, while his biological son continues to grieve about his father's choices. From www.life.com:

> "The heart wants what it wants." That now-famous line wasn't from one of director Woody Allen's movies, but rather was his defense for beginning a relationship with Soon-Yi Previn, the 22-year-old adopted daughter of his longtime girlfriend Mia Farrow, back in 1992. (Farrow discovered the relationship after stumbling across nude photos of Soon-Yi that Allen had taken.) Though he was never legally Soon-Yi's stepfather, Allen was described in the media as a father figure to her. An ugly court battle between Farrow and Allen over custody of their three children together (two adopted, one biological) then played out in the national media, with Farrow alleging that Allen molested their 7-year-old daughter Dylan. A judge said there was inconclusive evidence for that allegation, but Farrow still won her custody requests, and Allen has been estranged from their kids since: After Allen and Soon-Yi wed in 1997, his biological son Ronan Seamus Farrow said, "He's my father married to my sister. That makes me his son and his brother-in-law. That is such a moral transgression. . . . I cannot have a relationship with my father and be morally consistent."[20]

Is marrying an adopted daughter that Allen helped raise any less incestuous than if she were a blood relative? Incest occurs with authority figures—it is about impulse, power, and control—like rape, it is not about sexuality. Does a powerful societal avoidance keep us looking the other way?

Parenting is the easiest job in the world to get, and the hardest job in the world to do well. We owe it to ourselves, and to our children, and to our communities, to accomplish all that we can as individuals, families, and as therapists to heal ourselves and each other, and to stop neglecting neglect.

Chapter Thirteen

Grief and Its Relationship to Neglect and Abuse

Physician and author Elisabeth Kubler-Ross (1969) compiled the Five Stages of Death and Dying—the most familiar and widely-utilized phases that assist us in explaining the process of grief. Each individual grieves in a different way, and each stage is fluid. There is no order to grief, and no "right way" to grieve. Although this list was created to describe and define the five stages of terminal illness for the dying patient, the stages can be representative of all losses in life.

The stages are as follows:

- Denial
- Anger
- Bargaining
- Depression
- Acceptance[1]

All losses can trigger these stages. Let me give you an example. You are speeding on a remote mountain road. Your eye catches a police officer behind you. His lights are not yet on, and no siren is blaring. You are focused on your *denial*. You think you slowed down in time. You think maybe he's speeding up to catch up to that other speeding vehicle—there's no way he wants to stop you.

Next, the police siren blares, the light on the roof of the unmarked car begins to flicker on and off. You are *angry*. You are angry with yourself for speeding, or you may be angry at the police officer for catching you. His unmarked car closes in; you stop your vehicle.

As you slow down, you think about what you might say to the officer. Perhaps you would like to convince him to give you a warning instead of a ticket. Perhaps you can *bargain* with him about this—your first offense in years. You bargain with yourself, or with God. If I can just avoid the ticket this time, I promise I will stop speeding altogether. I might stop driving altogether! If I don't get this ticket, I'll use the $75.00 to buy a bus pass and help save the environment. I promise!

When all attempts at bargaining fail, you watch as the officer writes your ticket. You are *depressed.* You don't have the $75.00 that you need to pay the ticket. You shouldn't have been speeding. You knew this could happen. You should have known better. Self-blame sets in. Depression continues to cloud your mind.

Finally, you drive away. You leave the officer in your rearview mirror. You have some relief. You hate being on the side of the road, waiting for your ticket, watching other motorists peer into your vehicle's windows. You promise to change your driving habits. You continue on the mountain road, moving closer to your destination. With a final sigh about the incident, you have reached the phase of *acceptance.*

Of course, getting a ticket for speeding is much less traumatic than coping with neglect or abuse. The extent of the trauma can predict the depth of the phases. Some survivors become fixated in one phase or another. The characteristics of normal grief are juxtaposed against the characteristics of post-traumatic stress in table 13.1:

Table 13.1.

Grief	*PTSD*
Sleep disturbance (difficulty falling or staying asleep)	Sleep disturbance
Disbelief; shock	Disbelief; shock
Physical symptoms	Body memory
Confusion	Confusion
Anxiety	Anxiety
Lack of concentration	Lack of concentration
Acting or feeling as if the loved one will return	Acting or feeling as if the neglect is still happening
Depression	Depression
Idealization/identification with the deceased	Coping with the negative introject
Lowered self-esteem and loss of identity	Lack of self-esteem; identity crisis
Guilt	Guilt
Anger	Rage
Loneliness and despair; Missing the loved one's presence	Loneliness and despair; grieving for love lost due to betrayal/neglect
Helplessness	Victimization
Wanting to join the loved one in death	Suicidal ideation
Dreams of the deceased	Nightmares of abuse/neglect
Absent-mindedness	Dissociation

In the last phase of grief, hope emerges. There are struggles with new life patterns, and life is worth living again. People who come to accept their loss are able to reinvest energy into other loving relationships. After resolution of post-traumatic stress, aftereffects are overcome. Exposure and vulnerability are not obstacles to connection. Sexuality can be expressed without fear of victimization and flashbacks. Trust is either rebuilt, or built for the first time. Boundaries are solid. Caregiving is by choice. And, as with the loss of a loved one, new hope eventually emerges. A new identity is groomed; a love of the self blossoms, and a cycle of neglect and abuse is broken.

In a lecture given by Elisabeth Kubler-Ross, a story was told about a young girl. This child came to her mother after playing with her friend. The friend's doll had broken during their play. The doll had a porcelain face. The child reported helping her friend.

Mother: Did you help her put the doll back together?

Child: No, it was in a million pieces.

Mother: Then how did you help her?

Child: I sat down with her, and I helped her to cry.

One of the most important aspects of healing work for therapist and client is to sit with silence, to sit with tears, to sit with all expressions of loss. We need to stay where our clients are. Therapists need not try to rescue, give advice, or move someone to a "better place." During the course of healing, the best place to be is where you are. Grieving takes time and energy. Be patient and kind to yourself and your clients. Help your clients to separate their criticisms of self as much as possible from their pure grief. There is no need to judge themselves. Feelings will shift on their own. Grief is like the tide; it ebbs and flows in a natural rhythm. Trust your clients. They will arrive at their destination in their own time.

The last task of mourning, according to J. William Worden, Ph.D., in *Grief Counseling and Grief Therapy,* is to withdraw emotional energy and reinvest it in others, "one primary person, life itself."[2] The last task of mourning a neglect and abuse history is similar. We withdraw the emotional energy from feeling victimized, from feeling abandoned, and we reinvest it in self-love, in exploring passions, and in finding the safe home within ourselves.

The last task of mourning can be very difficult to reach, however. It can take years of constant focus, and many obstacles can reroute the journey.

Unresolved grief can pervade our consciousness in many ways. We may experience anniversaries of loved ones' deaths. In the same way, we can also experience anniversaries surrounding trauma. Dana, a former client mentioned in chapter 3, had an incest history that she had buried very deep inside.

Her grandfather had molested her, and he attached an enormous threat to his warning not to tell. When Dana was five years old, her grandfather nearly drowned her in her own bathtub, after the sexual molestation ended. Dana blocked the memory as fast as she could.

At ten years old, in the same month that her grandfather molested her, Dana tried to kill herself. She took a lot of aspirin that she found in her parents' medicine cabinet. Her stomach was pumped. She told her family it was an accident. At fifteen, the same incident occurred again. This time, her parents forced Dana to seek help from a professional. But with no conscious memory of the abuse, she was unable to resolve her grief during that episode of treatment. A psychiatrist prescribed antidepressants, however, and Dana-did experience some relief from them.

Dana made her last serious attempt at suicide when she was twenty years old. This time, during her hospital stay, the memory of her betrayal and near-death experience in the bathtub resurfaced. She was horrified at the thought that she re-experienced her abuse, at her own hand, every five years. Dana began therapy with me soon afterward. She was able to piece together her history and make sense of her past once this memory surfaced. She was able to grieve for the little girl who was so tortured and abused. She was able to experience gratitude that her life was spared three times. Dana went on to attend and graduate college magna cum laude. There was no suicide attempt at age twenty-five.

Examples of unresolved grief are also numerous in the lives of those adults who experienced the early childhood loss of a parent. Death is very difficult to conceptualize for young children, and they often create belief systems about themselves, or transference responses in the world, that affect their adulthoods.

Dorothy, mentioned in chapter 8, had to cope with her father's death when she was only four years old. She loved her father dearly. She made a promise to God on the day that the family buried her father. She promised God that she would never love another man as much as she loved her father. This promise to God stayed with Dorothy throughout her adolescence and into early adulthood. She had difficulty maintaining monogamous relationships, and in making commitments to men. Once Dorothy entered therapy, she was able to explore her promise to God, say goodbye to her father once again, and reinvest love and commitment into a lifelong partner.

Larry copes with anticipatory grief in his adult life on a daily basis. His mother died when he was nine years old. A drunk driver killed her as she walked from the subway station to her home in New York. Larry was the last person to see his mother. He said goodbye as she left the house, and she was gone forever. Larry integrated this loss by blaming himself. Like most children, he was unable to conceptualize the finality of her death. Days later, after the funeral and burial of his mother, he asked his uncle, "But when is Mommy coming back?" This memory of walking hand and hand with his uncle is still acutely painful to Larry, decades later. He believes he should have understood more, should have been there for her in his mother's last moments on earth, should have loved her more, and shown her more affection. As a young adult, Larry lost his father to cancer. He was attentive at his father's hospice bedside, but on the last day of his father's life, Larry was not with him. Larry and his father had had very loving conversations prior to his father's passing. In one of these conversations, Larry asked his father to "send me a sign to let me know that you're okay, once you cross over." On the same night of his father's passing, Larry had a unique spiritual experience. His father came to him, while Larry was crying about the loss. Larry actually felt the extreme love, bliss, and euphoria that people describe after near-death experiences. But even after this momentary glimpse of heaven and the integration of loving memories of his father, Larry's guilt was not soothed. He still harbors guilt about not being present at the moment of his father's death.

As an adult, Larry has lost three of his beloved cats. Larry's pets have always been like family members to him. Prior to the loss of each cat, and as he continued to watch them age, he would have strong desires to spend more and more time at home with them. When they became sick, he would monitor their every move, supervising their eating, their movements, and even their excretions on a regular basis. Larry would dream of their deaths before they occurred, and they each came to him in his dreams after passing. The most difficult loss to bear was Larry's cat Gizzy. Larry came home one Sunday to find Gizzy lying on the floor. At first, it looked like he was asleep, but soon Larry realized that Gizzy was no longer breathing. This loss was most difficult because, once again, Larry was not present when Gizzy passed.

This sense of feeling out-of-control about death is very common. Feeling out-of-control is especially common after a death from suicide. Guilt is pervasive when there are many questions following a death. People think they could have done more, or could have said something differently, or could have been more present for their loved ones. This self-blame is a way of taking control of the death. It is not unlike an incest survivor blaming herself for the trauma of sexual abuse. Both death and trauma are often out of our realm of control. It is sometimes easier to feel that we were responsible for them, than to feel that we were totally helpless. Self-blame, in death and in recovery from trauma, can prohibit pure grief. If the focus of grief is an obsession about guilt, there is not enough room left in one's mind or heart to grieve a loss fully.

Larry has two younger cats in his home at this writing. Although they are both healthy and spry, Larry experiences fear about their passing on a regular basis. If either cat shows signs of not feeling perfectly well, he feels out of control when leaving the house. Recently, one of the cats was sleeping soundly, and Larry began to pet him gently. The cat did not stir. Larry's panic about death immediately set in. He was a bit more forceful, woke the cat, and the cat was fine. It took Larry some time to recover from this incident, however. It is crucial that grieving people work at separating their self-blame from their bereavement, so that they can more fully connect to life and relieve their intense fear of recurrent loss. This process is very similar to survivors of neglect. We need to assist our clients in separating their self-blame from their grief about being neglected and abused as children.

Another example of unresolved grief is beautifully depicted in a story called "Fat Lady" in Irvin Yalom's book *Love's Executioner,* mentioned in an earlier chapter. If you can get past the title of the chapter, the story is well worth reading. A young woman begins therapy with Dr. Yalom to deal with weight loss, and inadvertently deals with unresolved grief.

"At first it seemed that these flashbacks," Yalom reports, "as well as the accompanying extreme mood swings, were chaotic, random occurrences; but after several weeks, Betty realized that they were following a coherent pattern: as she lost weight she *re-experienced the major traumatic or unresolved events of her life that had occurred when she was at a particular weight.* Thus her descent from two hundred fifty pounds set her spinning backward in time through the emotionally charged events of her life: leaving Texas for New York (210 pounds), her college graduation (190 pounds), her decision to drop the pre-med curriculum (and to give up the dream of discovering the cure for the cancer that had killed her father) (180 pounds), her loneliness at her high school graduation—her envy of other daughters and fathers, her inability to get a date for the senior prom (170 pounds), her junior high graduation and how much she missed her father at that graduation (155 pounds). What a wonderful proof of the unconscious realm! Betty's body had remembered what her mind had long forgotten."[3]

Betty also comes to grips with the transference response that she had to her father's death. Betty discusses with Dr. Yalom that "when I meet a new person whom I like, I start right away to imagine what it will be like to say goodbye to them."[4]

Dr. Yalom comments to his readers: "I knew this was an important issue, and that we would return to it." Otto Rank described this life stance with a wonderful phrase: "Refusing the loan of life in order to avoid the debt of death."[5]

Betty was clearly on the road to resolution of the grief that she was unable to access as a young child, when her father died.

As practitioners, we used to think that a child under three years old would not have any memory of grief or loss. We have since learned differently. Although memory may not be visual or concrete, beliefs do evolve into adulthood from early childhood loss.

Tim lost his father when he was less than two years old. He died in the hospital, during a routine surgery. One day Tim's father was there; the next day, he was gone. Soon, Tim's mother remarried, and his alcoholic stepfather would beat him regularly for making noise in the morning. Tim learned quickly to be very quiet indeed. Tim has memories of his beloved father, from as far back as when he learned to walk. He has images in his mind of a kind, caring, loving man by his side. The feeling memory that Tim has of his father is very solid. He can still feel his father's love. One of Tim's habits is very interesting in terms of early childhood loss. When Tim spends money on himself, which is an infrequent occurrence, he doesn't buy one item. He purchases two. If Tim likes something a lot, he will buy one thing to use, and another to save. The second one remains in plastic, at the top of a closet, just in case the first item disappears.

Fifteen years ago, I volunteered at a battered women's shelter. A young woman arrived at the shelter during my shift, and I helped her to settle into a room. She had an infant son, just six months old. Her son had never slept through the night, and he cried throughout the day, most days. His ears had witnessed his mother's verbal abuse, as well as his father's loud voice, and the sounds of his mother being physically hurt.

When this infant arrived at the shelter, his crying stopped. He began to sleep through the night. His mother was thrilled, as she was able to sleep as well. There seemed to be no resemblance to the infant that first came to the shelter. About a month after the family's arrival, there was a problem with the plumbing at the shelter. A plumber was contacted, and he arrived at the shelter promptly. He had a loud, booming voice. He only had time to speak a few sentences before a baby boy started wailing in the background.

Chapter Fourteen

Understanding Developmental Theory in Relation to Neglect

Margaret Mahler

In her book *The Psychological Birth of the Human Infant* (1975), Margaret Mahler discusses the concept of "rapprochement"—the initial successes a toddler achieves in holding on and letting go.[1] Success at this stage of life requires that a caregiver remains accessible. It certainly makes things easier if toddlers receive encouragement as they take their first steps in the world. If you have witnessed toddlers taking their first steps *in healthy circumstances,* you have no doubt witnessed the toddler's need to step forward, and then look back, to ensure that a parent or nurturer is still there. This looking back ("holding on") creates the safety necessary for the child to move forward again ("letting go"). Trauma occurring at this time of life can be devastating into adulthood. I have worked with clients who actually remember teaching themselves to walk. They held on to the bars of a crib or a playpen, and pulled themselves up on their own. They took tentative steps, fell, and got up again, with no witness to their challenge. What did they learn? What might you observe about their relationships?

A client may not value relationships at all. A client might feel more productive alone. She or he might trust people on the surface, but not be able to share true intimacy. She may feel that no one is ever "there for me"; everyone has their own agenda. And, people with neglect histories struggle with experiencing happiness—since in their prior experience, it goes away, so why bother? The *counterdependent* response to early childhood neglect is totally understandable: "I don't need anyone."

Counterdependence, Dependence, and Interdependence

Sarah, from chapter 1, recently told me: "I used to think people were weak and lame when they described feeling loved by their partners. Now I realize they were describing happiness, not neediness."

It is ego-syntonic for clients with neglect histories to withdraw into themselves. They are likely to be reserved and introverted, but even if they are attention-seeking, neither style meets their needs. It is, after all, counterintuitive for them to acknowledge their needs in the first place.

Counterdependence[2] is the opposite of dependence. It is the set of beliefs that develops when neglected individuals cannot allow themselves the feeling of dependence on their caretakers. After enough history of rejection and of being ignored, any individual could easily become counterdependent. Sarah relies on no one. She believes that she does not need anyone's help. She doesn't bother to ask for her needs to be met, because she assumes that no one can meet them. She stays isolated in relationships, which, of course, are rarely mutual. Sarah takes care of other people, but no one takes care of her. She always has "an out"—an escape route, to leave people behind and bask in the comfort of being alone. The escape scenario, however, is always preceded by feelings of abandonment and betrayal.

As therapists, we need to be wise about detecting counterdependence in our clients. Our clients can wrongfully assume that counterdependence is synonymous with independence. It is not. Independence entails knowing one's needs, asking for help when it is appropriate to do so, allowing love and nurturing into one's life, and being *interdependent* in the world. It entails trust in others, and trust in oneself. It does not arise from abandonment feelings, but from connection. When the initial connection to one's caretaker is absent, neglect survivors need to re-learn connection and dependence in a healthy way.

This re-learning can occur in therapy. Clients with neglect histories can become frightened when they start to feel dependent on their therapists. If their dependency needs are not acknowledged, they might even bolt from treatment for a while. The pain of abandonment remains fresh for survivors, and their assumption is that their clinicians will leave them as well. Sometimes, clients will leave treatment rather than acknowledge the need for dependence. They might need to leave therapy before the threat of abandonment can be resolved. If your client remains in treatment, however, this transference response can be discussed and resolved with the help of the counterdependence-interdependence-dependence scale.

Many neglect survivors will start out in treatment as counterdependent. As they enhance their ability to trust, they may allow themselves an experience of dependence on their therapist. As a result of allowing dependence that works for them, clients can stop hiding behind the mask of counterdependence.

They become able to graduate to interdependence. Of course, there may be sadness and grief to overcome during this process, since interdependence was not learned, as it should have been, from a loving caregiver early in life. Finally, though, this interdependence can enhance the quality of every relationship in the client's life.

Erik Erikson

Erik Erikson discusses his eight-stage model of development in his pivotal work *Childhood and Society* (1963). These stages also require optimal circumstances in order to be adequately achieved. If there is disruption or trauma in any of the stages, there is the danger of a child remaining fixated at that time and place. Erikson's first stage, *Basic Trust vs. Basic Mistrust*,[3] occurs successfully if there is a majority of positive experience with one's parent. Unfortunately for survivors of neglect, the inverse is also true. If there are few positive experiences, or if there is a severe absence of contact, that child will not graduate from this stage, and will most likely develop a mistrustful overview of people and relationships.

Erikson's second stage, *Autonomy vs. Shame and Doubt*,[4] occurs during the same phase of life as "rapprochement." This phase can emphasize a child's pleasure in discovery, as toddlers manage mobility and maturation of muscle control. Success means pleasure in independence and self-discovery; failure in this stage can create a multi-leveled, pervasive doubt.

If there is damage that occurs during rapprochement, children may develop coping strategies to defend themselves against perceived abandonment and loss. These same coping strategies may follow them into adolescence. Perhaps you have heard that if a child takes many risks as a toddler, he may also take many risks as an adolescent. Behaviors during toddlerhood are likely to be replicated during adolescence. Adolescence is the second phase of life that includes a literal and figurative "holding on and letting go." Adolescents learn to drive; they become more mobile; they separate and individuate—*in the best of all possible worlds.* They also ask themselves some very important existential questions at this phase of life. Who am I? What am I doing here? What do I want to take from my childhood, and what do I want to leave behind?

If adolescents start drinking alcohol or using drugs, or if they remain dissociated from childhood neglect, then—you guessed it—the tasks of adolescence cannot be accomplished. No questions are asked; no answers are found. A man who started drinking at age thirteen told me that he was an adult with three years of sobriety before he could start asking those questions of himself. It was several more years before he had answers. What are the implications of a lack of individuation that may pertain to the therapeutic alliance?

Your client may not trust you at all. It may take years to establish basic trust. Your client may try to push you away, to use criticism or ridicule in an attempt to rebel against an absent parent. Or, the opposite may be true. Your client may hang on to your every word. Your client may rely on you to define who she is. She may ask you for the answers because of a lack of trust in finding them within herself.

During the "terrible twos" of toddlerhood, children learn to say "no." They test the parental waters with partial rebellions against their caretakers, and ideally, they learn that their rebellions are accepted. *Ideally,* they are loved unconditionally. But what if children are ignored, or rejected, or physically hurt, when they attempt their minor rebellions? That child might respond in extreme ways. The child might stop asserting himself and succumb to being ignored. Withdrawal might occur. The child might try to dissociate from his or her feelings.

In adolescence, a young adult must feel safe in order to rebel. Adolescents that were neglected, or ignored, or rejected are often not able to assert their identities as separate from their parents in any way. In other words, they may not rebel at all. Unfortunately, those neglected young people often stay stuck in Erikson's *Identity vs. Role Confusion*[5] phase. They cannot ask themselves the important questions of that age, and as a result, they do not individuate. They remain underconfident, lost souls, with little sense of self, low self-esteem, and little motivation to achieve. They don't trust themselves any more than they trust anyone else. For these young people, love and nurturance are like tools in a locked shed. They can't access the key from either parent, and in the worst-case scenario, they don't even know that a key exists.

Masochism and Codependence

Many female clients that you will encounter may attempt to overachieve in their relationships. They may give much more than they receive. This may be due in part to a neglect history. Decades ago, women with this pattern in relationships were called "masochistic." Our masochism was potentially the result of women's stereotypical indoctrination into the culture of selflessness, taken to an extreme. But that extreme could easily have been a result of an unacknowledged and unresolved neglect history. In the late 1980s and early 1990s, we began to define this same behavior as codependent. Melody Beattie describes patterns in relationships in her classic book from that era, *Codependent No More,* in relation to addiction and recovery.[6] Codependent people were those who sacrificed their own needs for the sake of others, again, to an extreme. In my experience with clients who labeled themselves in this way, I learned that many codependents were survivors of abandonment and neglect. They formed selves that could not tolerate being alone, jumped from relationship to relationship without any time to grieve, and existed in their minds only to help others, with the goal of rescuing their partners. They drew needy people to themselves—the needier the better. In this way, they could take care of a partner without fear of being abandoned again. The foundations of their partnerships were rooted in unresolved neglect histories. These relationships served to attempt to master the experience of neglect without dealing with it directly. Our partners became stand-ins for our neglectful parents. We attempted to fix what was broken in our biological families, but it never seemed to work. The labels of "masochism" and "codependence" remained superficial themes in comparison to all that was occurring in these relationships. Robin Norwood's self-help book *Women Who Love Too Much: When You Keep Wishing and Hoping He'll Change* has maintained popularity throughout the decades since it was first published in 1985, as testament to the numbers of women who remain in this relationship cycle.[7]

In 1990, Bepko and Krestan published *Too Good for Her Own Good.* This book debates the efficacy of the term *codependence*. Evolving out of their work with alcoholic family systems, Bepko and Krestan discussed neglect without naming it, in describing this typical family dynamic:

> Triangles often occur between parents and children when a "ledger of justice" needs balancing. In other words, if either one of our parents was deprived of some important developmental need in childhood, and if they don't feel that need is met by their marital relationship, our parent may look to us or to our siblings to make up for the missing emotional contact. In effect, our parent says, "You be my missing mother or my missing father." This parent develops a close bond with us that leaves the other parent and perhaps our other siblings on the outside of the relationship. Eventually, all the relationships between other family members become unbalanced as a result.
>
> Loyalty triangles are ways of asking a child to take too much responsibility, to be too good. Having too close a tie with one family member puts pressure on us that prevents our relating easily to all the other important people in our lives.[8]

Clearly, the authors are not advocating for this particular parenting style. They are simply observing the frequency of its occurrence in families coping with addiction. Addiction itself can be seen as an aftereffect of neglect or loss. As long as neglect histories are unresolved, they risk being repeated.

Chapter Fifteen

Developing Object Constancy in Adults

In *Attachment and Dynamic Practice* (2007), authors Brandell and Ringel discuss "object constancy," Margaret Mahler's "fourth and final subphase of the separation-individuation process."[1] The subphase of object constancy is thought to occur during the third year of life. Mahler thought of object constancy "as consisting of two vital and interrelated tasks: the formation of stable images or mental representations of the self and of the other."[2] How do we apply this concept to neglect?

To simplify a bit, let's look at how puppies play. In their adorable puppyhoods, they will run after an object like a ball, for example. They will not yet fetch the object, but they seem to find endless pleasure in chasing it. If you grab the ball and hide it from a very young puppy, the puppy may run around in circles for a while, searching for the ball. The puppy will not know to search behind your back, in your closed fists, for the ball. To that puppy in that moment, the ball cannot be seen, so it no longer exists. The play may stop there, until you bring the ball back into the puppy's field of vision. Later, in normal puppy development, the puppy learns that the ball still exists when it can't be seen, and the dog will eagerly search for the ball throughout the area until it is successfully found.

We have all seen infants with separation anxiety. If an infant's mother leaves temporarily, it can create anxiety, which leads quickly to tears. Many infants do not enjoy being held by strangers, especially if that stranger is a substitute for the known mother. Separation anxiety is considered a "normal" aspect of development. But, in the best of all possible worlds, there is someone available consistently enough in the child's life. If this is the case, the child feels safe enough to experience that person's temporary absence. Tears and frustration are reasonable accommodations to the temporary loss of mother. When mother returns, the child learns that the mother still exists.

The child can start to learn to self-soothe, and develop the basic understanding that the pain of separation is temporary.

Neglect, however, creates a very different scenario. Clearly, in order to establish a separate sense of self, there has to be an "other" to separate from. What happens if there is no consistent other? Can there be a self? Perhaps not.

Jasmin Cori describes research conducted with infants in her book, *The Emotionally Absent Mother* (2010). "In the still-face experiments, these previously secure babies warmed up again to their mothers and returned to their former intimate relational dance, but what happens when Mother is often remote, dazed, and inexpressive? Or what happens if the young child has experienced other trauma—say, medical trauma, or physical or sexual abuse—and has learned to dissociate? Will it be so easy to reengage then?"

"Citing research, author Sue Gerhardt concludes, "For a baby, the most painful experience of all seems to be not being able to get Mother's attention." This seems even more unbearable than maltreatment. Mother, after all, is the baby's link to the world and the best hope for getting needs met, assuming Mother is the primary caretaker." [3]

How might this sound in your office?

A client might tell you that she doesn't feel real. That she doesn't belong, that she doesn't exist. Joelle, from Chapter Eight, told me that she had no opinions. You may hear that your client feels empty inside. Maybe she only knows who she is because of what others tell her, like in *Julie's Story*. She may say she's depressed all the time. She doesn't know what she wants or needs. She has 'no luck' in relationships. What does a lack of object constancy look like? How might a client behave?

A professor at Boston University told my Differential Diagnosis class: "If you think one thing is true about a client, remember that the opposite may also be true". I knew when I heard this statement that it was important, but at the time, I didn't understand exactly why. Here is why, as related to neglect.

Sue Gerhardt tells us:

> The dual nature of the defensive system seems to be built into our genetic programme: it's either fight or flight. Cry loudly or withdraw. Exaggerate feelings or minimise feelings. Be hyper-aroused or suppress arousal. These two basic strategies also underpin the insecure styles of attachment—the avoidant or the resistant. Whichever way the individual turns to find a solution (and these strategies may be used consistently or inconsistently), he or she will not have mastered the basic process of self-regulation and will remain prone to being overdemanding of others, or underdemanding. [4]

Clients may also fluctuate between two extremes. A client may trust haphazardly in relationships, for example, without clear boundaries around her self. She may later feel exploited, and become resentful. She may then end that relationship, stop trusting others, withdraw from the world, and develop impenetrable boundaries. Eventually, this strategy leads to loneliness and despair. The client may try to connect again, and revictimize herself, moving once again into relationships with no clear boundaries and a lack of awareness of her needs.

In treatment, your client may test you. Your client may schedule appointments and cancel them on a regular basis. She may consistently forget her checkbook. She may owe you a lot of money. Adolescent clients may sit in your office without saying a word. These may all be signs of a lack of object constancy. And over time, once trust is deeply established, these behaviors may change.

During my first internship in graduate school, I worked at a small elementary school in Malden, Massachusetts. My supervisor told me about a young boy that he worked with for several years. When my supervisor could not engage this young boy in talk therapy or art therapy, he decided to think outside the box. He brought in a chess set, and taught this young client to play the game. They played chess consistently for more than a year, during every session, and one day, the boy started talking. He spoke about a severe neglect history. Both of his parents were harsh with their words, and this young boy felt unloved and undervalued. The consistency of the chess game allowed this boy to develop object constancy.

Part III

OVERCOMING THE NEGLECT SCENARIO

Chapter Sixteen

Working through Transference in Relationships

At Boston University,[1] I was taught to consistently evaluate the therapeutic relationship *with my clients.* One of the most valuable tools to utilize during this ongoing evaluation is to remember to notice *process vs. content.* The process between the therapist and the client is often much more significant than the content of what is being said. This process includes visual evaluations of body language, eye contact, posture, and whether or not your client keeps her coat on throughout the session. But it also includes the more subtle and pervasive concept of *transference.* How are your clients transferring the attitudes and beliefs held about their histories onto you? If a client starts a sentence with, "You probably will think this is stupid, but . . . ," you can ask, "Did someone think your ideas were stupid? Is that familiar to you?" You can reassure your client that you don't think her ideas are stupid. And that they probably never were.

To quote Gerhardt (2004), from *Why Love Matters*: "Attachment literature has made it clear that children develop working models of relationships based on their own experiences, but that these are not simply models of how other people behave. They are models of one's self *with* another person; models of interaction between people, not static internal images of 'mother' or 'father'. This means that the inner pictures that we draw on to guide our behaviour are images that conjure up how it *feels* to be with another person. If the other person consistently treats you as if you were a fool, you feel like a fool. If your parents show little interest in your states of mind, you feel as if your states of mind are not of interest to others."[2]

A former client, Lizzie, was emotionally neglected by both parents. She was discouraged from feeling her feelings, and if she managed to cry in her parents' presence, she was nicknamed "Sarah Heartburn" (after the famous French actress, Sarah Bernhardt (1884–1923). Lizzie grew into adulthood with the feeling that she was boring to other people. Unfortunately, this client's belief was reinforced during her first therapy experience. During one of her first therapy sessions, Lizzie noticed that her therapist had actually fallen asleep! She woke him up, and he apologized to her. How is she supposed to believe that he was merely tired, or desperately in need of a caffeinated drink, without personalizing that experience? When Lizzie started working with me in therapy, she needed to process this experience fully before moving forward in treatment. She needed to know that the therapist's actions were not about her. Lizzie needed to feel interesting to others in order to combat her internalized beliefs and transference in relationships. Fortunately, it was very easy for me to show interest in all that Lizzie was about. By doing so, I aided her in her healing through the use of transference in our therapeutic relationship.

Once your client can resolve a negative transference in the therapeutic relationship, that client can then test her negative assumptions, with deeper awareness and interest in change, in all of her other important relationships.

The therapeutic alliance is a wonderful, albeit contrived, place to deal with transference in relationships. Ideally, we feel safe enough in therapy to explore the ways that we replicate our histories in our current relationships. Koren Zailckas (2010), in her recent book *Fury: A Memoir,* beautifully depicts one of her initial discoveries about replication and transference as she recaps a conversation with her therapist:

> Ever since I was a kid I've thought the world was divided between scapegoats and bullies."
>
> "So where did you get the idea that people had to be one thing or the other? Either always angry or always ingratiating?"
>
> "From my parents."
>
> "That's your blueprint," Alice says. "You model your relationships after how you've perceived your parents. Every time you enter into a new romantic relationship, or even a new friendship, you choose whether you want to play your father or your mother."
>
> "Whether I want to be all heart or all throat."
>
> Alice nods.
>
> Because I've been attempting to love without an awareness of my past, I've only been able to behave *as if* I were loving. Alice wants me to see how hypocritical and deceptive that is. How confusing it is to the people I might have used for this purpose.

Later, Koren comes to terms with the following realization: "All my life, in almost all of my interactions, I had either selected people who were controlling and critical to begin with or withheld my emotions, catered to these people, and tried to trick myself into thinking they were self-absorbed and stifling. Then I staged the rebellion I'd never been able to work up as a kid."[3]

Clearly, this type of realization regarding one's transference can be life-altering, and change one's relationships forever.

In the novel *While I Was Gone*, by Sue Miller (1999), the author created a fictional protagonist named Josie. Josie married a man with whom she shared no interests. She experienced no intimacy in marital communication. This lack of connection was partly due to the character lacking introspective ability, and partly due to her emotional needs being neglected during childhood. Josie was dissociated from her feelings. In that dissociated state, as a young adult, she "ran away" from her marriage. She moved to Massachusetts, rented a room with undergraduate students, and changed her identity. Josie had no idea why she made this drastic move; she only knew that it felt very necessary. Much later in the novel, we discover the transference response that led Josie to leave her marriage:

> I said earlier that running away from my first marriage was unique in my life, that it was hard for me to recognize or remember myself as I was then because the behavior was so foreign to me.
>
> But that was not, strictly, true. I ran away once as a girl, too, at perhaps eight or nine. I didn't get far, but if intentions had wings, I would have landed in Florida, in Brigadoon. In never-never land. As it was, I made several mistakes and was easily retrieved. The primary one was stealing my brother Fred's cowboy boots.
>
> I'd long coveted them. They were red, with white appliques stitched on them—crescent moons and stars. From the moment he'd unwrapped them the Christmas before, I felt that if there were any justice, any fairness in the world, I would have known about the existence of these boots. I would have asked for them for myself. They would be mine, not his. Now, on this dusty summer afternoon, I sneaked into Fred's room and found them in his closet. I carried them to the front porch. I pulled them on and set out on my journey: down to the corner and left onto the street that became the road that led out of town, the place where all journeys I'd ever known began.
>
> The boots swam freely around my feet as I walked. It was a hot day; my feet were damp with sweat. Within the equivalent of a few city blocks, I had blisters on both heels. At a point shortly after that, I took the boots off and left them in the tall grass that grew by the road. I went on, barefoot, slowed by pebbles and glass. I was hobbling and miserable when a neighbor saw me from her car and stopped. "Dearie," she called. "You've headed the wrong way!"
>
> I let her talk me into the car, I consented to let her drive me home. But nearly as soon as we started back, I burst into tears—at the thought of my failure, at my barefoot shame. At the enormity of my sin in stealing my brother's boots, at the fear of being punished. By the time we got home, I was inconsolable, so inconsolable that there was only sympathy for my bleeding bare feet, for my hysteria, for my having been—as they understood it—lost.

And what triggered that flight? What was the itch that time? This: My older brother had told me—it seems to me only a few days before, but it might have been weeks, or even months—about my father's previous life, his first marriage. I don't know why he chose the moment. Some smugness on my part he wanted to pierce. Some casual remark that seemed to claim ownership of our parents' history. Some minor offense to him. At any rate, he told. Cruelly, harshly, the correction being to my stupidity for not having known earlier—though how could I? No one had even hinted at it—that our father had had another wife, another whole existence, before he met our mother, before we were born. That if things had been as he first planned them, we never *would* have been born, there would have been other children living in our house, with another mother, with different rules, different notions of what was important in life.

This shattered my understanding of the universe, the feeling I'd had—I think every child has it until some point in life—that my life was somehow sacred and foreordained, the one absolutely necessary life I had to live.

Apparently not. Apparently I might never have been. Or I might have been other than what I was.

And it occurred to me then, mightn't I yet be? It seemed suddenly that what had been the cornerstone of my existence was shifting sand. That what had been a given was merely a whim. It seemed possible that there was another life waiting somewhere out there for me. This was not exactly how I thought of it, of course. Mostly I *felt* it: a yearning, suddenly justified, for something other for myself. Better. More real somehow. More like the lives I read about in my books.[4]

Sue Miller created a very plausible scenario of initial trauma and betrayal, and its effect on future relationships. She described Josie as lost and confused, while working through her transference response to her father's first marriage. Josie had no understanding of why she ran away from her first marriage, and later, why she thought about committing adultery in her second marriage—until she allowed this detailed memory to surface. Josie "played her father" in *While I Was Gone* in the same way that Koren Zailckas fluctuated between playing her mother and her father, in *Fury: A Memoir.*

Transference and Cross-Gender Neglect

Cross-gender neglect refers to young girls who are neglected by their fathers, or young boys who are neglected by their mothers. As you might imagine, the effect of cross-gender neglect on our adult lives can be very different than the effect of same-gender neglect.

In same-gender neglect, healing must involve working with *the introject*—the internalized messages from the same-sex parent, as discussed in chapter 11. In cross-gender neglect, the major issue that usually presents itself in the lives of neglected adults is the transference response to the opposite sex in adult heterosexual relationships.

Again, *transference*[5] is the phenomenon that we all bring to the table—the baggage and assumptions that we carry from our pasts, projected onto other people. Transference can be either positive or negative. If you were abused by a brother named Craig, for example, and you meet someone whose name is Craig, chances are, unless you have evolved past the abuse, the new Craig will have a lot to prove before you trust him.

We also tend to transfer our beliefs about how we expect to be treated. If, for example, you were told throughout your life that you were a "loser," and that you would amount to nothing, chances are that your expectation of a job interviewer would be that s/he would somehow glean this information about you, and not want to hire you for the position. This expectation could lead you to feel increased anxiety and upset before the interview, and perhaps you would not answer questions as comfortably as usual during the meeting. If you were not offered the position, it could reinforce your negative transference to people in authority, as well as confirm the old messages you had received in your family of origin.

What assumptions do you make about how other people will treat you? Are there ways that you may be contributing to this dynamic? If you have not explored your own transference responses, you will be less open to exploring them in the lives of your clients. Most significantly, you might be more reserved in discussing process vs. content with your clients.

Positive transference tends to be a bit more conscious than negative transference. Initially, upon meeting with a therapist who listens well and seems to understand your predicament, for example, a client might feel an immediate connection. This connection is somewhat intuitive, but it also has to do with the beliefs and hopes that they place on you as their therapist—despite the fact that you just met. Your client doesn't know you, but the transference response that your client develops can assist you in establishing the chemistry you will need to make the best of your sessions together.

Positive transference is often our initial reaction in meeting a potential new partner or friend. For most heterosexual men and women with cross-gender neglect histories, however, the transference carried from that history plays itself out most significantly in intimate relationships, no matter how great we might feel about the relationship at first.

It is the nature of transference that causes us to repeat patterns of neglect, until our patterns become more conscious. The type of neglect that we experienced in our childhood often dictates our adult repetition in relationships.

You can assist your clients in bringing their transference patterns to the surface, so that there is more opportunity for change.

Jill's Story

Jill is a current client whose father was an alcoholic during her younger years. He is sober today, and Jill has a cautiously optimistic relationship with him. She acknowledges in therapy, however, that she is still angry at him for making it so difficult for her to choose men who don't abandon her.

We all repeat patterns in relationships until our histories surface, and we take the opportunity to resolve those histories. Jill will be turning thirty next month, alone. She has had three fairly serious relationships with men; all three men have left her. The first young man left after a conversation about commitment. Jill was questioning her feelings for her partner, and that's when his commitment ended. He could not process her concerns about their relationship.

The second relationship was one in which Jill felt more connected than before. This young man had similar interests and goals, with a focus on health and wellness. Jill, working in the health industry and "addicted" to yoga and meditation, thought that "this was it". As the relationship progressed, however, Jill felt that she wanted to spend more time with her partner, and he pulled away as a result. He told her that she was "attached" (he meant this in a "yogic way, not a codependent way", according to Jill), and although she felt quite emotionally neglected after a while, she stayed with him. He continued his withdrawal from her, and they gradually spent less and less time together. Jill realized that her partner was not capable of intimacy in the way that she needed him to be. He also treated her as the problem, ridiculing her requests for more time and added commitment. This relationship ended as well.

Most recently, Jill was involved with a new man. Although the relationship was short-lived, this boyfriend seemed more emotionally evolved. He seemed able to process deep feelings with Jill, and she enjoyed the growth that she experienced in the relationship. After a month or so, her boyfriend admitted that he was an alcoholic. His mother had been an alcoholic as well. Jill spoke with her closest friends about what this admission meant to her. She did not want a relationship that repeated the pattern of her parents' marriage. She decided to be open-minded—her boyfriend's problem would not be a deal-breaker for her. There was one other problem, though. Although her boyfriend owned a home in the area, he worked for weeks at a time at out-of-state jobs. As he began to feel closer to Jill, he started to question the possibility of a future together. On the one hand, they talked about living together. On the other, he felt that his job was so consuming that he could not make a serious commitment at that time. He started drinking more in her presence, and the emotional neglect cycle began again. After a very difficult weekend together, they split up.

Jill has decided to take a hiatus from dating. She plans to travel, to work toward a promotion at the job she loves, and to create a home environment that feels comfortable, with some female roommates who are also her closest friends.

Jill has a strong sense of self. She does not suffer with low self-esteem. She felt loved by her mother, and she has no negative introject. During the course of Jill's treatment, however, she has realized that she does not trust men to stay with her. She has been very open to discovering where this negative transference came from.

Jill's father would leave home. He would one day decide to spend some time with his friends, and he would go on an alcoholic binge for days at a time. Before his leaving, there would be a loud argument between her parents, and Jill would usually retreat to her bedroom. She would wait until the fight ended, suspecting all along that her father would be gone when she left the comfort of her bedroom. He always was.

Then, there would be the waiting. Jill would try to act as if nothing was wrong. Days would go by, and Jill's anxiety would build. Sometimes, her father would return, and there would be no fighting, and all would be fine in the household. Other times, he would return angry, critical, and emotionally unavailable. There would be a slow recovery period for the family until things became comfortable again—and then the next binge would occur.

During this time period, Jill developed her capacity to read people. Like many daughters of alcoholic parents, Jill became hypervigilant. She is able to observe her world and predict mood and emotion in others practically flawlessly. Most daughters with this history can walk into a room of people, and understand and even absorb the feeling in that room within seconds.

In therapy, Jill realized that her hypervigilance was a special skill, honed during childhood. She reported that when she went out with her friends, especially to certain bars, Jill would sometimes walk through the entrance and almost immediately want to leave. She would remark to her friends that the feeling wasn't good in the building. Jill's friends initially thought that this was just one of her idiosyncrasies, but they started to observe something. When they refused to leave the bar with Jill, a fight would break out, or a bouncer would throw someone out of the bar. Jill's friends started to listen more openly to her requests, and validate her intuition. They leave now, whenever Jill is ready. Jill honed this sixth sense during the times she waited for her father to come home. She needed to assess his mood immediately upon his return, and she chose her behaviors in response to that mood. Although hypervigilance can serve Jill well, it is a by-product of Jill's neglect by her father.

Being emotionally neglected in relationship to men is all too familiar to Jill. She assumes abandonment by them, and she copes with her losses by distracting herself, working hard, attending yoga retreats, and nurturing herself through contact with friends.

The revelations Jill had in relation to her last boyfriend were quite significant. Whenever he left for an out-of-state job, she would pick a fight with him beforehand. They would usually be able to resolve her concerns before he left, but her anxiety would build while she waited for his return. She made some deep connections between her father's cycles of leaving, and her anxieties about how things would be when her boyfriend returned. Jill had thoughts that her boyfriend would abandon her, very consistently, for weeks at a time, while he traveled for work. She would feel possessive of him, despite his consistent contact with her while he was away. She could not learn to trust him fully with this dynamic present. When her boyfriend pulled away, there was some relief for Jill. She had been pushing against her limits, and staying in a relationship that felt counterintuitive to continue.

As she resolves the neglect surrounding her father's drinking, Jill will intuitively choose men who are more available emotionally as well as geographically.

Kevin's Story

A former client came to me with a desire to stop drinking. Often, when he drank beer with friends, he became a bully. Kevin was fiercely loyal to his friends, and when a friend was being threatened, and a fight started to brew in a bar, Kevin consistently threw the first punch.

Kevin's mother had a severe sexual abuse history. She had unresolved symptoms of Post-Traumatic Stress Disorder. She was anxious, with constant rumination and worry. Because of her own struggles, she had very little emotional energy to devote to her son. Kevin grew up feeling unprotected and abandoned by her.

Kevin did feel loved by his father, however. His father was a Vietnam veteran who returned from the war and became a car mechanic. He became passionate about restoring old vehicles. He took Kevin under his wing and taught him a great deal. Father and son spent a good deal of quality time together. When Kevin's father drank, however, he became violent. Kevin was physically abused when his father was drunk. During the course of the abuse, Kevin was not permitted to step away from the belt, or whatever object was being thrown at him. If he avoided the abuse, it would last longer and be more intense. Kevin learned to stand perfectly still, dissociate from the pain, and squelch his growing desire to fight back. His mother did not protect him. No one did. Kevin was helpless until his father regained his sobriety.

In therapy, Kevin discovered that his need to fight as an adult was representative of his accumulated anger and helplessness as a child. He was proving to himself, more than to his father, even, that he was able to protect himself. He utilized his loyalty to his friends as an excuse and an opportunity to fight the fight he was prevented from winning as a child. Kevin always won the brawls in the bars. He described feeling unable to stop fighting until he had won.

In Kevin's case, his mother's neglect contributed to his being unprotected. Kevin became a sensitive, introspective adult who integrated the violent alcohol-induced rages of his father, but those rages quickly became ego-dystonic for him. Once Kevin had an understanding of his need to prove he was no longer helpless, he was able to stop drinking. He continued to visit bars with his friends, but he remained sober, and he would walk out of the bar if a fight started. He was able to choose not to fight, consistently, and with pride. He was able to discuss his history with his father, and his father apologized to him for the physical abuse. His father also expressed gratitude to Kevin for making him accountable in the relationship. What a beautiful day that was for Kevin!

Oh, and one other thing. Before leaving therapy, Kevin broke up with his girlfriend of four years. She was an incest survivor, unwilling to "own" her promiscuous behavior and to take responsibility for this aftereffect of the sexual abuse. She had been emotionally neglecting Kevin for years.

From the work I have done, I have seen that there is usually an underlying reason why people choose to drink, abuse prescription medication, or take illicit drugs. Many people who choose to alter their realities as young adults have an unresolved childhood loss or a history of neglect, abuse, or trauma that they are trying to forget. Often, when people become sober or drug-free, it is this history that reveals itself. The way around one's history is through it. Altering one's reality is only a temporary fix, and that fix can produce many other problems for men and women with abuse histories.

I have worked with many women over the years that have used alcohol and drugs to comfort themselves while remaining in abusive relationships with men they love. They were often victims of abuse and neglect in their families of origin.

In listening to the partial histories of the men who batter them, through the eyes of their spouses and partners, I often hear similar themes. The majority of these men were emotionally neglected and often physically abused by their mothers. They use alcohol and other drugs to cope with feelings of insecurity. As with Joey's story in chapter 11, their insecurity about being abandoned is often disguised as rage. They push their partners away to block the pain of abandonment by their mothers. Often, abuse starts for battered women during pregnancy, when they are first becoming mothers. Their partners' rage surfaces in a misogynistic and symbolic negative transference to their mothers.

The Abandonment Struggle

Sometimes, when we struggle in relationships and they seem destined to end, we focus on the pain of the loss rather than the relationship itself. We tend to glorify the relationship in ways that fit our needs, in order to postpone the re-experiencing of abandonment. Sometimes, when people detach emotionally from us, we tend to latch on to them, to work harder to earn their love, so that we don't feel that familiar void in our hearts from early abandonment. In a partnership where the fear of abandonment is greater than the love between people, a couple may stay together in order to avoid their grief. This is part of the reason why some people break up and get back together, over and over again, until they can each cope with their own grief about ending. It is important to learn to separate our fears of abandonment from our love for another person, so that decisions can be made from a place of love, rather than fear of loss. We can help our clients to separate love from loss during the course of therapy.

Otto Rank (1936), an Austrian psychologist and philosopher, theorized that we can tell most things about a person by how they deal with beginnings and how they deal with endings.[6] Therapy can assist individuals immensely to cope with the inherent losses in life, and to access a full range of emotions to guide our journeys.

My work with women often entails helping them to access their anger. It is usually buried among their other difficult feelings—like sadness, helplessness, and feeling abandoned. The opposite is often true with my work with men. I usually need to help men to access their sadness, and their feelings of betrayal and helplessness, which are usually buried underneath their rage.

Perhaps because gay men, lesbians, and bisexual people are less bound by society's rigidity regarding gender identity, there may be some differences in the ways that they cope with an introject. Gay men, for example, who come from histories of abusive fathers and neglectful mothers, may be more likely to incorporate the introject of a victimized mother than an abusive father. Lesbians may be more in touch with their anger than heterosexual women, after surviving abuse by their male family members. Gay men and lesbians may still need to cope with their negative transference in relationships, however. I worked with a gay man named Marty many years ago. He identified with his victimized mother and cut off all ties with his abusive father. He consistently replayed his relationship with his father, however, in his selection of male partners.

In this chapter, I have focused primarily on heterosexual relationships. Although some transference issues remain the same with gay couples, some are different.

Sometimes, in working with gay couples in treatment, intimacy issues have just as much to do with socialization of men and women in our culture than with people's individual histories. Therapy is still about finding balance, but the dance between homosexual partners can vary from the heterosexual dance.

Between men and women, as described in Harriet Lerner's work *The Dance of Intimacy* (1989), closeness seems to happen in cycles.[7] A woman moves closer to her partner; he tends to be the one to eventually back away. If she withdraws, he feels safer to move close. Women are socialized to be other-oriented, and we need to learn as adults to nurture ourselves as we do others. Men are socialized to be more self-oriented, and they need to learn as adults to nurture others as they do themselves. Of course, there are many exceptions to these stereotypes, but in general, the heterosexual dance is still relevant in many couples' lives.

In treating gay male couples who seek professional help, the work is often about allowing intimacy into their lives. Lesbian couples, however, work toward allowing separateness. Intimacy can become overwhelming in lesbian couples, due to the other-orientation of both partners. This pattern is best described in an article about lesbian fusion, by Jo-Ann Krestan and Claudia Bepko (1980).[8]

At the same time, lesbians with histories of abuse and neglect by men can find great refuge in the arms of another woman. Gay men with histories of abuse and neglect by men, however, can struggle with transference and triggers to their histories, sometimes hindering their capacity for intimacy. The inverse of this dynamic is also true, if the abuse and neglect is by the mother. Gay men may find comfort in the arms of a man if the negative transference is due to a mother's abuse and neglect, and lesbians are often triggered inside their relationships with women if their neglect histories are with their mothers.

Lesbians who are other-oriented, with abuse histories by men, can find such healing in relationships that it is difficult to separate and individuate inside of the partnership. When Danielle came to see me following her sexual assault, her partner Hannah accompanied her for support. Hannah seldom spoke, but she sat with Danielle on the couch, holding her hand, helping her to remain present. Danielle and I conducted individual therapy sessions with Hannah present for several months, before Danielle would occasionally choose to come to treatment on her own. Clearly, their intimacy was about a deep love and commitment to each other, as well as a "fusion" that worked for them. The dynamic of lesbian fusion only becomes a problem that may require treatment when one woman wants to separate and the other does not.

Many years ago, I worked with a gay man named Dave who struggled with intimacy in all of his relationships with men. His father sexually abused him from the time he was a small boy. His father was emotionally unavailable to Dave, and treated him as if he existed only to meet his father's needs. Dave was so isolated and neglected that he attempted suicide as a young man. He came to therapy after his outside wounds had healed, to examine his inner wounds.

Dave had recently been involved in a long-term relationship with an emotionally unavailable man, who exploited him for sex, much like his father did. Dave wanted so badly to be able to be intimate with a male partner, but he was suffering from the repetition of his past, and choosing men who triggered all of his negative transference. Dave's father, like many other parents, was too focused on his own needs to conceptualize how he was damaging his son's future.

Dave acquired HIV in the mid-eighties, before medications could slow the progression of the virus. He was unable to resolve his history, and experienced very little love and nurturing in his life, before his tragic, untimely death. I sincerely hope that he is in a place where unconditional love is finally available to him. He was a kind, generous soul who deserved love all along.

Chapter Seventeen

Working through Countertransference Issues

Countertransference involves the beliefs and assumptions that therapists carry with them into the treatment room. It also involves the patterns that we repeat in relationships. Although many of us learn to keep our egos out of the room while conducting therapy sessions with clients, we often remain unaware of our own transference issues. Without awareness, we continue to replicate these familiar patterns. If we as therapists have unresolved histories of neglect or trauma, then we need to be particularly astute about how our patterns may affect our clients, as well as our own work.

Recently, I supervised a young woman named Angela as she completed her first year of graduate school in social work. Angela worked hard in supervision to gain greater understanding of her past relationships, and challenged her own limits in the process, thereby reducing her need for defenses. Angela started school with the belief that her family of origin had not impacted her choice of career. Her biggest obstacle, Angela told me, was processing the grief about her brother's sudden death in a car accident—an accident that occurred more than five years earlier. Whenever Angela spoke about her brother, her acute grief was enormous, and her tears seemed infinite. Angela had never spoken, however, about her role in the family when her brother died. As we explored her patterns in relationships, we learned together that Angela felt the need to walk on eggshells, especially with authority figures, due to her deep desire not to hurt others. She kept her feelings under lock and key, except in regard to her brother's death. When Angela was able to begin discussing her role in her family, I learned that Angela had been attempting to modulate others' feelings for many years. Angela was raised by an emotionally labile mother who prioritized her own needs over those of her children. Sometimes, when Angela attempted to express her pain, her mother would compete with her; while at other times, her mother would ridicule or embarrass her. Even in relation to Angela's brother's death, it was not okay to express her upset. When Angela would cry, her mother would say, "You have no idea what it's like to lose a son", and invalidate her daughter's pain.

Through supervision, Angela learned that her role in her family of origin was that of emotional caretaker. The caretaking role persisted after her brother's death, and Angela began to parent her younger brother. Her mother was too withdrawn in her grief to assist, and Angela was left to cope with her loss and parent her brother simultaneously.

During her young adulthood, Angela pressured herself constantly to overachieve. When she attempted to overachieve in her supervision sessions, however, I was able to notice and reflect this behavior back to her. She was confused at first, not knowing how to be in relationship to me without having to please me, to provide caretaking, or to read my moods and expectations. Once Angela relaxed into the relationship and began to trust me, she was able to refocus that energy back on herself.

Angela discovered through supervision that underneath her grief and loss, was a history of emotional neglect that began long before her brother died. Angela's mother would often act wounded and hurt when Angela expressed herself, or when she disagreed with her parents. Angela learned to dissociate from her own feelings in order to take care of others. She was unsure of her choice of career, and felt especially wary of doing clinical work with bereaved people. When asked to think about where her insecurity might have come from, a memory was retrieved by Angela. Her mother had told Angela that she was too "sensitive" to work with people. And that she "would never be good at it". Angela had integrated those words on a very deep level, and she questioned and doubted her choices as a result.

In beginning treatment with clients, Angela became aware of how to monitor her own countertransference. She would have trouble finding the right words to empathize with her clients, out of her concern about hurting their feelings. She had trouble trusting her own intuition, although Angela could read people's moods very well. Most significantly, Angela discovered her own elusive introject. Because her mother felt so hurt by Angela's expression of emotion, Angela assumed that she would unintentionally hurt her clients. She believed that she could become her mother. For example, she believed that she would say the wrong thing, become emotional as her clients spoke about their histories, or reflect inaccurate insights about what her clients revealed to her.

Because Angela was very dedicated to her own journey toward awareness, she was able to work through her transference patterns as well as the issues surrounding her internalized parent, or introject. She found that through her own personal exploration, her countertransference issues gradually lifted away. Angela chose an internship in her second year of graduate school that enabled her to prioritize clinical work and enhance her skill level. I have no doubt that Angela is on the path to trusting her intuition, insight, and astute awareness of others, now that she has found compassion for herself.

Countertransference responses can also be individualized and complex in relation to particular clients. Years ago, I supervised a student named Sandra. Sandra was an agnostic. Her client, Kyra, was a devout Catholic who went to church every day. Kyra would consistently recite Bible verses during her therapy sessions. For Kyra, the verses were very significant, and she relied on the Bible to soothe herself as she spoke about a severe neglect history. Sandra, however, had no interest in the Bible, and found herself dissociating during the sessions. She could not be helpful to her client for the first month of treatment. In supervision, Sandra needed to resolve her own personal issues regarding religion and spirituality before she could be mindful and present with her client. Once she was able to resolve her countertransference response, Sandra developed a deeper understanding of her own spirituality due to her openness and resilience in working with Kyra.[1]

In his book *Love's Executioner,* Irvin Yalom (1989) helps therapists to resolve countertransference issues by openly disclosing his own. I refer again to the chapter of Yalom's book entitled "Fat Lady." This chapter openly discusses Yalom's countertransference during his treatment of an overweight client.[2] Yalom's own mother was overweight, and he had a conflictual relationship with her. As he grapples with his beliefs and opinions about his client in "Fat Lady," Yalom acknowledges the triggers to his own relationship with his mother. Interestingly, as the client succeeds at losing weight, Yalom also succeeds at separating her from his mother.

Chapter Eighteen

Correction by Projection

Here is the essence of the quote that appears in chapter 12, as it applies to the repetition of neglect:

> Anyone addressing the problem of child abuse is likely to be faced with a very strange finding: it has been observed again and again that parents who tend to maltreat and neglect their children do it in ways that resemble the treatment they endured in their own childhood, without any conscious memory of their early experiences. . . . The explanation of this fact is that information about the cruelty suffered during childhood remains stored in the brain in the form of unconscious memories.[1]

Men and Women as Victims

When parents are narcissistic, they often treat children as extensions of themselves. Skye described her relationship with her mother in this way: “I feel like she sees me as her right arm. I help her constantly, listen to her woes, and I’m not separate from her in any way. I move with her; I’m attached to her.”

Skye’s mother grew up in a household where both parents worked. She had caretaking responsibilities for her two younger siblings from the time she was five years old. Her mother felt neglected and ignored by both of her parents. Although she loved her little sisters, she resented taking care of them full-time. Her mother had no time to play, no time to socialize with friends, no time for herself. Her mother left home to marry Skye’s father when she was only nineteen years old, to escape the neglect and criticism of her childhood. The couple gave birth to Skye in the late 1950s, and moved to a suburb of Connecticut.

With very little money and a lack of support from Skye’s grandparents, Skye’s father began to commute to NYC by train to pursue employment. The family could only afford one car. When her father found work, Skye's mother would drive her father to and from the train station. Skye would ride in the back seat, before seat belts and car seats were required. Skye and her mother spent quality time together while they waited for the train's whistle, signaling her father's arrival home.

When Skye was two years old, her brother was born. As an infant, Skye's brother slept during the drives to and from the train station. But as a toddler, he became more difficult to manage. Skye's mother would frequently feel the need to stop the car, pull over to the curb, and try to quell the fighting in the back seat. Skye's brother would continue to create havoc, and her mother would raise her voice, to no avail. Her brother's behavior became extremely upsetting to Skye's mother. One day, Skye was told she would not be going to the train station. "You're a good girl, so you get to stay home alone." Skye was told to stay in the family's den. The room contained a lamp, a television, a couch and a window. Skye was told not to look out the window, not to answer the phone or the door. She could watch television, if the volume was very low. If the train was late, or if they needed groceries, the trip could last hours. It always felt like hours to Skye. After quite a while, Skye's parents brought home a puppy. The puppy was allowed to stay with Skye in the dark den. She was no longer alone.

Throughout Skye's childhood, she was never asked to watch her brother. She was not involved in helping to raise him in any way. Skye's mother was able to correct her own history through Skye, by creating this separateness between siblings. It is the way her mother would have preferred to be raised—without responsibility for siblings. Her mother was very young herself, and she did not have the introspective ability to understand how leaving Skye alone might affect her. Skye's mother may have experienced an anniversary of being left alone at five years old. It may not be a coincidence that this was Skye's age when her mother repeated the abandonment she felt as a child. Skye's mother was incapable of prioritizing her child's needs over her own. She could not search within herself for a different solution to her own trauma history.

Skye chose to explore this memory further through *brainspotting.* For those of you who are unfamiliar with this technique, here is a blurb about it from a presentation in 2009 in Boulder, CO:

> Brainspotting, a recent therapeutic technique developed by EMDR therapist David Grand, has an almost magical capacity for resolving traumas that are stuck in the mid-brain. Engaging in the Brainspotting process can link together other life events and issues in a healing network, in a unique spontaneous manner, and can also surprise both therapist and client. Sometimes recipients may have profound

spiritual experiences that are comparable to prayer and meditation, even if the client has no particular religious faith.[2]

Skye had a transformational experience through brainspotting in her first session. She relived the traumatic memory in her therapist's office. As soon as she left the room, the connections to other aspects of her life became clearer. Skye realized the huge impact of the trauma. Whenever Skye was abandoned by a partner, she would experience a deep chasm of devastation and emptiness. The chasm felt much larger, and symbolized much more, than Skye's recent relationship ending. This is the type of overreaction that is usually a representation of prior trauma. Many clients with abandonment histories will stay with a partner that is neglectful and even abusive, because they do not want to trigger the initial memories of abandonment they felt as children. Skye also connected her anxiety about driving a car to this memory. She had watched from the den window as her mother drove away with her brother. She never knew when they would be back. Skye had intense anxiety about *waiting* for anything or anyone as a result of this abandonment. Skye had attached a post-traumatic stress response to the act of waiting.

Skye's mother did the opposite of what was done to her, by leaving Skye alone instead of forcing her to care for her younger brother. Doing the opposite of what was done to us might feel quite healing and therapeutic. But doing the opposite may still be a reaction to our neglect histories. Therapy can assist clients to become proactive, to make choices that are not based in their childhood histories. Clients can find a compromise, or a new path. Doing the opposite makes total sense if clients have abuse histories. Choosing not to physically or sexually abuse one's child is equivalent to breaking the cycle of violence. But for adults with neglect histories, the issue is more obtuse, and much harder to define. The opposite of what happened to us is not always the best thing for our children. We need to see our children more clearly, without the lens of PTSD to cloud our vision.

Through therapy and brainspotting, Skye realized that her mother had no intent to harm her, or to neglect her feelings, by leaving Skye alone. This realization helped Skye to find compassion for her neglected mother. In the years prior to Skye's treatment, she argued frequently with her mother over petty things. Once she discovered the source of her anger at her mother, Skye was able to access forgiveness for her mother's limitations as a young parent.

When there is intent to harm, however, forgiveness comes less easily.

Even when men identify as victims and not aggressors, there is still tremendous difficulty in integrating the negative introject of a neglectful or critical father. There is often a different type of repetition that occurs under these circumstances. If an abuse or neglect history is unresolved, men, like women, may try to correct their histories with their own children. Whether or not this correction involves neglect, I will leave the reader to decide.

Correction through our children may involve a defense called *projection*. It is the unconscious mental process by which we externalize our emotions and beliefs onto others. Sometimes, we are barely aware of our own feelings and needs, although we manage to project those needs onto our children. We treat them in the way we wanted to be treated, but often, that treatment is not what our children need.

Recently, Michael Jackson has come to the forefront of our minds as an example of a man who felt victimized and unresolved about his past. In his television interview with Martin Bashir from 2003, aired again after Jackson's untimely death, he recalled the details of a childhood of neglect and severe physical abuse.[3]

He tearfully remembered his father beating the Jackson brothers as they performed, with ironing cords and belts, when mistakes were made. Jackson recalls feeling faint on occasion, and actually regurgitating as a result of the anxiety associated with his father's presence. Although Michael traveled with a bodyguard, that bodyguard could not protect him from his own father.

In public, Michael described feeling extremely self-conscious. His father was critical and emotionally neglectful at home. In this interview, Michael recalled that his father would be very critical of his face, the size of his nose, and his acne. Michael reported that it was painful for him to appear in public, when he was not performing on stage. Is there a big leap between this childhood of intense self-consciousness, and his desire to have his children wear masks in public? Perhaps this is an example of an attempt at correcting Michael's own history through the raising of his children. Perhaps he attempted to heal from his own upbringing by vicariously creating the life he would have preferred to live—through the masks on his children's faces. Michael told the media that the masks were worn so that his children were not recognizable by the public. He felt that this technique could avert a kidnapping. Maybe his children felt protected and nurtured by his efforts. Maybe they did not.

In this candid interview, Michael also discussed his life on the road during his performance tours. He remembered that his older brothers would frequently have sex with women on the road, while Michael tried to sleep in the same room. As a young boy, Jackson witnessed sexual intercourse while making valiant attempts to get to sleep, so that he could rise early to practice and perform the next day. Any hope of a carefree childhood was robbed from him.

As an adult, Jackson created Neverland, his flight into fantasy and the dreams of his childhood. He invited young boys to sleepovers at Neverland, and according to Jackson, did nothing inappropriate with them. If this were in fact a repetition to correct Jackson's history, his only need would have been to help these young boys to get some sleep. He discussed reading to them, telling stories, and serving milk and cookies. In Jackson's eyes, he may have created the nurturing environment for others that he so sorely missed. There was something lacking in his frame of reference, however. He was unaware of the effect that remaining in bed with the young boys, while helping them to fall asleep, might have had on *their* psyches. Perhaps it helped Michael, but for some of his young friends and their parents, the behavior was unacceptable. When a neglect and abuse history is unresolved, it is difficult for the some affected adults to see past their own history, and into the separate sensitivities of another child.

Michael Jackson identified himself as a victim. He did not block memory. He may have been unable to utilize the defense of dissociation to help him to cope with his history. He remained a very sensitive individual, always conscious of his hurtful past. We know about Jackson's use of pain medications. We will never know how much of his pain remained in his body, however, from his years of physical abuse and emotional neglect. Perhaps he was altering his reality in order to manage his painful past.

Although men sometimes identify as victims, it is more common for women. As in Skye's story, mothers can correct their own histories through their children. Although there may not be a conscious intent to neglect or to do harm, the harm penetrates our wellbeing nonetheless.

There is one other pattern of repetition that is worth mentioning. This pattern is worth exploring if you are working with clients with neglect histories who are in neglectful or abusive relationships with partners. The problem with this pattern is that it can be very internalized and covert, and therefore, very difficult for clinicians to recognize. Many adult children of neglect stay in painful relationships because they cannot tolerate the concept of *abandoning another person* in the ways that they were abandoned. The internal belief is that they could cause the same extent of harm that devastated them as children. This belief represents a covert way of doing the opposite of what was done to them. Staying in an unhealthy relationship because of our own need to *not* replay the abandonment dynamic is synonymous with living our past neglect histories.

Once clients can identify this pattern of staying in unhealthy relationships, they can realize that there are other options. They can prioritize their own needs. They can learn to understand that no termination of an adult relationship can cause the same effect as the abandonment of a helpless child. Therapists can help their clients to see that although the abandonment might feel the same, it is very different.

Therapists must also be very conscious about our own need to project. We cannot fix what was broken in our own families by projecting our needs onto our clients. There is no healing through projection.

Chapter Nineteen

Therapeutic Tools for Working with Adult Survivors of Neglect

Guided Imagery

Your clients may request to explore relaxation and visualization work through the use of guided imagery. The most important initial undertaking in guided imagery is to help your clients to find a safe space. It is best if you utilize this exercise prior to any other visualization that you do. Inform your clients that when they start this process, there is no need to become perfectly relaxed. This is a skill that is developed over time. If their minds wander away from the visualization, that's fine. It's like falling asleep during a massage; your body still benefits from the healing touch. So invite them to enjoy their journey, and let's begin by reviewing some helpful exercises.

The following exercises have been rewritten for use with neglect survivors. They originally appeared in a wonderful book entitled *Mother Wit: A Feminist Guide to Psychic Development* (1981) by Diane Mariechild.

Safe Space Exercise[1]

Lie down comfortably now, close your eyes and begin to relax. Let your body relax now. Allow yourself to become more and more relaxed. Breathe very deeply now, and send your breath into your toes and feet. And let your breath like a healing massage break up any strain or tension, and as you exhale let the tension drain away. Breathe deeply now and send your breath into your ankles, and let your breath like a healing massage break up any strain or tension there, and as you exhale let the tension drain away. Breathe deeply now and send your breath into your knees and thighs, and let your breath, like a warm, healing massage break up any strain or tension in your legs, and as you exhale, let the tension drain away.

Breathe into your internal organs now; all of your internal organs are soothed and relaxed as your breath like a gentle, healing massage breaks up any tension, and as you exhale, let the tension drain away. Let your breath flow into your entire torso; let it soothe you like a gentle healing massage. Breathe into your back and spine now; your breath like a healing massage is breaking up any strain in your back and spine, and as you exhale, the tension drains away. The deep relaxing energy is flowing through your back, into each vertebra as each vertebra assumes its proper alignment. And the healing breath is flowing into all of your muscles and tendons and you are relaxed, very fully relaxed. Feel yourself sinking deeper and deeper into a state of total relaxation. Breathe now into your shoulders and neck; your breath like a healing massage is breaking up any strain or tension and as you exhale the tension is draining away. You shoulders do not need to carry any weight or responsibility right now; your neck and shoulders are becoming more and more relaxed.

And the deep relaxing energy is flowing into your arms; your upper arms, your elbows, your forearms, your wrists, your hands, your fingers are fully relaxed. Breathe into your shoulders and neck again and let them relax. Breathe into any area that carries your stress, and let that area become more fully relaxed. Become more and more relaxed. And let that relaxing energy wash up over your throat, and your lips, your jaw, your cheeks are fully relaxed. As you breathe into your face, the muscles around your eyes, your forehead, your scalp are relaxed. Any strain or tension is draining away. You are relaxed, most completely relaxed.

Picture three slender trees, three slender trees dancing in the wind. And as you focus on these trees, you become like the trees, firmly grounded. You have given yourself roots. You are safely grounded.

And let your mind clear; let it become relaxed, clear, and calm. Picture two beautiful butterflies. And as you focus on these butterflies, you become like the butterflies, light and free. And you have given yourself wings, wings to travel between dimensions. And now you have roots and wings. (*Pause for about one minute.*)

And now float to your space; move between dimensions and travel to your space, a meadow, a mountain, a forest, the seashore, wherever your mind is safe and free. Go to that space now. And you are in your space, the space you have created, a space sacred and apart. A space where you are bathed in a golden glow that protects you from all harm. And here in this world you are developing your natural healing abilities. Here in this space you are free from all tension and stress. You are in touch with the calm, expansive power within you. Here in this space you are in touch with your body, and able to help heal whatever is wrong. Here in this space you have access to spiritual information and energy. Here is the space where you can communicate with your soul, and with your spirit guides. Your flow is in harmony with the flow of the universe. Here you are pure and free.

Stay in this space a while and when you are ready let yourself drift up and back to your usual waking reality. (*Pause about two minutes.*) You will return relaxed, refreshed, and filled with energy. And you will return now, gently and easily. When you are ready, open your eyes and stretch your body.

Shedding the Cloak of Negativity[2]

Relax, deepen, and protect yourself. Here in this space out of time you are becoming conscious of the garment you are wearing, a cloak, a heavy, black cloak. This dark, hooded robe is the cloak of your negativity. It symbolizes all the negative thoughts, feelings, and experiences you carry with you. This is the negativity you have integrated into your being, from the most critical voices of your parents, to the least supportive people in your life. It is the negativity from your past and your present life. Feel the heaviness of this cloak of negativity that surrounds you. Become aware of the texture and the feel of the cloth. Feel the weight on your shoulders, your whole body cloaked in negativity and despair. (*Pause about one minute.*)

And now, become aware that the cloak is gradually lifting up and away from your body, and with it, your negativity and despair. Stay with this image until you are watching the cloak vanish. (*Pause.*) Now the cloak has vanished.

And your attention is drawn to a fountain, a fountain of light, an incredible fountain of light. And the shimmering light is bubbling up and spilling over. A shower of light, a shower of tiny stars, thousands of tiny stars, is streaming down upon you. The whole space is filled with a brilliant light.

And you realize that you are gowned in a new garment, a sheer translucent cloak of light woven from the stars. And you are wearing this robe of love, joy, and protection. It is the symbol of your womansoul, the loving connections you feel and sense and see. Wear it now and always. *To end this visualization*:

(When you are ready, drift up and back to your waking reality, filled with light and love.) Or, to move deeper from this visualization to inner wisdom and positive change:

- Wise Old Woman Visualization
- Theater Visualization for:
  - A. Inner Child Work
  - B. Positive Change
- Hot Air Balloon—Letting Go Visualization

Wise Old Woman Visualization[3]

Relax, deepen, and protect yourself. And now let yourself sink deeply into the realm of intuitions and images. Deep in this sea of images is the image of a wise old woman. She lives very deeply within you. You may uncover her and enjoy the benefit of her great wisdom and love. And now you will begin the process of unfolding and opening, of moving toward the old woman and her wisdom, the wisdom of the ages that is unfolding within you.

And now you are at the foot of a mountain. And you begin to climb this mountain, making your way along the stony mountain path. Climbing higher and higher now and the ascent is becoming steeper but you are drawing on an inner strength and the climb is almost effortless. The air is getting thinner now, yet it is clean and clear and rejuvenating. And you eagerly make your way upward, almost running the last few steps of the journey as you reach the door to the cabin. Here in this cabin lives the wise old woman. She is here to greet you now. Feel the warmth of her love and the power of her wisdom as you enter her home. Let her loving presence envelop you like a glove, protecting you from cold and storms, from your fears, and from your criticisms of yourself. You will spend some very important time with her until you hear my voice again. *(Pause about five minutes.)*

And now you thank the old woman for her advice and support and you leave the cabin and descend the mountain. Moving down the mountain path and back to your usual waking reality. Return now, relaxed, refreshed, and filled with energy. Open your eyes and stretch your body.

The following visualization is from Dan Brown's advanced hypnosis training:

Theater Visualization[4]

Relax, deepen and protect yourself. Imagine now that you are seated in a very comfortable chair, in a very old and beautiful theater. You are the only person in this audience, and you feel safe and comfortable in your theater. As you sit in this chair, notice the beautiful details of your theater surroundings, and the large velvet curtain in front of the stage. The curtain is closed. As you sit in this chair, notice how much more relaxed you are becoming—relaxed and comfortable. The longer you sit, the more you sink deeper and deeper into the chair. Soon you will be very relaxed. *(Pause about one minute)*

When you are feeling ready, watch the curtain open. Soon a play will begin taking place on the stage. You will be curious to know exactly what kind of play you will see.

Inner Child Work:

The play will be about your inner child. The little girl you once were, and how she survived her hurt, betrayal, and pain. Although it may not be clear to you right away just how this play is about her, nevertheless, it will be about that little girl you once were. You will be able to watch the play with interest. No matter what you see on the stage, you'll remain comfortably relaxed as if you are just watching a play. The curtain opens when you are ready, and the play begins. *(Pause about three minutes.)*

Before the play ends, imagine that the little girl on stage is beckoning you to join her. She is calling to your adult self, the only one in the audience, to join her on the stage. You can go to her now, and ask her what she needs from you. You can greet her in whatever way is comfortable for you both. She will be delighted to meet you, and she will tell you what she needs from you now. *(Pause about three minutes.)*

And now the curtain begins to close. Notice that you become aware of sitting in the chair once again, alone with the memory of the little girl inside you, and her insights and requests of you. She is inside you now, and you feel your compassion for her. *(Pause.)*

When you are ready, watch yourself rise from your chair, and begin to leave the theater. Knowing that you can return here at any time, to revisit your inner child, you return to your waking reality, awake and refreshed, filled with compassion and peace.

Positive Change:

The play will be about the life that you want. A life free of neglect, abuse, and fear. A life free of negativity, self-criticism, and doubt. A life that envisions your powerful woman self, living to your potential, overcoming all obstacles, and finding peace and purpose.

When you are feeling ready, watch the velvet curtain open. The play begins. You are comfortable and safe in your chair, and you watch the play begin. You are ready to embrace your future. You are ready to embrace your true self. You will see yourself achieving your lasting peace, and you will learn a great deal about crossing the bridge from here to there. *(Pause about three minutes.)*

And now the curtain begins to close. Notice that you become more aware of sitting in the chair once again, relaxed and calm. When you are ready, return to your waking reality, with the knowledge of how to get to where you want to be, filled with love and compassion.

Hot Air Balloon—Letting Go Visualization

Relax, deepen, and protect yourself. Imagine that you are walking in a large green field, a field filled with beautiful flowers. There may be a soft breeze that feels very good on your skin. The smell of the flowers brings you peace and contentment. It is a beautiful day.

Up in the distance, you see a large, colorful hot air balloon. The hot air balloon is attached to a woven basket, anchored to the ground with four thick cords fastened to four posts. As you move closer to the balloon, you see the balloon's basket. As you move closer to this basket, you are filled with the hope that this basket can lift away all of your hurt and pain from the past, all of the obstacles to your success, all of the negative aftereffects of your history that continue to block your emotional evolution.

Now you are able to reach the basket. When you are ready, watch yourself place the obstacles and unresolved problems from your past into this basket. You are easily able to give each obstacle a shape, a color, a texture, and place it in the basket. You may choose to invite other people, animals, fictional characters into this image, to assist you in filling your basket. As you watch the basket filling up, notice how it feels to give yourself credit for succeeding at this task, as I pause for a moment. *(Pause about one minute.)*

This hot air balloon is strong enough to lift away all of the obstacles in your life. It is a powerful vehicle that will assist you in letting go of your past. As the balloon becomes full, begin the walk around the balloon, removing each of the four posts from the soil. You are surprised at how easily each post is released. First one, then the second, the third, and finally, the last. As you remove the last post, watch the balloon as it rises from the ground, taking with it all of your despair, all of the unresolved problems and obstacles to your potential. Continue to watch the balloon moving higher and higher into the sky, until it vanishes from your view. (*Pause.)*

Now you have a sense of letting go, of release of pain and hardship, and you are ready to face the day with a new intent. When you are ready, return to your waking reality, filled with joy and relief at your accomplishment.

Family Sculpture

The technique of family sculpture is described in this article from *Psychology Today* online:

> When psychologists or marriage and family therapists hear the term "family sculpture," an expressive technique invented by experiential family therapists David Kantor, Fred Duhl, and Bunny Duhl often comes to mind. They think of a nonverbal method whereby a family member is asked to physically place other family members in positions in relation to one another—a three dimensional, in vivo arrangement of actual people. Virginia Satir, psychotherapist and author of the classic *Peoplemaking*, also had each family member "sculpt" the other in a similar way. Satir believed that it was easier for families to accurately see their situations rather than just talk about them.[5]

Just as the technique of *psychodrama* can assist therapists and their clients to monitor and change negative internal voices, *family sculpture* can assist us in exploring transference patterns in relationships that originated in our biological families. Although family sculpting is often successful with all family members present, the act of sculpting can be achieved in individual psychotherapy as well. A client can place objects around the room, each object representing a family member. The client places the objects close to her, or farther away, depending on the quality of each relationship, and its importance to her. The client then develops a choreographed group of steps, or simple moves, to symbolically describe her role in relation to her other family members. For example, if she was the peacemaker in her alcoholic family of origin, she might stand in between both of her parents, swaying between the two objects that represented them. She might stretch out a hand toward one, and then the other, back and forth. The dance continues in this manner for a few minutes, and the client is instructed during the course of the exercise to concentrate on what the role feels like inside her body. After the dance ends, the client describes her insights into her role, and any feelings that she has developed in her body from her own choreography. Perhaps, for example, she develops new insight into the exhaustion involved in peacemaking.

Clients may be unfamiliar with the patterns and roles that they played in their families of origin. Family sculpting can assist them to externalize those roles, in order to see them more clearly, explore them more deeply, and let go of the roles in their current relationships that may be familiar, but unproductive.

Chronological Anger List[6]

If your clients are creative and artistic, you might focus on helping them to access their anger about their neglect histories through painting or photography. If they are very athletic, you might suggest the use of a punching bag, or a long jog to help to dissipate anger. If your clients are more successful at utilizing cognitive behavioral techniques, then you might suggest the creation of a chronological anger list.

Ask your clients to make a list of those things that they would have been angry about, if they could have expressed that anger, as they were growing up. Divide the list into four sections: ages zero to five, six to ten, eleven to fifteen, and sixteen to twenty. Clients can start making the list in session, and therapists may participate by recalling some of the memories of neglect that have already surfaced in previous sessions. It may take months for the list to be completed. Once it is completed, clients may choose to review each incident with you, or to review the generalized feelings from those years, or just to refer to the list as needed.

The chronological anger list helps clients to externalize their anger, instead of turning it against themselves. It can help people to stop blaming themselves for their neglect histories, and to integrate the extent of their neglect on a deeper level.

Utilizing the History of Parental Neglect Questionnaire in Treatment

The History of Parental Neglect Questionnaire can be very useful in treatment. Perhaps you are not sure if your client has a neglect history, but you are aware of some behaviors or defenses that are congruent with that history. You can utilize the questionnaire as a tool to help decipher your client's past, with that client's permission. Each "yes" response on the questionnaire can be explored at length during the client's sessions. Sometimes, the questionnaire assists clients to redefine their histories. They may start to acknowledge that *something* happened to cause their aftereffects. They may begin to have other memories resurface about their neglect. By establishing tangible effects of emotional neglect, the questionnaire may also assist clients to stop minimizing their histories. They may be able to lift the burden of self-blame as they consciously acknowledge the severity of their neglect. I have found that if clients answer "yes" to at least five of the twenty questions, it may be time to further explore a history of neglect in treatment. Some clients answer "yes" to all twenty questions. This suggests that the issue of severity be examined at length in treatment.

If your clients are already aware of a history of neglect, then the questionnaire can be utilized to validate and universalize the client's experience. With continued awareness, your clients may be able to acknowledge other aftereffects specific to their own histories, and explore them further with you when they are ready.

Chapter Twenty

The Therapeutic Environment

While experiencing so many aftereffects of abuse and neglect, many sexual abuse survivors actually manage to seek help. The act of walking through a therapist's door is difficult for anyone. But for a sexual abuse survivor, the act of seeking help from a professional therapist may feel like a repetition of the experience of incest—at least initially. This is why:

- The survivor is asked to enter an unfamiliar room.
- An authority figure is in control of the surroundings.
- The door is closed behind her.
- The survivor is asked to make herself vulnerable, expose intimacies and details about her life, while the therapist shares next to nothing.

To avoid this sense of replication of the trauma, or re-victimization, therapists can:

- Attempt to take the mystery out of the therapeutic process.
- Avoid hierarchy and authority.
- Share appropriately.
- Answer her questions appropriately, without turning the question around to her.
- Explain interventions prior to using them.
- Ask what the client needs in order to feel safe.
- Turn control over to the survivor. Let the client create her own agenda.
- Be extremely mindful about boundaries.

Do not offer to hug your client, or make any physical contact at all, unless you discuss her needs first.

If your client eventually shares that she is feeling sexually attracted to you, acknowledge what she is experiencing, and help her to understand that this response is about her history in some way. Maybe she learned that if she feels cared for, she must meet other people's sexual needs. This is a connection that therapy can help to break.

Do not accept referrals of close friends or family members of your sexually abused client, while she is in the midst of her own healing. This is a boundary that needs to be respected by individual therapists, even if the client is insistent.

Remember that many sexual abuse survivors have an extraordinary ability to observe the details of their surroundings. A colleague of mine in New York[1] worked with a survivor who noticed that the sign on the door—"Therapist"—contained all of the same letters, in the same order, as "the rapist".

Please try to maintain consistency with appointments. Most survivors assume that people will be inconsistent, as their abusers were. If you need to cancel an appointment, please give your client some rescheduling options within the same week of the cancellation. Do not cancel an appointment with a survivor if circumstances arise in your life where other options are available to you. The importance of consistency with this population cannot be measured.

The consistency issue also applies to being on time. In the few ways that you can be consistently available to your survivor client, it is important that you remain so. If you find that you run late on a regular basis, and your prior client takes time away from the survivor, try to schedule your client hours with a cushion of at least 15 minutes or longer between appointment times. If you have a personal concern about your ability to manage your time, please allow yourself the opportunity to get to the root of that concern, and resolve it, prior to working with survivors.

And if you work with a large population of abuse survivors with post-traumatic stress symptoms, consider placing your most comfortable seating near the exit door, or facing the exit. Many abuse survivors tend to survey a room for the nearest escape route in order to develop a level of comfort.

Hiding and escaping, as well as ambivalence about committing to this work, can be seen in many forms. If a survivor has difficulty with connection, and with opening up the Pandora's box of her history, she might benefit from coming in every other week at first, rather than weekly. Although weekly therapy is usually advised in order to help to establish a sense of trust, when trust has been severely damaged, it is sometimes wise to start more slowly.

A former client of mine started therapy when she was in her twenties. She had a severe incest history; her abuser was an uncle who lived with the family. This client made a point of scoping out the room for a long while before she sat down. She tried out different chairs. She refused to sit in the designated spot on the couch. Eventually, she made herself comfortable in an armchair that was placed very close to the door.

I facilitated a group for incest survivors in 1986, in a counseling center in Westhampton Beach, New York. Four women attended the first meeting. The initial discussion among the women was actually about where each person would sit. They all stood until they could assess where each woman would feel most comfortable. The unanimous criteria for sitting in the room had to do with either visual or physical proximity to the door. Their names, and other modes of introduction, were superfluous.

This group later provided a very unique experience for all of us. One of the women was a member of a small church in the area. The church had a cozy, beautiful chapel. This church member asked if we could use the chapel for a funeral service, and each group member wrote a eulogy for her abuser. Whether their abuser(s) were alive or deceased, group members felt that their perpetrators still lived inside of them, and they wanted to create an exercise to exorcise them.

We all sat in the pews, while one by one, each of the four women stood to read her eulogy. One of the women played the organ. Most of the eulogies were not kind. But they were cathartic. The experience touched all of us. It remains one of the most powerful group experiences I have ever witnessed, more than twenty years later.

Sexual Identity and Incest

In chapter 8, we met Gary, a heterosexual man who had a sexual abuse history. It is possible that part of the reason that Gary committed adultery was that he was coping with internalized homophobia secondary to his incest history with a same-gender relative.

As therapists working with gay people, we need to be aware of another aftereffect of incest. When gay men, lesbians, and bisexual people have sexual abuse and trauma histories, there can be another difficult component added to the coming-out process. Of course, gender identity and sexual preference can be negatively affected by a history of incest. I am not advocating that there is a causal relationship between incest and coming out. But, gay people with incest histories by same-gender relatives can integrate a sense of guilt, fear, and even repulsion about being with same-sex partners. The reminders of the abuse are numerous, and sexuality is always affected. Gay people may have integrated a negative introject from the same-gender perpetrator. This complicated internal battle may also exist for lesbians with histories of abuse, emotional incest, or even inappropriate touching by female relatives. Internalized homophobia is even more difficult to cope with as a gay person—if you're straight, you can try to ignore it; if you're gay, you're forced to deal with the issue in order to make peace with your lifestyle and your relationships.

If you are working with gay people who were abused by same-gender perpetrators, it is important to help them to separate pedophilia from love. They are not perverse because their abusers were of the same gender. Their sexual abuse did not in any way cause them to feel attracted to people of the same sex. Separating their histories from their current, loving feelings for their partners will help to free them to express intimacy. We would do something similar for a heterosexual woman who wants to have an intimate relationship with her husband again, following a violent rape. We might help her to make a list of the ways her husband is different than her rapist.

Keep this in mind: if a perpetrator is of the same gender as his victim, then we need to acknowledge that there may be an internalized abuser, or negative introject, inside our gay clients' minds and hearts. This internalized abuser could potentially inhibit the coming out process. If a perpetrator is the opposite gender of the victim, then it is the externalized transference response that we treat. After rape, for example, we would help a woman to stop defining all men as evil.

Chapter Twenty-one

For Therapists with Neglect Histories

If you have been in the field of mental health for even a short while, I imagine that you may have already realized that many of your colleagues come to this field from a history of neglect or abuse. Initially, in helping others, we may be attempting to fix what was broken in our families of origin. Since we couldn't necessarily fix the problems at their source, we gravitated toward a field that would enable us to resolve our histories through helping others with theirs. At least this time around, we could tell ourselves, our clients *want* our help. If we felt undervalued in our families, or disrespected and thwarted in our efforts to create change, then the act of providing a service to those who need it can be quite healing. We replace the helplessness of childhood with the power of becoming a catalyst for others.

When I am confronted by acquaintances about this dynamic amongst therapists, a comment is often made about how therapists are more "screwed up" than their clients. My response is always similar to this: I don't think we're any more or less screwed up than anyone else; we're just more aware of it!

A therapist's level of awareness will directly and positively impact the clients that therapist serves. Compassion for the self also creates patience and mindfulness in working with others. These concepts may sound simplistic at first, but the road to awareness is often very rocky, and gravel can easily accumulate in our shoes, no matter how hard we try to extricate it. Sometimes, we can remove our shoes and let the stone slip out, only to discover that another stone has buried itself in the same shoe, even larger than the last one. Many of us stop walking the walk because of the stones. We don't reach the destination of awareness, and we may do unintentional damage to others by stifling our own journeys.

We have discussed how a lack of awareness of our pasts contributes to repetition of neglect. This is also true within the therapist/client relationship.

If we are unaware of our own neglect histories, we may collude with our clients in minimizing theirs. We would be less likely to recognize their defensive structures, or their use of survival skills, or their camouflage when discussing relationships. We would be more likely to stay with them in their discussions of present relationships, validating their concerns, without recognizing their behaviors as patterns stemming from their histories of neglect. We would not be searching for an elusive introject in our clients' minds, because we would not yet have discovered and embraced our own introjects with compassion. We would be able to provide support to our clients, but not necessarily therapy.

We are also likely to err in other ways as a result of providing treatment without resolving our histories. Often, in loving partnerships, people give love by treating others the way they themselves want to be treated. This is most often witnessed in couples' therapy with heterosexual couples. Stereotypically, women want to process their feelings with their male partners, while men want solutions. So, when women talk about their feelings, it is very foreign for men to just witness their pain, and offer supportive responses. Men pressure themselves to come up with immediate solutions. They may have difficulty in just listening. They are goal-oriented, not process-oriented. The last thing many women need when they are upset is to be given an immediate solution to their problem. The "problem" may just be a need for a kind and gentle ear. In the opposite manner, men may have no intention of processing their feelings with their female partners. They may want their wives or girlfriends to tell them what to do, or come up with a solution, so that they can focus on the solution rather than the emotions that the problem may trigger. Men may be asked supportive questions by their wives, in an effort to facilitate an in-depth conversation about the issue, when all they really want is an answer. This type of dynamic can be involved in therapist/client relationships as well.

Some therapists will give clients advice about a particular concern, from their own perspectives. This may be experienced as nurturing by some clients, at least on the surface. Underneath that nurturing experience, however, is the belief that the therapist does not respect the client's own path. If we offer help in decision-making when clients request it, we are giving them this double message:

- I care about you.
- I don't think you're capable of figuring this out on your own.

This double message may actually be a replication of messages received during the course of a client's neglectful childhood. Ask instead:

- What's the hardest part about this decision for you?
- How can I help you to get to where you want to be?
- What's missing for you, in being able to make this decision on your own?

In this way, you empower your clients to feel capable, albeit confused. You trust them to be able to find answers within themselves. If they are angry with you about not giving advice, utilize this emotion clinically to delve into transference patterns in relationships. Perhaps they are angry at a neglectful parent who did not provide any guidance?

If our histories are unresolved, we may be more likely as therapists to project our own issues onto our clients. If a client has a similar history to yours, beware. You may be making assumptions about their healing process that are not accurate. What worked for you may not be appropriate at all for them. Take care to visualize this need to project. Where is it coming from? Were you isolated in your own healing? Are you searching for a sense of belonging through your work?

Remember that clients do not usually enter therapy with the goal of resolving their neglect histories. Their presenting problems will be many and varied, and it is your job to resolve your own history in order to better redefine theirs. Remember that neglected adults have felt ignored, devalued and disrespected. You can easily continue to ignore their needs—especially the ones they're not yet conscious of—if you are not aware of the intersection of your own neglect history with your therapeutic work with others.

Let's not replicate in the therapeutic environment the toxic silence that exists in some neglectful families. In *The Source of All Things,* Tracy Ross (2011) compares this silence with the abuse and molestation she suffered:

> More and more, I also began to feel the deep, abiding betrayal of my entire family. Dad had created the lie, but Mom and Chris had let me carry it all. Never once did either of them ask me what had happened during all the years I'd been molested. In some ways, their refusal to ask was more painful to me than the actual abuse. [1]

Let's ask our clients the questions about their histories that will help them to enhance their self-awareness. There is no need to ask for graphic details. Giving details may feel too vulnerable or retraumatizing to victims of abuse and neglect. But we can ask about how they integrated what happened to them. What beliefs do they hold about themselves because of their histories? How do their histories negatively affect their current relationships? If they had been born into families without neglectful parents, how might they be different today?

It takes practice to be able to leave your ego and your past at the door of the therapy room. It takes time and history as a therapist to see that people move toward health in their own way, at their own pace. It is easy to forget that we help clients by listening more than responding, by witnessing their pain more than giving advice. Over time, clinicians become more astute at *differentiation of self*—the ability to separate enough from one's own ego to become the therapist that each particular client needs you to be.[2] It is important to encourage your clients to ask for what they need from you as well. The act of asking can be healing in itself for neglected adults. First, you are helping them to discover their needs, and then, to verbalize them to you. And ideally, through the process of therapy, you provide your clients with a comparison to a trusting, consistently caring adult, who *sees* them and *hears* them and understands. You provide good parenting, in a therapeutic way. You enable your clients to change their expectations of relationships. You observe as they begin to let down the walls around their hearts, alleviating the need for their unproductive defenses, their negative introjects, and their transference responses, outside of the therapist's office.

It is a very sacred role we play with our clients. We must be diligent, and we must be dedicated. We must provide consistency where there was none. We must be trustworthy. It helps to keep appointments at the same day and time each week, and certainly, to start and end sessions on time. If you are working with clients who have histories of abandonment, imagine how they might feel if the client before them runs late, and they are patiently awaiting their session in the waiting room. If you have time to do so, schedule clients with at least 15 minutes between them, so that you can center yourself, write notes if you choose to, and refocus your energies on the next session. Think about the symbolic nature of everything you do in relation to your clients. If you are working with hypervigilant, sensitive, neglected adults, you can be sure that they are getting your covert messages.

Most significantly, we need to heighten our own awareness of ourselves, in order to help others to heal from their neglect histories. There is always more to learn. The process of self-discovery can be very enlightening. As we observe our own growth and enhance our introspective skills, our connections may become more epiphanous. There is a wonderful story about a child who watches as a sculptor chips away for months at a block of marble. When the sculpture, a beautiful horse, is finally revealed, the child asks in wonder, "How did you know that was inside there?"[3] Discovering more about our blocks of marble can help our clients to chip away at theirs.

Self-discovery can bring relief as well. Consider this insight from a sermon given by Daniel, the minister in *While I Was Gone*: "Loss brings pain. Yes. But pain triggers memory. And memory is a kind of new birth, within each of us. And it is that new birth after long pain, that resurrection—in *memory*—that, to our surprise, perhaps, comforts us."[4]

In order to explore your memories further, find good, accessible supervision. Work with a supervisor who is willing and able to help you to see yourself in relation to your clients. Find someone who can lift the traditional boundary between therapy and supervision. A supervisor with traditional and alternative training can provide a combination of both, by helping you to process your countertransference issues.

In his book *Momma and the Meaning of Life* (1999), Irvin Yalom recorded a conversation with one of his long-term psychotherapy clients. He asked his client, Irene, to describe why her therapy was successful. Irene spoke in a very eloquent manner about the importance of connection:

> "Tell me, from your perspective, what was the real center, the core of our work?"
>
> "Engagement," she said at once. "You were always there, leaning forward, getting closer. . . ."
>
> "In your face, you mean?"
>
> "Right! But in a good way. And not in any fancy metaphysical way. I needed just one thing: *for you to stay with me and be willing to expose yourself to the lethal stuff radiating from me.* That was your task."

Irene continues:

> "You had good staying power. You hung in there close to me. More than just staying close, you kept pushing for more and more, urging me to talk about everything, no matter how macabre. And if I didn't, you were likely to guess—pretty accurately, I'll hand it to you—what I was feeling."
>
> "And your actions were important—words alone wouldn't have done it. That's why one of the best single things you did was to tell me I had to see you an extra session every time I got really enraged with you."[5]

Focus less on diagnosis, and more on connection. No matter what a client's diagnosis might be, the ability to engage that client is tantamount to healing. Many neglected adults have a very difficult time with connection and intimacy of any kind. Eye contact can be strained. Stay in tune with the relationships that you have with each of your clients. In gentle ways, notice how they have had to protect themselves through distancing. If they begin to cry or become angry, move closer to them in some way. Lean forward. Don't hesitate to nod in agreement with their insights and realizations. Active affirmation is a powerful tool to utilize with hypervigilant clients, who may be watching for any clues about what their therapists are thinking and feeling.[6]

Our culture has many ways of disconnecting from emotion. You will find it easier to hold this emotional space for your clients if you have taken the opportunity to resolve any intimacy issues from your own neglect history.

When we work with neglect survivors, we become vessels for our clients' pain. Our job is to hold onto their pain, until they can take it back from us, in a different form. Until they can carry it differently within themselves. If we are carrying too much of our own pain, our vessels are too full to be helpful to others.

Sue Bender (1995) created this symbolic image of healing in her book, *Everyday Sacred*:

> I saw a strikingly handsome Japanese tea bowl that had been broken and pieced together. The image of that bowl made a lasting impression. Instead of trying to hide the flaws, the cracks were emphasized—filled with silver. The bowl was even more precious after it had been mended.[7]

It is an immensely difficult but rewarding task to mend the bowls of our youth. To access the pain and the heartache, the devastation, violation and betrayal, that comes from neglect and abuse. Neglect is often, as we have seen, a prerequisite for abuse of all types. It sets the foundation for victimization. Neglect forces us into keeping our secrets.

Resolution of neglect allows us to journey to a much better place. We can live to our full potential. We can feel whole. We can create a very long-deserved peace. And best of all, we can assist others to find peace as well.

By resolving your own history, you are helping others to break the cycle of neglect. Know that there will be children born to loving, mindful, grounded parents, partly because of your successful work.

Notes

PREFACE

1. Moshe Talmon, *Single Session Therapy* (San Francisco: Jossey-Bass, 1990).
2. More information about Bill O'Hanlon and solution-focused therapy can be found at his website, www.billohanlon.com, accessed August 19, 2011.

INTRODUCTION

1. "Signs of Neglect," www.childwelfare.gov, accessed July 10, 2010.
2. This is my paraphrase of several topics discussed in a lecture by Dr. Dan Siegel on March 2, 2011, which was aired on National Public Radio. For more information about Dr. Dan Siegel's events, visit www.drdansiegel.com.

CHAPTER 1: "BUT NOTHING HAPPENED!": REDEFINING CHILDHOOD NEGLECT

1. My sincere thanks to Sarah for telling her powerful story of her earliest memories of neglect, and for granting me permission to print her words in chapter 1.
2. Alice Miller, *The Drama of the Gifted Child: The Search for the True Self* (New York: Basic Books, 1997), 12.
3. The concepts of being *parentified* and *pseudo-mature* were first introduced to me during my internship at Tapestry, a feminist therapy collective in Cambridge, MA, 1982–1984.
4. These commonalities among survivors of neglect were collected in individual and group meetings with clients, graduate students, and beginning clinicians from

1990 through 2008. My special thanks to Elizabeth, a current client who has taught me a great deal about overachieving as an aftereffect of neglect.

CHAPTER 2: POST-TRAUMATIC STRESS REVISITED

1. "Rock-a-bye Baby," *Wikipedia,* http://en.wikipedia.org/wiki/Rock-a-bye_Baby, accessed March 24, 2011.
2. American Psychiatric Association, *Quick Reference to the Diagnostic Criteria from DSM IV-TR* (Washington, D.C.: American Psychiatric Association, 2000), 218.
3. Sue Gerhardt, *Why Love Matters: How Affection Shapes a Baby's Brain* (NewYork: Brunner Routledge, 2004), 143.
4. Jasmin Lee Cori, *Healing from Trauma* (Cambridge, MA: Marlowe & Company, 2007), 28.
5. Cori, *Healing from Trauma,* 43.
6. Diane Poole Heller and Laurence S. Heller, *Crash Course: A Self-Healing Guide to Auto Accident Trauma and Recovery* (Berkeley, CA: North Atlantic Books, 2001), 59.

CHAPTER 3: MAGICAL THINKING: FINDING POWER IN HELPLESSNESS

1. Jean Piaget, *The Psychology of the Child* (New York: Basic Books, 2000), 96–99.
2. Information about this reference can be found at www.kideo.com.
3. Eric Clapton, "Conor," in *Clapton: The Autobiography* (New York: Broadway Books, 2007), 229–36.
4. Jeannette Walls, *The Glass Castle* (New York: Simon & Schuster, 2005), 40–41.
5. Agnes Wohl and Bobbie Kaufman, *Silent Screams and Hidden Cries: An Interpretation of Artwork by Children of Violent Homes* (New York: Brunner/Mazel, 1985), 22–23.

CHAPTER 4: WEIGHT MATTERS: USING FOOD FOR COMFORT

1. Geneen Roth, *Feeding the Hungry Heart: The Experience of Compulsive Eating* (New York: Penguin Books, 1982), 34–35.
2. Katherine E. Krohn, *Oprah Winfrey* (Minneapolis, MN: Lerner, 2002), 23–32.
3. Evelyn Silten Bassoff, *Mothering Ourselves: Help and Healing for Adult Daughters* (New York: Dutton/Penguin, 1991), 52.

CHAPTER 5: GONE TOO SOON: WHEN DEATH LEADS TO NEGLECT

1. Evelyn Silten Bassoff, *Mothering Ourselves: Help and Healing for Adult Daughters* (New York: Dutton/Penguin, 1991), 135.
2. The self-help exercises throughout Julie's story were initially taught to me by my own therapist, Barbara Mantel, LICSW, in Cambridge, Massachusetts, during my treatment in the 1980s. This book is dedicated to her.

CHAPTER 6: AT HOME WITH INCEST: THE PAVED ROAD FROM NEGLECT TO ABUSE

1. Ellen Bass and Laura Davis, *The Courage to Heal* (New York: HarperCollins, 1988).
2. Jasmin Lee Cori, *Healing from Trauma* (Cambridge, MA: Marlowe), 28.
3. I want to thank Kathy for her courage in writing her story, and for the honor of being her witness throughout her healing process.

CHAPTER 7: THE BROKEN PROMISE OF LOVE: ADDICTED PARENTS AND NEGLECT

1. Tatum O'Neal, *A Paper Life* (New York: HarperCollins, 2004).
2. "Ryan O'Neal Hit on Daughter Tatum at Farrah Fawcett's Funeral," *UsMagazine.com,* www.usmagazine.com/celebritynews/news/ryan-oneal-hit-on-daughter-tatum-at-farrah-fawcetts-funeral-200938, accessed March 24, 2011.
3. O'Neal, *A Paper Life,* 116–17.
4. O'Neal, *A Paper Life,* 116–17.
5. Tara was the first client I worked with online, through a psychotherapy service available at www.Find-A-Therapist.com. I have never met Tara, nor spoken with her on the telephone. And yet, her healing was profound and powerful.
6. Tracy Ross, *The Source of All Things* (New York: Free Press, 2011).

CHAPTER 8: ADOPTION AND NEGLECT

1. Betty Jean Lifton, *Lost and Found: The Adoption Experience* (New York: The Dial Press, 1979).
2. I was Joelle's psychotherapist for five years in the late 1980s. We are still in contact today. I am grateful to her for granting me permission to include her adoption story.

3. Dorothy has taught me a great deal in the decades we have known each other. She has been a consistent source of support and encouragement during the writing of this book.

CHAPTER 9: "IT WASN'T THAT BAD!": WORKING WITH DEFENSIVE STRUCTURE

1. Sigmund Freud, *Three Essays on the Theory of Sexuality* (New York: Basic Books, 1962).
2. Jeffrey M. Masson, *The Assault on Truth: Freud's Suppression of the Seduction Theory* (New York: Simon & Schuster, 2003).
3. The concept that defenses are developmental was initially introduced to me in class at Boston University School of Social Work, during my study of Freud's theories and defensive structure.
4. Elisabeth Kubler-Ross, "First Stage: Denial and Isolation," in *On Death and Dying* (New York: MacMillan, 1969), 51–63.
5. Anna Freud, *The Ego and the Mechanisms of Defense* (Madison, CT: International Universities Press, 1937).
6. Margaret S. Mahler, "The Third Subphase: Rapprochement," in *The Psychological Birth of the Human Infant: Symbiosis and Individuation* (New York: Basic Books, I1975), 76–109.
7. "Denial," *Wikipedia*, http://en.wikipedia.org/wiki/Denial accessed March 24, 2011.
8. A reference is made by an e-therapy client to *The Courage to Heal*, by Ellen Bass and Laura Davis (New York: HarperCollins, 1988).
9. The reference I have made to the *Diagnostic and Statistical Manual of Mental Disorders* and my own defensiveness about its use comes from my early years as a clinician. The manuals are numbered; in my early years of practice, I utilized the *DSM III-R*.
10. Virginia Norton, "Artworks Symbolize Woman's Healing," *Augusta Chronicle,* November 16, 2002, http://chronicle.augusta.com/stories/2002/11/16/rel_358937.shtml, accessed August 14, 2011
11. E. Sue Blume, *Secret Survivors: Uncovering Incest and Its Aftereffects in Women* (New York: Random House, 1990), xxvii.
12. This definition was accessed on August 28, 2011, at www.thefreedictionary.com/dissociation.
13. Donald A. Misch, "Basic Strategies of Dynamic Supportive Therapy," *Journal of Psychotherapy Practice and Research* 9 (2000): 173–89.

CHAPTER 10: THE INTEGRATION OF DEPRIVATION: INTRUSIVE THOUGHTS AND HYPERVIGILANCE

1. According to *Wikipedia,* accessed August 16, 2011, Niccolo Machiavelli was an Italian historian, philosopher, humanist, and writer, 1469–1527.

2. Sue Bender, *Everyday Sacred: A Woman's Journey Home* (New York: HarperCollins, 1995), 86–88.

3. American Psychiatric Association, *DSM IV-TR* (Washington, D.C.: A.P.A., 2000).

4. Karyl McBride, *Will I Ever Be Good Enough? Healing the Daughters of Narcissistic Mothers* (New York: Simon & Schuster, 2008), 8–10.

5. This definition of psychodrama was accessed on August 16, 2011, at the American Society of Group Psychotherapy and Psychodrama website, www.asgpp.org/pdrama1.htm.

CHAPTER 11: WORKING WITH THE *INTROJECT*

1. This is my paraphrase of a definition of *introject* from www.definitionof.net/introject, accessed August 16, 2011.

2. Anna Freud, *The Ego and the Mechanisms of Defense—Revised Edition* (Connecticut: International Universities Press, 1966), 43.

3. Ellen Bass and Laura Davis, *The Courage to Heal* (New York: HarperCollins, 1988), 109.

4. Karyl McBride, *Will I Ever Be Good Enough?* (New York: Simon & Schuster, 2008), 119–20.

5. In Belle's story, she references a children's book called *The Once and Future King* by Terence Hanbury White (New York: Berkeley, 1966).

6. Belle also references a book entitled *Fat Is a Feminist Issue,* by Susie Orbach (New York: Berkeley Books, 1990).

7. This quote by Barack Obama during his presidential campaign was accessed on April 22, 2009, www.thedisplacedafrican.com/2008/11/barrack-husein-obama-is-president-of-the-usa/.

8. Barack Obama, *Dreams from My Father: A Story of Race and Inheritance* (New York: Random House, 2004).

9. EMERGE information can be accessed at: www.emergedv.com/. This group has been in existence for decades, and has helped men through counseling and education to stop domestic violence.

10. Scott D. Krugman, and Howard Dubowitz, "Failure to Thrive," *American Family Physician* 68 (2003): 879–84.

11. Justin A. Frank, *Bush on the Couch: Inside the Mind of the President* (New York: HarperCollins, 2004), 3.

12. Frank, *Bush on the Couch,* 105.

13. Frank, *Bush on the Couch,* 105.

CHAPTER 12: NEGLECT IN THE NEWS

1. Scott Brown, *Against All Odds: My Life of Hardship, Fast Breaks and Second Chances* (New York, HarperCollins, 2011), 33.

2. Brown, *Against All Odds,* 14.

3. Brown, *Against All Odds,* 128.
4. Brown, *Against All Odds,* 93.
5. Brown, *Against All Odds*, 54.
6. Brown, *Against All Odds*, 70.
7. Brown, *Against All Odds*, 79.
8. Tracy Ross, prologue, in *The Source of All Things: A Memoir* (New York: Free Press, 2011), 2.
9. Ross, *The Source of All Things*, 29.
10. Ross, *The Source of All Things*, 139.
11. Ross, *The Source of All Things*, 260.
12. Ross, *The Source of All Things*, 50.
13. Ross, *The Source of All Things,* 201.
14. Ross, *The Source of All Things,* 274.
15. Dena Kleiman, *A Deadly Silence: The Ordeal of Cheryl Pierson* (New York: Signet, 1988).
16. Betty Rollin, "The Girl Who Stopped Feeling Nothing," *New York Times,* October 9, 1988, www.nytimes.com/1988/10/09/books/crime-mystery-the-girl-who-stopped-feeling-nothing.html, accessed August 7, 2011.
17. Andrea Peyser, *Mother Love, Deadly Love: The Susan Smith Murders* (New York: HarperCollins, 1995), 47.
18. Charles Montaldo, "The Dear John Letter Sent by Tom Findlay," http://crime.about.com/od/murder/a/susan_smith_4.htm, accessed August 7, 2011.
19. Alice Miller, "The Childhood Trauma," lecture presented at the Lexington 92nd Street YWHA, New York City, New York, October 22, 1998.
20. This quotation was accessed from *Life Magazine* online, on August 28, 2011, at www.life.com/gallery/50441/image/50611439/creepiest-hollywood-hook-ups#index/1.

CHAPTER 13: GRIEF AND ITS RELATIONSHIP TO NEGLECT AND ABUSE

1. Elisabeth Kubler-Ross, *On Death and Dying* (New York: MacMillan, 1969), 51–146.
2. J. William Worden, *Grief Counseling and Grief Therapy: A Handbook for the Mental Health Practitioner* (New York: Springer, 1991), 77.
3. Irvin Yalom, "Fat Lady," in *Love's Executioner and Other Tales of Psychotherapy* (New York: Basic Books, 1989), 93–125.
4. Yalom, *Love's Executioner,* 93–125.
5. Yalom, *Love's Executioner,* 10.

CHAPTER 14: UNDERSTANDING DEVELOPMENTAL THEORY IN RELATION TO NEGLECT

1. Margaret S. Mahler, *The Psychological Birth of the Human Infant: Symbiosis and Individuation* (New York: Basic Books, 1975), 76–108.

2. Janae B. Weinhold, and Barry K. Weinhold, *Counter-dependency: The Flight from Intimacy* (Colorado: CICRCL, 2004).

3. Erik H. Erikson, *Childhood and Society* (New York: W.W. Norton 1963), 247–50.

4. Erikson, *Childhood and Society,* 251–54.

5. Erikson, *Childhood and Society,* 261–62.

6. Melody Beattie, *Codependent No More* (Center City, MN: Hazelden Foundation, 1986).

7. Robin Norwood, *Women Who Love Too Much* (New York: Simon & Schuster, 1985).

8. Claudia Bepko and Jo-Ann Krestan, *Too Good for Her Own Good: Searching for Self and Intimacy in Important Relationships* (New York: HarperCollins, 1990), 124.

CHAPTER 15: DEVELOPING OBJECT CONSTANCY IN ADULTS

1. Jerrold R. Brandell and Shoshana Ringel, *Attachment and Dynamic Practice: An Integrative Guide for Social Workers and Other Clinicians* (New York: Columbia University Press, 2007), 65.

2. Brandell and Ringel, *Attachment and Dynamic Practice,* 66.

3. Jasmin Cori, *The Emotionally Absent Mother: A Guide to Self-Healing and Getting the Love You Missed* (New York: The Experiment, 2010), 79–80.

4. Sue Gerhardt, *Why Love Matters: How Affection Shapes a Baby's Brain* (New York: Brunner-Routledge, 2004), 92.

CHAPTER 16: WORKING THROUGH TRANSFERENCE IN RELATIONSHIPS

1. I attended Boston University School of Social Work from 1981–1983. The concepts mentioned in this chapter were taught in a course entitled "Differential Diagnosis."

2. Sue Gerhardt, "Active Harm: The Links Between Trauma in Babyhood and Trauma in Adult Life," in *Why Love Matters: How Affection Shapes a Baby's Brain* (New York: Brumer-Routledge, 2004), 146–47.

3. Koren Zailckas, *Fury: A Memoir* (New York: Penguin, 2010), 170–71.

4. Sue Miller, *While I Was Gone* (New York: Random House, 1999), 206–7.

5. The concept of the *introject,* and the skills I developed in working with transference, were initially introduced to me in my second year internship at Tapestry, a feminist therapy collective in Cambridge, Massachusetts.

6. Otto Rank, *Truth and Reality* (New York: W.W. Norton, 1936).

7. Harriet Lerner, *The Dance of Intimacy* (New York: HarperCollins, 1989).

8. Jo-Ann Krestan and Claudia Bepko, "The Problem of Fusion in the Lesbian Relationship," *Family Process* 19 (3): 277–89, doi: 10.1111/j.1545-5300.1980.00277.x, accessed August 9, 2011.

CHAPTER 17: WORKING THROUGH COUNTERTRANSFERENCE ISSUES

1. I would like to extend my thanks to three very special graduate student interns for permitting me to record their words and experiences: Lindsey, Sandra, and Angela. It has been an absolute pleasure to supervise them for the past several years.
2. Irvin D. Yalom, "Fat Lady," in *Love's Executioner and Other Tales of Psychotherapy* (New York: Basic Books, 1989), 93–125.

CHAPTER 18: CORRECTION BY PROJECTION

1. Alice Miller, "The Childhood Trauma," lecture presented at the Lexington 92nd Street YWHA, New York City, New York, October 22, 1998.
2. Laurie Branch and Susan Hubbard, "Brainspotting: A Magic Window to Release Trauma and Receive Spirit," lecture presented at the Mapleton Center, Boulder, Colorado, June 17, 2009.
3. "Living with Michael Jackson," *Wikipedia,* accessed August 16, 2011.

CHAPTER 19: THERAPEUTIC TOOLS FOR WORKING WITH ADULT SURVIVORS OF NEGLECT

1. Diane Mariechild, *Mother Wit: A Feminist Guide to Psychic Development* (New York: The Crossing Press, 1981), 6–8.
2. Mariechild, *Mother Wit,* 20.
3. Mariechild, *Mother Wit,* 78.
4. Daniel Brown et al., "Theater Visualization," *Advanced Hypnosis and Post Traumatic Stress Disorder*, Newton, MA, conference and training workshop, 1991.
5. Cathy Malchiodi, "Family Sculpture: Bringing Family Relationships to Life in Clay," *Psychology Today,* accessed online August 16, 2011, www.psychologytoday.com/blog/the-healing-arts/201002/cool-art-therapy-intervention-9-family-sculpture.
6. I learned about the Chronological Anger List during the course of my own psychotherapy with Barbara Mantel, LICSW, in Cambridge, Massachusetts.

CHAPTER 20: THE THERAPEUTIC ENVIRONMENT

1. I refer to a colleague in this chapter, and her sign, "Therapist." Gail Michele, M.A., M.S., is a practicing psychotherapist and hypnotherapist in Hauppauge, New York. I have referred clients with neglect and abuse histories to Gail, for conjoint hypnosis work over the years. I have been consistently impressed with Gail's outcomes. Her personal and professional support has been a blessing to me.

CHAPTER 21: FOR THERAPISTS WITH NEGLECT HISTORIES

1. Tracy Ross, *The Source of All Things* (New York: Free Press, 2011), 265.

2. The concept of *differentiation of self* was developed by Murray Bowen, an American psychiatrist and innovative family therapist. Bowen's theories were taught at Boston University School of Social Work.

3. This is my paraphrase of a story by Jostein Gaarder, in *Sophie's World: A Novel About the History of Philosophy* (New York: Farrar, Straus & Giroux, 1994), 109.

4. Sue Miller, *While I Was Gone* (New York: Random House, 1999), 110.

5. Irvin D. Yalom, *Momma and the Meaning of Life* (New York: Basic Books, 1999), 144–45.

6. My colleague, Ann Norris, L.C.S.W., encouraged me to include active affirmations in this chapter. She assisted me in editing this chapter as well.

7. Sue Bender, *Everyday Sacred: A Woman's Journey Home* (New York: HarperCollins, 1995), 13.

Resources

National Child Abuse Information Websites:
www.NationalCASA.org
www.childhelp.org
www.preventchildabuse.org
www.childwelfare.gov

Therapy for Daughters of Narcissistic Mothers:
www.nevergoodenough.com
(Dr. Karyl McBride's website, author of *Will I Ever Be Good Enough?*)

National Therapy Directory:
www.psychologytoday.com
(This site lists providers in your area with profiles and details about each practitioner's areas of expertise)

E-Therapy Online:
www.etherapistsonline.com
(This is a very reputable site, with practitioners that have at least ten years of experience in their fields.)

Adult Children of Alcoholics:
www.nacoa.net
www.adultchildren.org

Help for Battered Women:
www.ndvh.org
24-hour hotline 1-(800) 799-7233

For Men who Batter:
www.emergedv.com

For Sexual Abuse Survivors:
www.siawso.org

EMDR and Brainspotting Information and Referrals for EDMR (Eye Movement Desensitization and Reprocessing):
www.emdr.com

Brainspotting:
http://emdrworks.com/brainspotting.html
www.biolateral.com/brainspotting.htm

Bibliography

American Psychiatric Association. *Diagnostic and Statistical Manual of Mental Disorders, Fourth Edition, DSM IV-TR*. Washington, D.C.: American Psychiatric Association, 2000.

Bass, Ellen, and Laura Davis. *The Courage to Heal*. New York: HarperCollins, 1988.

Bassoff, Evelyn Silten. *Between Mothers and Sons: The Making of Vital and Loving Men*. New York: Penguin, 1995.

———. *Mothering Ourselves: Help and Healing for Adult Daughters*. New York: Dutton/Penguin, 1991.

Beattie, Melody. *Codependent No More*. Center City, MN: Hazelden Foundation, 1986.

Bender, Sue. *Everyday Sacred: A Woman's Journey Home*. New York: HarperCollins, 1995.

Bepko, Claudia, and Jo-Ann Krestan. "The Problem of Fusion in the Lesbian Relationship." *Family Process*, 19 (3): 277–79. doi: 10.1111/j.1545-5300.1980.00277.

———. *Too Good for Her Own Good: Searching for Self and Intimacy in Important Relationships*. New York: HarperCollins, 1990.

Black, Claudia. *It Will Never Happen to Me*. New York: Ballantine Books, 1981.

Blanck, Gertrude, and Rubin Blanck. *Ego Psychology: Theory and Practice*. New York: Columbia University Press, 1974.

Blume, E. Sue. "Secret Survivors: Uncovering Incest and Its Aftereffects in Women." *Incest Survivors Aftereffects Checklist.* New York: Random House, 1990.

Brandell, Jerrold R., and Shoshana Ringel. *Attachment and Dynamic Practice*. New York: Columbia University Press, 2007.

Brown, Daniel, et al. "Advanced Hypnosis and Post-Traumatic Stress Disorder." Newton, MA, conference and training workshop, 1991.

Brown, Scott. *Against All Odds: My Life of Hardship, Fast Breaks and Second Chances*. New York: HarperCollins, 2011.

Clapton, Eric. *Clapton: An Autobiography*. New York: Broadway Books, 2007.

Cori, Jasmin Lee. *The Emotionally Absent Mother: A Guide to Self-Healing and Getting the Love You Missed.* New York: The Experiment, 2010.

———. *Healing from Trauma: A Survivor's Guide to Understanding Your Symptoms and Reclaiming Your Life*. New York: Marlowe, 2007.

Erikson, Erik H. *Childhood and Society*. New York: W.W. Norton, 1963.

Frank, Justin A. *Bush on the Couch: Inside the Mind of the President*. New York: HarperCollins, 2004.

Freud, Anna. *The Ego and the Mechanisms of Defense*. *Revised Edition.* Connecticut: International Universities Press, 1966 [1937].

Gaarder, Jostein. *Sophie's World: A Novel about the History of Philosophy*. New York: Farrar, Straus & Giroux, 1994.

Gerhardt, Sue. *Why Love Matters: How Affection Shapes a Baby's Brain*. New York: Brunner-Routledge, 2004.

Kleiman, Dena. *A Deadly Silence: A Case of Incest and Murder*. New York: New American Library, 1988.

Krestan, J. A., and C. S. Bepko. "The Problem of Fusion in the Lesbian Relationship." *Family Process* 19 (1980): 277–89.

Krohn, Katherine E. *Oprah Winfrey*. Minneapolis: Lerner, 2002.

Kubler-Ross, Elisabeth. *On Death and Dying*. New York: MacMillan, 1969.

Lerner, Harrie. *The Dance of Anger*. New York: HarperCollins, 1985.

———. *The Dance of Intimacy*. New York: HarperCollins, 1989.

Lifton, Betty Jean. *Lost and Found: The Adoption Experience*. New York: The Dial Press, 1979.

Mahler, Margaret S. *The Psychological Birth of the Human Infant: Symbiosis and Individuation*. New York: Basic Books, 1975.

Mariechild, Diane. *Mother Wit: A Feminist Guide to Psychic Development*. New York: The Crossing Press, 1981.

Masson, Jeffrey M. *The Assault on Truth: Freud's Suppression of the Seduction Theory*. New York: Simon & Schuster, 2003.

McBride, Karyl. *Will I Ever Be Good Enough?* New York: Simon & Schuster,2008.

McNaron, Toni A. H., and Yarrow Morgan. *Voices in the Night*. Pittsburgh: Cleis Press, 1982.

Miller, Alice. "Alice Miller: The Childhood Trauma." New York, transcript from Lecture at Lexington 92nd Street YWHA, October 22, 1998.

———. *Banished Knowledge*. New York: Random House, 1991.

———. *The Drama of the Gifted Child: The Search for the True Self.* New York: Basic Books, 1997.

———. *For Your Own Good: Hidden Cruelty in Child-Rearing and the Roots of Violence*. New York: Farrar, Straus & Giroux, 1983.

———. *Thou Shalt Not Be Aware: Society's Betrayal of the Child.* New York: Farrar, Straus & Giroux, 1998.

Miller, Sue. *While I Was Gone*. New York: Random House, 2000.

Norwood, Robin. *Women Who Love Too Much*. New York: Simon & Schuster, 1985.

Obama, Barack. *Dreams from My Father: A Story of Race and Inheritance*. New York: Random House, 2004.

O'Neal, Tatum. *A Paper Life*. New York: HarperCollins, 2004.
Orbach, Susie. *Fat Is a Feminist Issue*. New York: Berkley Books, 1990.
Peyser, Andrea. *Mother Love, Deadly Love: The Susan Smith Murders*. New York: HarperCollins Publishers, 1995.
Piaget, Jean. *The Psychology of the Child*. New York: Basic Books, 2000.
Ross, Tracy. *The Source of All Things*. New York: Free Press, Simon & Schuster, 2011.
Roth, Geneen. *Feeding the Hungry Heart: The Experience of Compulsive Eating*. New York: Penguin Books, 1982.
———. *When Food Is Love*. New York: Penguin Books, 1991.
———. *Women, Food and God: An Unexpected Path to Almost Everything*. New York: Simon & Schuster, 2010.
Walls, Jeannette. *The Glass Castle*. New York: Simon & Schuster, 2005.
Weinhold, Janae B., and Barry K. Weinhold. *Counter-dependency: The Flight from Intimacy*. Colorado Springs, CO: CICRCL, 2004.
Wohl, Agnes and Bobbie Kaufman. *Silent Screams and Hidden Cries: An Interpretation of Artwork by Children from Violent Homes*. New York: Brunner/Mazel,1985.
Worden, J. William. *Grief Counseling and Grief Therapy: A Handbook for the Mental Health Practitioner*. New York: Springer, 1991.
Yalom, Irvin D. *Love's Executioner and Other Tales of Psychotherapy*. New York: Basic Books, 1989.
———. *Momma and the Meaning of Life*. New York: Basic Books, 1999.
Zailckas, Koren. *Fury: A Memoir*. New York: Penguin, 2010.

Index

www.ingramcontent.com/pod-product-compliance
Lightning Source LLC
Chambersburg PA
CBHW051252200926
51612CB00001B/23
* 9 7 8 0 7 6 5 7 0 8 9 2 2 *